World Encyclopedia of
DOGS

Happy Birthday. 1979.

Clive ~

World Encyclopedia of
DOGS

Edited by
Mary Crosby

octopus

Contents

First published 1977 by Octopus Books Limited
59 Grosvenor Street, London W1

© 1977 Octopus Books Limited

ISBN 0 7064 0623 0

Produced by Mandarin Publishers Limited
22a Westlands Road, Quarry Bay, Hong Kong
Printed in Hong Kong

Know Your Dog

IF asked what it is that has won the dog its unique position in its relationship with Man, the usual answer is that a dog is more intelligent and affectionate than other animals. But those who have worked with and studied other animals know this is not true. The cat, for instance, has just as much intelligence as a dog, but she uses it to her own ends, not her master's. She is also just as affectionate, but when she wants affection, not always when her master wants affection. Many wild animals taken from the nest at an early age and imprinted on a human foster mother are more affectionate and devoted than the average dog.

In fact, the dog has been such a wonderful servant and friend to Man because of its instincts, rather than its intelligence. This does not mean that dogs are not intelligent – far from it – but, contrary to common belief, intelligence does not make a dog trainable. Indeed, exceptional intelligence is the cause of many dogs being quite untrainable. Most difficult and disobedient dogs are very intelligent, and in some cases the whole problem arises from the fact that their intelligence surpasses that of their owners!

The first instinct to make itself apparent is the instinct for survival. Immediately it is born, the young puppy squirms about until it finds a teat and then sucks it. Intelligence or learning by association of ideas plays no part in this process; it is pure instinct that drives the puppy to find food.

Similarly, it is the maternal instinct which tells the bitch to clean up the foetal membrane and fluid and to stir the puppy into action by licking it. She does not have to be taught how to do it and she is unlikely to have seen another bitch doing it. Indeed, a maiden bitch is unlikely ever to have seen a newborn puppy before her own.

A dog's instincts vary enormously in strength between different breeds and individuals of the same breed. Again taking the maternal instinct as an example, we find that in some bitches it is so strong that they will happily adopt other puppies, kittens, lion cubs, piglets and other orphaned babies. On the other hand, some bitches which look after their own offspring very well will, if given the chance, kill newborn puppies belonging to another bitch, and some bitches are so devoid of maternal instinct that they simply walk off

and leave their puppies to die. Intelligence has no connection with their behaviour, and it is surprising to observe how really 'stupid' an exceptionally intelligent bitch can be when it comes to looking after a family. Likewise, many bitches of low intelligence make most efficient mothers.

Most instincts provide pleasure to the dog, and consequently they grow stronger, with usage. The maiden bitch will usually look with amazement at her first puppy, refusing to touch it for quite some time. As soon as she starts licking it she will become more and more enthusiastic, sometimes almost frantic, in her efforts to clean it. She will start licking her second puppy immediately, and when she has her next litter there will be no hesitation at all in cleaning the first puppy.

Another example of the dog's instinctive behaviour is a puppy retrieving a ball in response to the retrieving/hunting instinct with which we shall be dealing more fully later on. Many puppies will run after a ball and pick it up, sometimes bringing it back and sometimes running off to play with it. The first time it sees the ball 'running away', the puppy will usually lollop after it only half seriously. But if the game is continued, it will quickly become more and more enthusiastic until it can be relied on to fetch a ball every time it is thrown. This is one instinct which can grow stronger with usage to the extent of becoming overdeveloped and many dogs are completely obsessed by balls, sticks, stones or anything else they can carry.

There seems to be an age at which a dog's instincts tend to develop. A puppy which has shown no previous inclination to retrieve may suddenly decide to do so. If encouraged at this stage the instinct will quickly develop, but if discouraged it will weaken and possibly die out altogether. A dog which has never been allowed to play with a ball as a puppy is very unlikely to do so as an adult. Whether or not instincts flourish depends to a great extent on the strength of the instinct in the first place. Some dogs, particularly the gun dog breeds, have very strong retrieving instincts which will survive under very adverse conditions. At the opposite extreme, other dogs are so completely devoid of the retrieving instinct that it is impossible to persuade them to pick up anything at all. In between are the majority of dogs, which require training to develop the retrieving instinct or to keep it under control, as the case may be.

Instinct is something which is either there or not there. It can be strengthened, weakened or diverted, but it cannot be put there and it cannot be taken away. It may lie dormant throughout a dog's life, but once developed it can never be weakened again. A dog with an obsession for chasing balls may be controlled by training and by providing other outlets for its energy, but the basic obsession will always remain.

The canine instincts most important in a dog's relationship with Man are the pack instinct, the hunting instinct, the guarding instinct, the instinct to keep the nest clean, the sex instinct and the instinct of fear arising out of the instinct of self-preservation. Some of these will be dealt with in later chapters, but we will start here with the pack instinct. All animals have what is known as a 'pecking order', so called because it was first studied scientifically on poultry. A 'pecking order' simply means that in a flock of 26 animals,

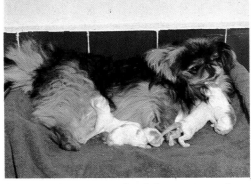

Above: The strength of the maternal instinct varies enormously between individual bitches. Here a Pekingese which has lost her puppies is suckling a litter of Turkish Van kittens, which were four days old when the picture was taken.

Opposite: French shepherds with their dogs. Although the sheepdog's most important role is to herd and/or guard the flocks, most shepherds also value it as a faithful companion.

Overleaf: This Great Dane demonstrates how gentle so large a dog can be if it is well trained.

Right: Some bitches are very possessive about their puppies, especially in the early stages, but they are often pleased to show off their offspring to people they know and trust.

Below: Puppies normally enjoy playing together and get far more exercise this way than their owner is likely to provide. Care should be taken, however, to ensure that they do not become more attached to each other than to their owner.

Right: A dog chases and carries a ball in response to the hunting instinct. Chasing a ball gives your dog both an outlet for the instinct and at the same time plenty of physical exercise.

Below right: The herding instinct is only a slight deviation of the hunting instinct. In well-bred Border Collies the herding instinct is often strong enough to make the dog herd, or try to herd, literally anything that moves.

A can peck anyone from B–Z, B pecks anyone from C–Z but not A, C pecks anyone from D – Z but not A or B, and so on until we come to poor Z who can peck no one but is pecked by everyone. In dogs it is not nearly so simple, although at first sight the principle is very similar. The pack leader does not simply dominate his subordinates, he actually keeps them all in order and tells them what to do. When the leader says 'Let's go hunting', they all go hunting; and when he says 'It's time to go home', they all go home. The majority of pack leaders are dogs, but a bitch can, and quite often does, take on the role.

Although every dog pack has a leader, the other members of the pack do not follow in a straightforward pecking order from A–Z. Often there are quite a number of dogs who neither dominate nor are dominated. Age also plays an important part and quite often one senior member of the pack will become more and more dominant until he attains the position of second-in-command; very often he will wait for an opportunity to overthrow the leader and take over that position for himself. If a pack leader dies without leaving a successor, there is considerable fighting and confusion for some time until a new leader emerges to take control.

Large packs of dogs are normally only found in the wild but, having kept quite a large and varied pack of domestic dogs for some thirty years, we have seen that this pack instinct is still very much alive.

Dogs are not 'almost human' and great suffering can be caused to them by people who think they are. But in some ways we are almost canine! Human and canine social habits have many similarities and it is this which enables Man to take over the role of pack leader. The dog's willingness to accept a human master as a substitute for a canine pack leader makes it easier to train than most other animals. Not only is it willing to be trained, it actually wants to be trained, and owners who neglect this can cause just as much suffering as those who starve their dogs.

The instinct of self-preservation which makes most wild dogs furtive and afraid of the unfamiliar is one of the instincts which is of little or no benefit to Man. It is from this instinct in the wild dog that nervousness in the domestic dog has evolved, and nervousness is the major cause of most dog problems. Nearly all cases of children being attacked by dogs and people being bitten by their own dogs arise from

nervousness; the dog is afraid it is going to be hurt and attacks first. In the evolution of the domestic dog, the instinct of self-preservation has been considerably weakened by simply breeding from bold dogs rather than nervous ones, but it has never been entirely removed.

Although essential if we are to continue breeding dogs, the sex instinct is another instinct which is of no benefit to Man and, under present-day conditions, is rarely of any benefit to the dog itself. Perhaps the saddest aspect of all this is that it is unnecessary, for the sex instinct is the only instinct which can be removed by a simple surgical operation: castrating the dog and spaying the bitch. The castrated dog is not only a happier dog, free from the worry and frustration of local bitches, it is also a much

nicer animal to have around. It will lose some of its pack leader instinct, which will only make it less likely to mark its territory by urinating on your furniture, less likely to fight other dogs and more submissive to the wishes of its human pack leader. We have not found that it alters any of the other instincts at all, and dogs guard, hunt, work sheep and retrieve game just as well after castration as before.

It is most important that dogs should be castrated after they have reached maturity, otherwise they lack character and initiative and become lazy, fat 'eunuchs'. The age at which a dog reaches sexual maturity varies enormously between individuals. Generally speaking, small breeds mature more quickly than large ones. The first clear indication is when the dog starts 'lifting its leg', which

may be as early as six months or as late as eighteen months. It is usually better to castrate too late than too early, and I have known dogs castrated at six or seven years old with no ill effects. It is better to leave a submissive dog until it is older, while a dominant one should be operated on much sooner.

Similarly, bitches should not be spayed until they have come in season at least once. Bitches spayed too early tend to be overweight and obese, which affects them mentally just as much as physically. Unlike castration, spaying done at the right time does not change a bitch's character at all. The owner who does not want to breed is saved a great deal of trouble and worry, and the bitch is spared the ordeal of being confined for three weeks twice a year. There is also some evidence to suggest that spayed bitches may be healthier, with less uterine disorders and no risk of false pregnancies.

The dog's various instincts can be strengthened or weakened by careful selective breeding. Through the ages Man has bred dogs to suit his own purposes, and in the process different breeds have evolved with their own characteristics. For many, but not all, of Man's purposes, the submissive aspect of the pack instinct is more important than the dominant aspect. We find breeds where the majority are submissive and willing to learn, while in others the majority are dominant and anxious to lead rather than be led.

A Greyhound chases a hare in response to the same instinct as a sheepdog works sheep. But as a result of selective breeding, various breeds of sheepdog have emerged where the majority are willing, even

anxious, to be trained. The same applies to gun dogs. With Greyhounds, Afghan Hounds and other hunting breeds the picture is a very different one. Once a hound has been unleashed to pursue its quarry, its master ceases to play any part. In many cases he simply follows it, so that in fact we have the dog leading and the master following. It is obvious that for this type of work a strong submissive instinct is not required, and hounds, and terriers too, are therefore generally much more difficult to train than gun dogs and sheepdogs. This is not due to lack of intelligence, and of course many hounds and terriers can be and are trained to be obedient, well-behaved animals.

Whether or not a dominant breed can be trained raises an aspect of the pack instinct which is often overlooked. It is easy for Man to take over as pack leader to his dog or dogs, but only if he is capable of leading. Nearly anyone can train a submissive dog, but a dominant dog can only be trained by a dominant person. Within a household, it is common to find a dog will obey some members of the family but not others. In recent years, trainers have tried more and more to study and practise the methods used by the canine pack leaders, with very successful results.

A good pack leader commands respect without bullying. He does not need to keep proving how big and strong he is, and therefore does not put himself in a position to be challenged. The most important lesson for the human owner to learn from the canine pack leader is that by gaining the respect of his subordinates he will also gain their affection and loyalty. The bully who

rules by force may obtain implicit obedience, but at the loss of friendship or affection.

Unfortunately a large number of trainers (including very successful trainers in trials and competitions of various types) adopt the latter policy. Never having trained by any other method, they have no idea of the pleasure they are losing in not having a dog which works *with* its master rather than *for* him – a dog which is a good servant *and* a loyal friend.

Above: These wolves are showing typical dominant and submissive attitudes. The submissive wolf exposes its throat to its dominant companion.

Right: Husky puppies in summer. This type of dog was developed to pull sledges in the Arctic, and in the past they were vital to the way of life of both the native Eskimo trappers and foreign explorers. Huskies were bred for the survival of the fittest and they will endure incredible conditions. At one time the Eskimos sometimes even cross-bred their Huskies with wolves. Although mechanical transport is gradually replacing the Huskies, they are still used in large numbers. Some are now kept as show dogs and companions, with varying degrees of success.

Overleaf: In many ways, Man has taken over the role of the pack leader.

The Dog's Ancestry

In contrast to the horse, whose prehistoric evolution is well documented by archaeological evidence, the evolution of the dog remains much more of a mystery. There is no chain of fossil evidence reaching back and connecting the dog and its wild relatives with their prehistoric ancestors. Granted that the domestic dog was a development from a wild dog species, there were, until recently, conflicting views about which of these species could possibly have been the basic stock. Most scientific opinion now tends to regard the wolf as the sole ancestor of the domestic dog, not the great grey timber wolf of the north but a smaller, reddish wolf of the Indian plains.

Where and when domestication took place is also highly speculative. Possibly it was in the Middle East that man took the first tentative steps to domesticate the wolf. This, however, took place at a time so far distant that guesses at the date vary between authorities by some tens of thousands of years. On somewhat surer archaeological evidence, we know that man reached Europe in Neolithic times and that with him came an already domesticated dog.

Why the relationship was such a successful one is easier to answer and also gives some clues as to how the working partnership might have started. Nearly all the animals which man has been able to domesticate are social in behaviour, those whose life is spent mainly with small groups of their own kind. In every such group there is a leader and a hierarchy below him of younger or weaker animals. Within the group there is a certain amount of co-operation—a recognition of social obligations, perhaps—which enables a pack to work together towards a common goal. In this way, packs of predators can prey upon creatures larger and stronger than themselves. Individual pack animals can follow a scent in relays, minimizing the chance of losing it, while the whole pack co-operates to pull down and kill a victim. When teamwork like this is evident, it follows that the younger members of the pack must be teachable and submissive. Most pack animals have also a sense of territory, an instinct for possession and consequently protection of a home ground.

The ability to co-operate for a common good, the submission of a weaker animal to a stronger, and the idea of possession, are all basic characteristics shared by man and dog and are the foundations of the relationship between the two. It seems likely that when this first occurred tribes of men and packs of wild dogs roamed over large, loosely defined territories hunting the same prey. Man, already developing a greater intelligence and beginning to use weapons, was possibly slightly more successful and the dogs would be attracted to the camp sites to scavenge the leftovers. Here they would act as an early warning system, alerting their probably unwilling hosts to the presence of the large carnivores feared by man, as well as to that of game undetected by the tribe. We cannot know whether man first followed dog or dog first followed man on a hunting expedition, but co-operation between the two must have grown from this sort of mutual foray.

Perhaps later in time puppies would be taken into the camps and reared, to be used as a source of warmth on chilly nights, as playmates for the children and doubtless as a source of food when times were hard. These animals, in which the fear of man would be lessened, would be more reliable hunting companions and their added usefulness give impetus to the whole process of domestication.

Once the bond was formed, the dog went where man went. Man at that time was a nomad. This does not necessarily mean he wandered at will. Most nomadic peoples travel over a wide territory following an annual migration pattern. When man reached new areas it was often due to climatic

Left: A scene from the Bear and Boar Hunting Tapestry dating from the Middle Ages which shows huge mastiffs in studded collars on the point of attacking a wild boar.

changes affecting his food supply, though no doubt the spirit of exploration which has led mankind so far was also responsible for some tribes breaking new ground. It was a change in the climatic conditions which enabled the dingo to reach Australia with the aborigines in late Palaeolithic times. The dingo arrived on the Australian mainland as a domesticated animal and then reverted to the feral state, contributing to the extinction of the less efficient marsupial carnivores, and later becoming a major threat to the sheep farming white settlers. However, the aborigines still keep dogs of the dingo type as hunting animals and the situation of both a wild and a domestic form existing side by side must have been a familiar one in the distant past. Similarly the Maoris, who settled New Zealand, arrived there with their dogs. The carved and decorated staff which is an emblem of the Maori chieftain has a plume of dog's hair hanging from it, symbolizing that the chief is the guardian of his people.

If we look at the recorded history of the dog in general, we find scant reference to the utilitarian, all-purpose farm dog. Yet this must have been almost the first use of the domesticated animal. Once settlement began and agriculture developed, farmers would be using the dog to round up the stock, catch the vermin and act as a watchdog. These were not the highly specialized animals which the hunting hounds became, but 'jack of all trade' dogs expected to help in a variety of ways. They were of little or no interest to artists, potters or writers of any period and were beneath the notice of the rich who were the patrons of the arts.

What then did the early working dogs of the agriculturist look like? We know from archaeological evidence that one of the earliest types of dog in Europe was a medium-sized spitz dog kept in the Mesolithic Danish settlements. The spitz group of dogs all have wedge-shaped heads, erect and pointed ears, short compact bodies and a bushy tail usually carried over the back. The coat may vary in length but is always extremely dense. When such dogs are apprehensive the tail hangs down, thereby increasing their resemblance to a wolf or wild dog. There are many spitz breeds throughout the world and nearly all are considered indigenous, indicating that this is certainly a very early type of dog.

If we look at the history of some of the modern spitz breeds, we can appreciate their versatility. Japan has three sizes of the Akita, a dog used in the past for bear and deer hunting and now used for police work. American soldiers occupying Japan after World War II were so impressed by the largest Akitas that they took a number back to the U.S. where they are now firmly established as show and companion dogs. China has the Chow, pottery models of which have been found as far back as the Han dynasty (206 BC–AD 220). These pottery figures wear a heavy leather harness of a type in use in China almost up to the present day. This symbolizes the dog's role in leading the dead safely to the underworld, a widespread religious belief occurring among many peoples, including the American Indian. Chows in the past were used for hunting deer, putting up birds for the gun, as sledge dogs and guard dogs, and for the production of furs and meat. Gilbert White, the English naturalist, comments in 1802 on the first pair of Chows imported to Britain: 'such as are fattened in that country (i.e. China) for the purpose of being eaten; they are about the size of a moderate spaniel; of a pale yellow colour, with coarse bristling hair on their backs; sharp upright ears and peaked heads, which give them a very fox-like appearance. Their hind legs are unusually straight, without any bend at the hock or ham, to such a degree as to give them an awkward gait when they trot. When they are in motion their tails are curved high over their backs. . . . Their eyes are jet-black, small and piercing; the inside of their lips and mouths of the same colour, and their tongue blue. When taken out into a field the bitch showed some disposition for hunting, and dwelt on the scent of a covey of partridges till she sprung them, giving her tongue all the time. These dogs bark much, in a short, thick manner, like foxes, and have a surly, savage demeanour, like their ancestors, which are not domesticated but tied up in sties, where they are fed for the table with rice-meal and other farinaceous foods. These dogs did not relish flesh when they came to England.' Later importations of the breed also did not like meat and were prone to skin troubles on a high protein diet.

The flesh of carnivorous animals is not very palatable. Nevertheless eating dog flesh has been a fairly widespread practice, often having symbolic or superstitious connexions. Captain Cook in the eighteenth century ate dog when in Australasia, reporting that it tasted like lamb. The Romans ate dog, recommending that it be served with whey.

Further north than China, the sledge dogs are all of the spitz type. A fourteenth century account of travel in Mongolia by Ibn Batuta says: 'In that country they travel only with small vehicles drawn by great dogs. For the steppe is covered with ice, and the feet of men or the shoes of horses would slip, whereas the dogs having claws their paws don't slip upon the ice. . . . The guide of the travellers is a dog who has often made the journey before. The price of such a beast is sometimes as high as a thousand dinars or thereabouts. He is yoked to the vehicle by the neck, and three other dogs are harnessed along with him. He is the chief, and all the other dogs with their carts follow his guidance and stop when he stops. The master of this animal never ill-uses him or scolds him, and at feeding-time the dogs are always served before the men. If this be not attended to, the chief of the dogs will get sulky and run off, leaving the master to perdition.' This account is particularly interesting with regard to the treatment of the dogs, which contrasts very favourably with the excessive brutality often recorded as being meted out to Arctic sledge dogs by their masters.

Life in the Arctic circle was only possible with the help of the sledge dog. The peoples who used them have little in the way of recorded history but even until very recent times all exploration of the Polar regions depended on the dog as a draught animal. The Eskimos had a number of distinct types of sledge dog whose purity was maintained by the isolation of their communities. However, when the isolation of many of the Eskimo and Indian tribes was broken by the Yukon gold rush, which also brought an unprecedented demand for sledge dogs, many of these breeds disappeared for good. The modern sledge dog breeds include the Eskimo, the Alaskan Malamute and the Siberian Husky. The Samoyed, another Siberian draught dog, was also extensively used by the tribe of the same name as a herd dog for their reindeer.

Northern Europe has the Finnish Spitz, the most fox-like of the group often with brilliant red colouring, used by the Finns as a bird dog. The Elkhound, the larger of the two Norwegian spitz, was used, as the name

The early history of the dog may possibly go back to the time-phase between the Eocene and the Oligocene periods, some 35–40 million years ago. At this time there were few carnivorous mammals, and in fact all mammals were in a transitional stage of development being much smaller than their counterparts of today. There was certainly no dog on earth then as we know it today; but there was a creature known as *Miacis*, which was the forerunner of several forms from which the true dog evolved. This animal was arboreal, long-bodied and short-legged, with an elongated tail. In fact, it was rather like the Polecat of today. The form known as *Cynodictis* evolved from *Miacis* in the latter half of the Oligocene period, some 15–20 million years ago. This trunk-line flowed through two intermediate forms, the Miocene *Cynodesmus* and the Pliocene form *Tomarctus*. By the Pleistocene era, of about one million years ago, the dog had become larger and, now established as *Canis,* was already diversifying into the forms we now know as wolves, jackals and coyotes.

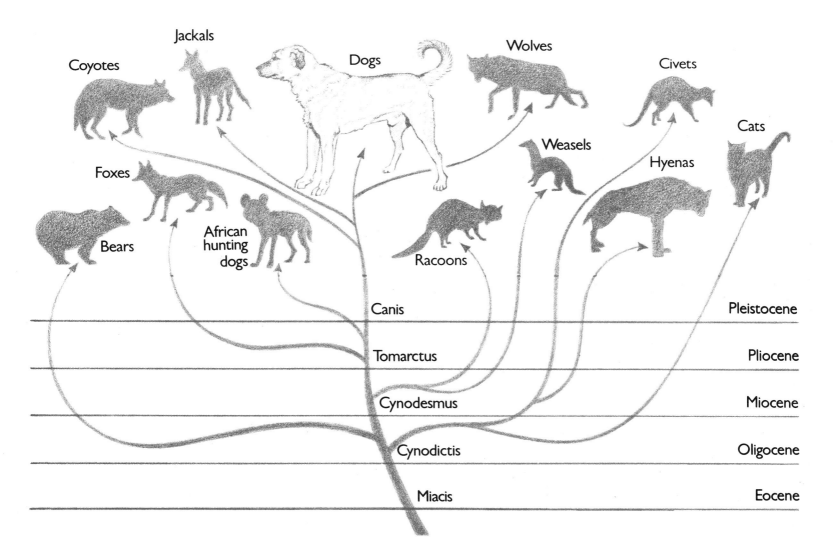

Coyotes

Jackals

Dogs

Wolves

Civets

Cats

Foxes

Weasels

Hyenas

Bears

African hunting dogs

Racoons

Canis — Pleistocene

Tomarctus — Pliocene

Cynodesmus — Miocene

Cynodictis — Oligocene

Miacis — Eocene

implies, for hunting elk. The Norwegian Buhund is a general all-purpose farm dog, a ratter, a watchdog and a herding animal. It seems likely that dogs of this type were taken to Iceland by the Vikings, for the Icelandic dog has many similarities. The Dutch Keeshond was also a watchdog, while the modern German spitz breeds are divided by size and coat colour.

German spitz seem to have reached popularity in the eighteenth century. They were mostly white and were called Pomeranians as they came from that district in Germany. Gainsborough painted a bitch and her puppy in 1777, and George Stubbs painted at least two portraits of a truly magnificent black and white dog called Fino. In 1816 *Ree's Encyclopaedia* described the Pomeranian as being 'larger than the common sheepdog'. In the mid-Victorian era white Pomeranians of about 9–10 kg (20 lbs) in weight were one of the most popular of ladies' pets. Then came a demand for a smaller variety and within a short space of time British breeders had produced a new toy Pomeranian averaging about 2 kg (4 lbs) in weight. Sometimes these were as small as 750 g (1½ lbs) when fully grown. The vivacity and charm of these tiny animals led to a decline of interest in their larger spitz relatives which are no longer seen in the U.S. or Britain. Most coat colours are accepted in Pomeranians today but, strangely enough, white which was once so fashionable has fallen completely out of favour.

Though it is possible that the spitz dogs have a better claim, members of the greyhound group are usually considered the oldest of pure-bred types. The evidence for this comes mainly from Ancient Egypt. The greyhounds, sometimes called gazehounds, are dogs which hunt by sight and rely on superior speed to catch their prey within a relatively short distance. The hot, dry desert air makes for bad scenting conditions but good visibility and with little vegetation for cover, the slightest movement of game can be seen over a long distance. These climatic conditions were instrumental in producing hunting dogs of the gazehound type. Bred for speed, the gazehound has a narrow, streamlined head, a long arched back and a long tail which acts as an efficient rudder when turning fast. It is deep-chested with room for well developed heart and lungs, long-limbed, and carries no

superfluous flesh. These dogs all appear to have originated in the Middle East whence they spread out along the trade routes of the ancient world.

Pictorial evidence from Ancient Egypt suggests that its peoples were skilled animal breeders as early as 2000 BC. Several distinct types of dog are apparent and some of these closely resemble modern breeds. Saluki-type hounds with dropped ears and long fringed tails are shown, among other places, on the walls of the tomb of Rekhma Ra, circa 1400 BC. Later these hounds were among the treasured possessions of the nomadic Bedouins who bred them with the same care as they bred the Arab horse. Though these tribes generally despised the dog as an unclean animal, the Saluki was considered an exception, being allowed to share the Arab tents where the puppies were reared by the women. On the longer treks the younger animals were carried on camel back to protect their feet from the burning sand. As with many animals valued by princely owners, Salukis were never sold, but were given away to those whom their masters wished to honour.

Greyhounds with large, upright ears looking like the modern Pharaoh and Ibizan hounds were also bred in Ancient Egypt. These types were spread throughout the Mediterranean basin in pre-Christian times by the Phoenician traders. Ibizan and

Pharaoh hounds, both extremely agile, use scent and hearing as well as sight when hunting, as does another breed whose likeness is seen on Egyptian tombs. This is the Basenji, rediscovered in the twentieth century as a hunting dog in the Congo basin. It seems likely that this dog also originated in the Middle East where early pictures show similar lightly built hounds with erect ears and the typical tightly curled tail of the breed.

A more typical gazehound is the Afghan. Although the tribesmen who owned these believed them indigenous to Afghanistan, it seems more likely that ancestral stock came there with the camel caravans going across 'the roof of the world' to collect spices from India and silks from China. Like the Bedouins with the Saluki, the Afghan tribesmen did not part lightly with their hounds. It was in the Afghan wars towards the end of the nineteenth century that British Army officers first saw these dogs. One or two were sent back to Britain where they were viewed with curiosity. Only when a number were imported by the wife of a British Army officer in the 1920s did the breed make any impact.

The history of the Afghan illustrates the two main influences on the spread of dog breeds during historical times. Dogs with specialized abilities or dogs with curiosity value have always been valuable trade commodities. They were taken as gifts by embassies travelling

Left: *Canis lupus* – the Woolly Wolf.
The family *Canidae* embraces the
true dog *(Canis familiaris)*, the wolf
(C. lupus), the jackal *(C. aureus)* and
various other forms. These true
members of the dog tribe are
structurally similar, with skeletal
and dental kinship.

Greyhounds, or gazehounds, were
bred to hunt in the desert. These
dogs hunted by sight and relied on
superior speed to catch their prey.
This engraving shows greyhounds
hunting the desert gazelle with the
aid of a falcon.

to far lands seeking trading
concessions, and they were exchanged
between the courts of ruling powers as
tokens of friendship and esteem. Wars
and the movement of armies have also
contributed to the spread of breeds.
Many invading armies took dogs with
them and these were often left behind
in occupied territories. The reverse
process also occurred – armies of
occupation admired native breeds and
took them back home with them.

When dogs of the greyhound type
first reached Britain is not very clear.
It is possible that a dog like the Irish
Wolfhound was brought by the Celtic
invaders in the sixth and seventh
centuries BC. The Wolfhound is referred
to in many Celtic legends and was
certainly known in Ireland at a very
early date. In 391 BC a gift of seven
Irish Wolfhounds was sent to Rome for
the circus organized by Consul Quintus
Aurelius Symmachus – dogs of a size
and courage which astonished the
Roman audience. Irish dogs went into
battle beside their masters, pulling
down the enemy horsemen. Wolves
were exterminated in Ireland by the
seventeenth century and, as happens
with so many breeds when their
function in life disappears, the
Wolfhound declined into virtual
oblivion. The breed was recreated in
the mid-nineteenth century by Captain
Graham. Oddly enough, we have no
evidence of what the earlier Wolfhound
looked like, although both rough- and
smooth-coated greyhound types had
been known in the British Isles for
many centuries. Captain Graham
assumed the Wolfhound to be a larger
and more massive version of the
Scottish Deerhound on the grounds
that when the Celts went from Ireland
to Scotland they took their dogs with
them· and that it was from these that
the Deerhound descended. By the end
of the eighteenth century, the

Deerhound itself had become scarce.
It had been used to bring to bay
wounded stags and to course deer
across open country. With the
improvement of the rifle, this method
of hunting declined and the Deerhound
lost the patronage of the owners of the
deer-forests. Luckily, interest in the
breed revived before numbers became
too low.

The Greyhound breed has also been
known for a very long time and it
seems likely that it arrived with the
Phoenician merchants whose wooden
ships carried goods round the Mediterranean ports and who are known to
have traded for Cornish tin in the
fourth century BC. The value of the
Greyhound was such that there were
constant references to the breed
in the early game laws with
restrictions on ownership. When
hunting was a monarch's chief
pleasure, poaching was a serious
crime. Much legislation was therefore
passed in an endeavour to protect
game from ending up in the stewpots
of the local inhabitants. By medieval
times the English Greyhound had
acquired a high reputation. There
are many references to gifts of
Greyhounds being sent as tokens of
esteem to foreign courts. The Councillor
to the Duke of Milan was sent to
England in 1471 with the following
instructions: 'We desire you to obtain
some fine English hackneys of those
called "hobby" for the use of ourself
and the Duchess our consort, as well
as some greyhounds for our hunting,
a laudable exercise in which we take
great delight, and so we have decided
to send you to England where we
understand that each of these things
is very plentiful and of rare excellence.
We are giving you a thousand gold
ducats for the purpose to buy the best
and finest horses you can find and dogs
also. In order that you may find and

buy them more easily we are sending with you el Rossetto, our master of horse, and two of our dog-keepers, who know our tastes and the quality of horses and dogs that we require.' When the East India Company opened up trade with Japan and China, the high reputation of British dogs made them a common article of export. In 1614 the East India Company was asked to send a 'fine greyhound' for the son of a Japanese nobleman and 'looking-glasses, figures of beasts or birds made of glass, mastiffs, greyhounds, spaniels, and little dogs' as presents for the Great Mogul. There is no doubt that the English Greyhound reached China at the same period.

Greyhounds have always been used for coursing hares although it was not until 1776 that the rules governing the sport were codified. A century later the show Greyhound and the coursing Greyhound constituted two distinct types, the former being larger and heavier with an extremely fine coat. In the twentieth century, as coursing declined, the Greyhound was given a

new lease of life by the popularity of Greyhound racing. More are being bred now for this purpose than at any other time in their history.

Surprisingly the Whippet is a comparatively modern greyhound breed produced by the colliers of the north of England in the nineteenth century for rabbit coursing and later racing. One of the dogs used in producing the new breed was the Italian Greyhound, a toy version of the Greyhound which first appeared in the fashionable portraits of sixteenth and seventeenth century artists. The history of the breed before this is not known although, as toy dogs have been kept and cherished from pre-Christian times, there seems little reason to suppose that they were not known earlier. The extreme delicacy of their appearance and their high stepping gait gives an unmistakable air of aristocratic distinction. This was not lost on King Lobengula of Matabeleland who, in the 1890s, saw one belonging to a South African theatrical manager and purchased it

Hare coursing was a popular sport for many years and the English Greyhound was highly prized for its hunting ability. When hare coursing declined in the twentieth century the Greyhound was given a new lease of life with the introduction of Greyhound racing.

for 200 head of cattle. Lobengula was following in the tradition of many other rulers throughout history when in return for a Great Dane which had taken his fancy he also offered another trader two wagon loads of ivory and as many women to sell into slavery as he desired. When asked why he wanted the Great Dane so much, Lobengula replied: 'He is a king among dogs and suitable as a companion of Lobengula, King of the Matabele. As he followed at your heels, he kept his head high and did not take any notice of the barkings and yappings of my people's curs. He is a king among dogs.'

Lobengula, one feels, would have been equally impressed had he ever seen a Borzoi or Russian Wolfhound. The Russian aristocracy used these for coursing hares and wolves. The ancestors of the breed came from the Mediterranean via Persia. As they were a working breed a number of crosses were used to give the original types more strength and a heavier coat more suitable for the Russian climate. The first book on Borzoi hunting was published in Russia in about 1650 but it was not for nearly another century that the type became established and colour and markings, as well as purity of blood, became important. A traveller in Russia in 1812 describes the Russian huntsmen in their gaily coloured liveries and large boots, who went wolf catching with a breed of greyhound of exceptional beauty, 'the fan-tailed greyhound'. Borzois were not expected to kill wolves: 'The perfect wolfhound must run up to the wolf, collar him by the neck, just under the ear, and when the two animals roll over, the hound must never lose his hold, or the wolf would turn round and snap him through the leg. Three of these hounds hold the best wolf powerless. The men can dismount from their horses and muzzle a wolf and take him alive.' Some wolf hunting was carried out on a very great scale. In the 1880s the Perchino hunt belonging to His Imperial Highness, the Grand Duke Nikolai Nikolaivitch, consisted of up to 150 Borzois, 15 English Greyhounds, and two packs of Foxhounds totalling 100. Liveried huntsmen on horseback surrounded an area from which the Foxhound pack was to flush the wolves and other game. Each held a leash of three Borzois, two dogs and a bitch, matched in colour and markings. These were slipped whenever a wolf broke cover. The Czars of Russia presented Borzois to Queen Victoria and later to

Edward VII, whose wife Queen Alexandra had a great fondness for the breed. Her patronage made the breed fashionable with the English aristocracy. America imported Borzois first from England and then direct from Russia. By the time of the Russian Revolution, both these countries had enough breeding stock for the Borzoi to survive.

The word 'greyhound' is thought by some to be a corruption of 'Greek hound', for the Ancient Greeks had a passion for hunting and have left us a number of works on hunting and the management of hounds. They used Greyhounds for coursing the hare but they also had a number of other types of hound, some of which hunted by scent. These were used for boar and deer hunting. Both the Greeks and the Romans after them imported many types of hunting dogs. These were often given the name of their country of origin, or supposed origin. Xenophon mentions hounds from India, Crete and Sparta. There are a great number of pictures of hunting scenes on frescoes, drinking vessels, vases, etc., but unfortunately no inscription tells us which hound is depicted. Consequently, although a Roman poet Gratius Faliscus, writing about the time of Christ, lists no less than 22 hunting breeds and the uses of some of them, we have little idea of what they looked like. What is remarkable is that only one of these breeds originated in Italy, all the rest coming from other parts of the Roman Empire, notably Germany and Gaul. Roman hunting followed similar lines to that of Ancient Greece. A single hound picked up the scent and led the field to where the game lay, when the rest of the pack was unleashed. This method of hunting, using lyam or leash dogs, continued until medieval times.

In the moister climate and heavier vegetation of Europe the sight hounds were not as useful as those which followed their prey by scent. These dogs did not need to rely on their speed, but, would wear down the game by their persistent pursuit. Gazehounds need all their breath for the chase but scent hounds give tongue when hunting a line. Although hounds and quarry may be out of sight in the undergrowth, the huntsman can still tell in which direction they are moving and whether the hounds have brought the game to bay.

Up to the time of the Revolution, the French probably had more distinct

types of hound than any other country, for the French nobility considered hunting to be almost an art form. Many of these pure-bred packs perished with their masters after the fall of the Bastille.

The patron saint of hunting is St Hubert who lived from AD 656 to 727. The son of the Duke of Guienne, he was a worldly youth with a passion for the chase. Legend says that while hunting on a Good Friday, he saw a white stag bearing a shining crucifix between its antlers. Contrite, the young man took holy orders, eventually becoming Bishop of Liège and founding an abbey in the Ardennes. He and his successors, however, continued to breed hounds which were famous for their scenting ability. There were two kinds of St Hubert hounds, an all white and a black or black and tan. Both were somewhat heavy hunting hounds with large pendulous ears and sonorous voices. From these developed many of the French hunting breeds, including dwarf-legged varieties such as the Basset Hound. Short-legged dogs are the result of a genetic mutation and this must have occurred relatively frequently since they were also known to the Ancient Egyptians and the Chinese. These slower dogs were much used by medieval falconers who wanted a smaller dog with a good nose to put up birds for the hawks.

Descendants of the St Hubert hounds reached Britain with the Norman conquest. The Normans imported these hounds for stag hunting, for they regarded deer as the proper quarry for a gentleman. From the black St Hubert is descended the modern Bloodhound. These dogs were first used as leash hounds in the manner of the Greeks to find the quarry. The Gentleman's Recreation of 1688 says: 'To find out the Hart or Stag where his harbour or Lare is, you must be provided with a Bloodhound, Draughthound, or Sluithound, which must be led in a Liam.' But they were also used for tracking men and this use became more frequent down the centuries, helping to counteract the menace of highway robbers, brigands and rebels. From the same stock the French settlers developed the Cuban bloodhound used to hunt runaway slaves from the West Indian sugar plantations. In the U.S. the Black-and-tan Coonhound comes from the same root.

The white St Hubert was known as the Talbot and was a common hound in the Middle Ages, but it had become extinct by the end of the seventeenth century and is now only remembered by some inn signs. However, from the Talbot came the Southern Hound, a slow working hound with the same excellent scenting powers and melodious voice as its ancestor. When fox hunting became the popular sport the Southern Hound formed the root stock from which the English Foxhound grew. American settlers in the seventeenth and eighteenth centuries took with them packs of hounds from Ireland and France as well as from England. From these evolved the American Foxhound, a leggier and more versatile beast than its English counterpart.

Another hunting dog known to the Greeks and Romans was the Molossus, a much larger, more robust beast than the hounds, and with a heavy, wide, square muzzle suggesting that it was of mastiff type. These dogs became famous for their ferocity and courage in tackling wild boar and other large game. The Greeks had known of them in the sixth century BC and it is interesting to speculate on the relationship between the Molossus and the Assyrian Mastiffs shown hunting lion and wild asses on the wall reliefs of the palace of Nineveh. These belonged to Assur-banipal who kept them for hunting and war in 625 BC. By Aristotle's time there were two strains of Molossus, the shepherd dogs guarding the flocks against predators, and the hunting dogs powerful and courageous enough to tackle anything. The Molossus is considered to be the archetype of the mastiff group of dogs. When they reached England we do not know, but it is possible again that the Phoenicians trading for Cornish tin brought these powerful hunting dogs, or that they came across with the Gauls. However, by the time the Romans invaded Britain, the British Mastiff was sufficiently impressive for it to be sent back to Rome to fight in the wild beast shows. Strabo, a contemporary of Caesar, wrote of Britain: 'It produces corn, cattle, gold, silver and iron, which it exports together with skins, slaves and dogs of a superior breed for the chase. The Gauls use these dogs for war as well as others of their own breed.' The export of mastiffs continued for the next seventeen hundred years, sometimes in astonishing numbers. Louis XI 'had a mighty curiosity for dogs and sent into foreign countries for them'. In the French court accounts for 1479, there is the line: 'To an Englishman who brought him a

great dog . . . ten gold crowns.' Henry VIII sent some 400 mastiffs to Charles V of Spain who used them in his war with France. These proved a valuable asset as they went out with reconnaissance parties tracking the enemy and warning of hidden ambushes. In 1540 Henry VII's envoy to the King of France wrote: 'The Constable took me to the King's dinner, whom we found speaking of certain "masties" you gave him at Calais, and how long it took to train them; for when he first let slip one at a wild-boar, he spied a white horse with a page upon him, and he took the horse by the throat and they could not pluck him off until he had strangled it. He laughed very heartily at telling this. . . .'

The reason why Britain bred such a quantity of these dogs was the popularity of baiting sports as public entertainment. Bulls and bears were the usual unfortunate victims but lions and even horses were baited for public amusement. The English Mastiff has, of course, changed over the years, the modern breed being much heavier and probably taller than its predecessor. It is still today a good guard dog, a purpose for which the Romans found it excellent and for which it has been used throughout its history. Barnaby Googe in 1631 gives the following description of the good guard dog: 'First the Mastie that keepeth the house; for this purpose you must provide you such a one, as hath a large and mightie body, a great and a shrill voyce, that both with his barking he may discover, and with his sight dismay the Theefe, yea, being not seene, with the horror of his voice put him to flight. His stature must neither be long nor short, but well set, his lippes blackish, neither turning up, nor hanging too much downe, his mouth blacke and wide, his neatheriawe fat, and comming out of it on either side a fang, appearing more outward than his other teeth; his upper teeth even with his neather, not hanging too much over, sharpe, and hidden with his lippes: his countenance like a Lion, his brest great and shagayrd, his shoulders broad, his legges bigge, his tayle short, his feet very great, his disposition must neither be too gentle, nor too curst, that he neither fawne upon a theefe, nor lavish of his mouth, barking without cause, neither maketh it any matter though he be not swift: for he is but to fight at home, and to give warning of the enemie.'

This description is interesting because the distinction between

mastiffs and bulldogs was not clear at that time, indeed, the word bulldog had only just started to come into use. Bull- and bear-baiting were immensely popular for a number of centuries. These events drew huge and disorderly crowds. Special performances were put on for visiting royalty. The meat from baited bulls was believed to be more tender because of the animal's exertions prior to its death. In the same way the flesh of a coursed hare is supposed to be sweeter than that of one shot dead. However, the attraction of the baiting sports lay really in its mixture of savagery, courage and cruelty, an irresistible formula for much of mankind and one which filled Roman amphitheatres for gladiatorial and wild beast fights just as it fills cinemas today when showing certain categories of film.

The dogs used were of any variety which would fight but chiefly those of a mastiff type, probably about 18–27 kg (40–60 lbs) in weight. An undershot jaw was desirable so that the lower teeth locked over the upper. If the nose was recessed or 'laid back' the dog could retain its grip and still be able to breathe. These features, which were finally to distinguish the Bulldog from the Mastiff, proved hard to stabilize and Pugs were supposed to have been used to improve the head shape. This experiment, however, was not an unqualified success as some Bulldogs inherited the gentle, comfortable nature of the Pug, a feature which was definitely not desired. The more horrifying excesses of baiting are best left alone but this account by John Houghton F.R.S. written in 1694 illustrates the danger for the dog: 'I have seen a dog tossed by a bull thirty, if not forty feet high–and the men strive to catch them on their shoulders lest the fall might mischief the dogs. I must tell you that the famed dogs have crosses or roses of various coloured ribbon stuck with pitch upon their foreheads; and such like the ladies are very ready to bestow on dogs that do valiantly. . . . The true courage and art is for the dog to hold the bull by the nose till he roars, which a courageous bull scorns to do.'

Bull-baiting was not banned in Britain until 1822 although it had been in decline for some time before this and continued surreptitiously in some country districts for some years after. The Bulldog naturally declined in numbers as no one who cared about dogs wanted anything to do with an animal of such ill repute and ferocity.

They lingered on as inn-keeper and tavern dogs until a few people, perturbed that such a breed of historical interest should die and realizing, too, that they had as much devotion to their masters as other breeds, started showing them. This might be called either the salvation or the death knell of the Bulldog according to one's point of view. Breeders, seizing on the salient points of the dog–the undershot jaw, the laid back nose and the broad chest– exaggerated them to the point where the breed became a caricature of its former self. Any prolonged exertion makes the breathing of a modern Bulldog so laboured that one realizes it would not even be able to escape a bull and certainly not fight one.

The old-fashioned type of bulldog was such a famous animal in its day that it is among the ancestors of a remarkable number of breeds, especially among the fighting and guard dogs. Dog-fighting, a gambling sport, has been known worldwide and still takes place in many countries even where it has been made illegal. Fighting dogs normally have their ears cropped, most of the ear being cut away so that an opponent cannot hang on to it. As ears bleed freely, cropping can be said to have had some point. Today many countries still cling to the practice because it is considered fashionable. Even with the development of anaesthetics, there does not seem any justification in cutting pieces from living animals merely to alter their appearance.

As greater speed was required in the fighting dog than in the bull-baiting dog, the latter was crossed with a terrier to produce the bull-and-terrier. At the end of the eighteenth and the beginning of the nineteenth century, the young dandies who had an interest in blood sports kept them for fighting, badger-baiting and for contests in the rat pit–indeed anything promising sport and the chance of a wager. Many of these dogs were black and tan or white with large patches of colour. In England in the 1860s, James Hinks,

An early illustration of a Mastiff with dogs of all descriptions pictured behind him. Mastiff-type dogs appear on many early pictures, Babylonian and Assyrian as well as Egyptian. They are shown pulling down large game and as guard and watch dogs. They were also used for war, their necks being protected with massive collars. From their size, relative to the men leading them, they were obviously quite capable of killing a man and later accounts tell of large numbers of such dogs appearing on the field of battle.

a well known dog breeder from the Birmingham area, produced an all white Bull Terrier smarter in appearance, better balanced and lighter in weight than those being shown. He seems to have achieved this by crossing the old bull-and-terrier with the white English Terrier, a breed now extinct. The story goes that Puss, a white bitch and the first of the strain to be shown, won her class first time out to the chagrin of the old guard. While conceding that she was smarter than the old type, they insisted that she would be no good as a fighting dog. Mr Hinks then backed her against the best known fighting dog present, the stakes being £5 and a case of champagne. Tradition has it that Puss killed her rival in 30 minutes while remaining almost unmarked. In passing it should be noted that dog-fighting at this time had already been illegal for some 27 years.

White Bull Terriers then swept the board for a number of years. As it is a recessive colour in the breed, they bred true. Colour was reintroduced by mating the whites back to the coloured side of their ancestry, a process which proved so full of snags that coloured bull terriers did not match their white counterparts in quality until World War I. It says much for the loyalty of the owners of this breed that Bull Terriers have survived two major set-backs in their history. The first was when the Kennel Club banned cropping in 1895. Uncropped dogs turned out to have soft, floppy ears but attempts to breed an erect ear finally succeeded. Congenital deafness also made its appearance amongst the white stock and this, too, was successfully bred out.

Probably the nearest modern breed to the old bull-and-terrier is an American type, the Staffordshire Terrier. Among other names this was known as the 'Pit dog' as it was a favourite fighting animal among the Pennsylvania coal miners. The English equivalent, the Staffordshire Bull Terrier, is an extremely powerful dog but somewhat shorter in the leg and

Dog-fighting continued surreptitiously for more than a century after it had been banned by law. This engraving, dated 1873, shows a dog-fight among Welsh miners.

lighter in weight. These, too, are descendants of the old bull-and-terrier. They were kept by ironworkers and chainmakers, tough and callous men who expected their dogs to be as courageous and indifferent to pain as they were themselves. Among close knit communities like these, dog-fighting continued surreptitiously for more than a century after it had been banned by law. The 'pit' where the dog fought was usually about 3 m (9 ft) across and had a line or 'scratch' marked through the centre. The dogs were matched at a weight and officially 'tasted' beforehand. The 'taster', for the modest sum of a shilling or so, ensured that no corrosive or poisonous chemical had been rubbed into the coats of the dogs. At the start of the fight the dog which had won the toss was loosed first to cross the scratch line and to attack his opponent. Rounds lasted until there was a 'fair go away', when one dog let go or attempted to avoid its rival. After a minute's rest they were loosed again and the first dog which did not come up to 'scratch' was the loser.

Both the American and English breeds of Staffordshire still look capable fighting dogs, unlike two further descendants from the old-fashioned Bulldog, the Boston Terrier and the French Bulldog. The latter was introduced into Britain at the end of the nineteenth century causing a great uproar from resentful and jingoistic English exhibitors who had been trying to breed a toy bulldog for a considerable time. The French breed, however, prospered at the expense of the Miniature English Bulldog which disappeared almost as soon as it had been produced.

Finally, mention must be made among the descendants of the Bulldog of two guard dogs, the Bullmastiff and the Boxer. The Bullmastiff, whose ancestry is clearly shown in the name, was produced by gamekeepers anxious to protect their masters' coverts against the nightly depredations of gangs of poachers. The early name of the breed was the 'gamekeeper's night-dog'. The dogs were expected to work silently, helping to catch poachers and protecting their masters in what were often bloody battles. As penalties for poaching were severe, poachers had little to lose in fighting it out with gamekeepers and it was a war sometimes resulting in deaths on both sides. The following account comes from *The Field* and was published in 1901: 'Mr Burton of Thorneywood Kennels brought to the show one night-dog (not for competition) and offered any person one pound, who could escape from it while securely muzzled. One of the spectators who had had experience with dogs volunteered and amused a large assembly of sportsmen and keepers who had gathered there. The man was given a long start and the muzzled dog slipped after him. The animal caught him immediately and knocked down his man at the first spring. The latter bravely tried to hold his own, but was floored every time he got on his feet, ultimately being kept to the ground until the owner of the dog released him.'

The German Boxer, a police dog on the continent but better known as a show and companion animal elsewhere, was produced from a mixture of types including German bull-baiting dogs and a white English Bulldog. Undesirable traces of the latter still crop up in the shape of white Boxer puppies, a colour not acceptable in the breed.

Although all the fighting and baiting dogs coming down from the Molossus are smooth-haired, there are many mastiff-type breeds which are long-haired, such as the Alpine Mastiff drawn by Landseer and now only remembered as an ancestor of the St Bernard. The portrait of a mastiff by Richard Ansdell, painted about 1840, also shows a long-coated dog. If the distinction which Aristotle made between the two types of Molossus, the hunting and the shepherd dog, is valid, then the shepherd dogs were often of a long-coated mastiff type. These sheepdogs were not expected to work sheep in the way of the modern border collie. They were merely guard dogs, keeping the flocks safe from thieves and wolves. They were often left to work on their own initiative and were equipped with iron collars from which protruded sharpened spikes. This type of collar protected the vulnerable area of the neck from the teeth of wolves and is an obvious adaptation of the collars worn by earlier dogs of war. These had spikes or knives attached to cut the legs of enemy horses and men alike. As countries became more law abiding and both sheep stealing and wolves declined, the value of these dogs remained appreciated and they were used to guard persons and property, finally becoming recognized show and companion breeds.

Some which did not make this transition have either died out or are on the verge of extinction. One of these is the Tibetan Mastiff, a black-and-tan animal reputed to be of surly aspect and ferocious temperament. It did not adapt well to temperate climates and presumably no longer survives in Tibet. Some authorities claim that this breed is the archetype from which many of the other mastiffs sprang but there seems little evidence for this view. On the other hand, many of the early trade routes between the Mediterranean and the Far East passed through the Himalayas and it seems more likely that mastiff guard dogs spread along these routes from their original homelands in Asia Minor.

Other pastoral guard dogs which are on the verge of extinction include the Estrella Mountain Dog from Portugal and the Anatolian Karabash from Turkey. What is happening to these breeds is a familiar story in the history of the dog. Protected by isolation, a breed type develops which is suited to local working conditions. The purity of the stock is not valued by the owner who merely wants a working animal, but it is virtually guaranteed by lack of communication with the outside world. Once the country becomes more accessible, law enforcement and the reduction in the numbers of predators removes much of the need for the larger type of guard dog, and the strain also becomes diluted with outside blood. Unless the breed becomes some sort of status symbol with those who value it for its purity, as for example the Great Pyrenees with the French aristocracy or the Kuvasz with the Hungarian nobility, or it survives long enough to be recognized as a show dog, it disappears into oblivion.

A surprising number of these large guarding breeds are white in colour, including the Great Pyrenees, the Maremma, the Kuvasz and the Komondor. There are two theories, perhaps complementary, as to why this should be so. One view is that it enabled the dogs to be distinguished easily from any attacking wild animal. The other view is that the colour may have been less alarming for the sheep, enabling the dog to guard the flock more closely without panicking them. In support of the latter theory is the belief held by some modern shepherds that too much white on a working collie is undesirable. They maintain that sheep will turn and stare at a white dog, as if mistaking it for one of themselves, instead of moving smartly away.

The Roman armies marching north over the Alps took dogs of the molossus type with them and the influence of these can be seen in the modern Swiss mountain dogs, the St Bernard, and the German breeds, the Rottweiler and the Great Dane. The latter used to be known as the German Boarhound, reminding us that this was one of the first uses of the Molossus.

The St Bernard is the best known of these breeds, a dog about which there are many myths and legends. The monks of the Hospice of St Bernard started breeding these dogs in about 1660. They were probably used more for finding paths obliterated by snow and for leading parties safely along them, than for locating benighted travellers in trackless wastes, which is the more popular view of their work. They were also used to carry necessities for the journeys undertaken by the monks, a fact which gave rise to the legend that they were sent out with casks of brandy round their necks. As working dogs, these animals were of a different type from the present show breed, being less cumbersome in build and often short-coated. Undoubtedly the monks and the dogs saved many hundreds of lives but it was Victorian enthusiasm for the breed which distorted the facts and produced the 'super dog' myth—a myth which, incidentally, received a great set back in 1937 when a child visitor to the Hospice was killed by the dogs in a tragic incident which has never been explained satisfactorily. Although dogs are still kept at the Hospice they are now more of a tourist attraction. The modern equivalent to the traditional role of the St Bernard is that of the trained avalanche rescue dog but the breed used for this purpose is usually the German Shepherd Dog.

Armies on the march often took dogs with them for use in a number of ways. When supplies were a problem, cattle droving dogs brought up the rear of the column, herding beef on the hoof to supplement the rations. In this way the ancestors of the Rottweiler are supposed to have reached the district of Württemberg in Germany. This area was a grain and cattle market place for Central Europe and the 'butcher's dog' of Rottweil acted as his master's guard, carried the purse of money round his neck for the purchase of the cattle, and drove the newly bought beasts back to the markets. The use of dogs as messengers and carriers of valuables has always been a widespread practice. First mentioned

by Homer, the tradition continues up to the despatch-carrying dogs of World War I. Abraham Fleming wrote in 1576: 'At his masters voyce and commaundement, he carrieth letters from place to place, wrapped up cunningly in his lether collar, fastened thereto, or sowed close therein, who, least he should be hindered in his passage useth these helpes very skilfully, namely resistaince in fighting if he be not over-matched, or else swiftnesse and readinesse in running away, if he be unable to buckle with the

The St Bernard is the breed most famous for bringing help to humans in distress. Kept by the monks of the Hospice of St Bernard, they were used as guide and rescue dogs. Contrary to romantic belief, they did not carry a keg of brandy around their necks, as shown in this engraving.

dogge that would faine have a snatch at his skinne.'

Breeds like the Rottweiler and the Bernese Mountain Dog were also used for draught purposes, although there is no European breed developed solely for freight work in the manner of the northern sledge dog. Dogs pulling carts were common in Switzerland and the Low Countries until recent times and though most of the dogs used were of a mastiff type, the only factors which really mattered were whether their size and temperament were suitable. Many small tradesmen depended on these animals for their living, especially those selling dairy produce and bread. By 1914 there were still enough draught dogs in Belgium for some thousands to be recruited to carry ammunition and pull light machine guns.

The use of draught dogs spread to other parts of Western Europe. Abraham Fleming tells us of the 'tinckers curre' in 1576: 'With marveilous pacience they beare bigge budgettes fraught with tinckers tooles, and metall meete to mend kettles, porridge pottes, skellets, and chafers, and other such like trumpery requisite for their occupacion and loytering trade, easing him of a great burthen which otherwise he himself should carry upon his shoulders, which condition hath challenged unto them the foresaid name.' In 1820 John Lawrence tells us that a Monsieur Chabert has recently arrived in London from Bath with his great Siberian wolf dog 'which would draw him thirty miles a day in his gig'. Dog-drawn carts took fish from the ports to the railheads at the beginning of the railway age. Some of these were teams of four Newfoundlands and they are reputed to have made Brighton to Portsmouth in a day. Costers went to the races in dog-drawn carts and the children of the well-to-do took the air in chaises drawn by Newfoundlands. This form of transport had its drawbacks. The dogs were noisy and frightened the horses. In 1839 draught dogs were banned within fifteen miles of Charing Cross by the Metropolitan Police as a measure to simplify traffic control. This led to 3000 dogs being destroyed in London alone. Later the practice was banned everywhere in Britain.

Although the Newfoundland achieved almost as much fame as the St Bernard in the nineteenth century as a life saving dog, it was used more for draught purposes in its native land, being expected to take nets and lines from boat to shore and to haul

loads of wood and salt fish. How the breed reached Newfoundland we do not know, although it is possible that the Basque fishermen who settled those coasts may have taken a large mastiff-type dog with them. The dogs reached Britain in the eighteenth century aboard the boats of the cod fishing fleets bringing their catch across the Atlantic to sell it at the southern English ports. The breed became well known not only in its working capacity but also as a companion of the famous. Admiral Collingwood had a Newfoundland called Bounce with him on his flagship at the Battle of Trafalgar. When the Admiral was made a peer, he wrote to his wife: 'I am out of patience with Bounce; the consequential airs he gives himself since he became a right honourable dog are insufferable. He considers it beneath his dignity to play with commoners' dogs. This, I think, is carrying the insolence of rank to the extreme.' Byron also had a famous Newfoundland, Boatswain, for which he wrote a much quoted epitaph carved on the monument raised to the dog at Newstead Abbey. The dogs, however, also continued to be used for their original work, as this extract from a government report on crab and lobster fisheries shows: 'The fishermen of Hall Sands keep four or five Newfoundland dogs for the purpose of carrying lines from the shore to the boats in rough weather. The surf is so heavy in certain winds, that the only possible way of landing is for the boat to be drawn through the surf by the friends of the fishermen on the shore, by means of the lines which the dogs take out to them. The fishermen think it a very great hardship that these dogs should be taxed.'

The early reports about the dogs from the Labrador coast are confusing because there were two quite distinct types both of which were called Newfoundlands by different writers. Blaine's *Encyclopaedia of Rural Sports* published in 1840 says: 'The Spaniel group includes the Setter, the Common Spaniel, the Newfoundland dog and the retriever. The Newfoundland dog is a spaniel much employed in the southern coasts of our kingdom and there appears to be two distinct breeds of them, one from Labrador and another from St Johns. The St Johns breed is to be preferred by the sportsman on every account, being smaller, more easily managed, and sagacious in the extreme. His scenting powers are also very great.' The St John's dog was in

fact the Labrador Retriever as is evidenced by the following eulogy from the diaries of Lieutenant Colonel Peter Hawker. He is lamenting the death of his favourite dog, Tiger, and the date is again about 1840. 'This dog was of the real St Johns breed, quite black with a long head, very fine action and something of an otter skin, not the curly-haired, heavy brute that so often and so commonly disgraces the name of Newfoundland dog. He was just in his prime (three years old) and from his sagacity, attachment, good temper, high courage and as a personal guard, as well as his excellence in the shooting fields, for cover, for the hedgerows, for the marshes and above all for night work with the wild fowl, I may not disgrace the lines of our immortal poet by saying: "Take him all in all, We ne'er shall look upon his like again." '

Retrievers were in fact the last group of gundogs to be developed for a specialized role in the shooting field. It only became necessary to employ dogs for the purpose of picking up dead and wounded game when game preservation was successful enough, and guns accurate enough, to ensure that many sportsmen were able to account for a large number of birds by the end of the day. Shooting flying instead of sitting game only became possible with the production of more sophisticated firearms in the mid-eighteenth century and by the early 1800s all sorts of dogs were being tried out in the shooting field as retrievers, including bloodhounds, mastiffs and sheepdogs. Many experiments were undertaken by sportsmen anxious to get the best types of dog and it seems likely that most of the retriever breeds sprang from fortuitous crosses between different sporting dogs. The frontispiece to a book called *Dog Breaking* published in 1848 and written by General Hutchinson shows various cross-bred dogs listed as 'various retrievers'. The engraving of the water spaniel/Newfoundland cross shows something very similar to the Curly-coat Retriever, a really tough breed that was very popular by the end of the nineteenth century. The following incident taken from the reminiscences of Dr Salter, an eminent Victorian sportsman, shows how hardy both dogs and men were. He was out shooting on ice-covered marshes with a dog called Prince Rupert, 'a big, strong, curly brown retriever'. At the end of the day the dog went out on the ice to fetch a fallen teal and fell through into the freezing water. Rather than watch his dog drown, Dr Salter threw off his coat and managed to crawl out far enough to seize the dog by its topknot and tow it back to shore. 'The dog was apparently dead. Coated with ice, he was an ice-dog–ice all over him in a great, big mass. We had to kick it off him. We carried him down to the decoy house, laid him in front of the fire, gave him brandy, kept rubbing him of course–and he lived for years after.' So incidentally did Dr Salter, who died at the age of 92.

Bearing in mind that the Newfoundland referred to in the illustrations from *Dog Breaking* is probably the St John's dog of Labrador, we get further confirmation that the Flat-coat Retriever resulted from crossing the Newfoundland with a setter. The origin of one of the most popular of modern retrievers, the Golden Retriever, is rather more obscure. These seem to have been developed in the kennels of Lord Tweedmouth who mated an exceptional yellow puppy from a Flat-coat litter to the now extinct Tweed Water Spaniel.

Spaniels are the oldest amongst the gundog breeds. The name is first mentioned in the Irish Laws of AD 17 and spaniels were widely used in the Middle Ages by falconers to find and spring birds for the hawks. They were also used for netting wild birds. The spaniel located the birds on the ground by scent and indicated their position to the huntsman by crouching down, whereupon a net would be drawn over the covey of partridges or whatever was found. Because of the way they crouched, these spaniels were said to 'sett' and were known as 'setting spaniells'. Spaniels were also used to catch duck by the simple and unsporting process of swimming out after fledglings and unflighted adults. The earliest division in the spaniel family is between the land and water spaniels. By 1790, land spaniels were divided into Springers and Cockers, the difference in size rather than breed type being the deciding factor. Springers found and sprang game for the gun. Cockers were rather smaller and used to push out woodcock from the thick undergrowth preferred by this bird. By the second half of the nineteenth century a large number of spaniel varieties were in existence, some of which have prospered and others of which have declined.

The history of the family of water

spaniels, in which we must include the Poodle, is really a mystery. The obvious similarities in type between the Portuguese Water Dog, the Irish Water Spaniel, the American Water Spaniel, and the Poodle, suggest some common early ancestor of which we know little. Possibly it was the Great Rough Water Dog shown in some of the earliest dog illustrations as a large dog covered with loose curls and with typical spaniel ears. A woodcut of 1621 shows 'The Water Dogge' already clipped in the manner of a show Poodle. This clipping was to facilitate swimming. Germany, Russia and France all claim the Poodle as a national breed which suggests that this type of wild fowling dog was widespread at an early date. In 1540 Madame de Bours sent to England for 'poodles for the crossbow and hackbut'. The letter accompanying the one sent back says: 'He is very good at retrieving the head or bolt of a crossbow, both in the water and on land, and will fetch a tennis ball or glove put on the end of a stick, and other tricks.' Pictures by George Stubbs and James Ward show typical Poodles existing in the eighteenth century. The breed by then had already ceased being a gundog and was better known as a companion and a showman's dog. The clipping, originally utilitarian in origin, became more fantastic as the dog became fashionable. Smart owners had their dogs clipped to show the family coat of arms or emblems such as the shamrock.

The pointer family is also widespread and complex, although most of these breeds are believed to have stemmed at least in part from the Spanish Pointer. When Spain was at the height of her power, Spanish hunting methods and Spanish dogs were fashionable throughout Europe and the New World. The Spanish Pointer was a massively built dog with an excellent nose. The work of pointers and setters in the field is to range in great sweeps in front of the sportsman, quartering the ground until they catch the airborne scent of game birds. They then freeze into the classic point which indicates where the birds are lying. Methods vary about the rest of the procedure. Some pointing breeds are expected to flush the birds when the guns have caught up with them. However, some sportsmen flush the birds themselves considering that the pointer's work is done when it has found the sitting game, while many of the continental pointing breeds are expected to point,

flush and retrieve the game after it has been shot.

The various pointer breeds were developed to suit local conditions and local preferences. The Spanish Pointer was a slow working animal, suitable for the time when loading and firing a gun was a lengthy business. As the sporting rifle improved a faster dog was needed. In England Foxhounds were crossed with Pointers to improve the speed of the latter. The effect of this was not all that was desired. Foxhounds hunt with their heads down on a ground scent and some of the improved Pointers did this instead of ranging with head up sampling the air. Many Victorian dog trainers resorted to a device called a puzzle peg when training dogs which showed this fault. The puzzle peg was fastened to the dog's collar in such a way that the sharpened end dug into the dog's chin when it attempted to put its nose to the ground. Selective breeding, however, finally established the English Pointer as one of the fastest and most graceful of the pointing breeds. Economic change then brought the decline of the grouse moors where Pointers are seen at their best. The space needed to appreciate the bird dogs at work is now more often found in America than in England.

Another breed which, like the Poodle, is no longer considered a gundog, is the Dalmatian, which is probably of continental origin. A picture called 'The Hunting Party' by Jan Fyt (1609–1661) shows a group of dogs including spaniels, greyhounds and a dalmatian. The breed may be Italian in origin as it was certainly used as a Papist symbol on the broadsheets of the time of Oliver Cromwell. It is believed to have reached England at the heels of the young gentlemen of quality who had been on the 'Grand Tour' of Europe as a way of finishing their education. Dalmatians became fashionable as coach dogs, first as guards but later as decorative accompaniments to a gentleman's turnout. Some dogs trotted between the wheels under the carriage but others preferred a place under the pole between the lead pair of horses. The gaily spotted appearance of the dog made it popular as a circus performer and it became somewhat of a mascot in the days of horse-drawn fire engines. However it took the Disney film *101 Dalmatians* to rocket it to real public popularity.

So far these breed histories have detailed dogs which were developed to

breed as they have been called by a
variety of names including shock
dogs, Barbichon, Bolognese, Havanese
and Tenerife Dogs. The surviving
modern breeds from this group include
the Maltese, the Lowchen and the
Bichon Frise. In many of the portraits
showing these dogs, such as that of
Dorothy Brereton in 1615, they are
clipped or shaved in a variety of styles
as the fashion of the moment dictated.

Although we cannot trace their
history back so far, by the sixteenth
century Toy Spaniels were equally
popular with ladies of quality. Dr
Caius wrote of these in 1570: 'Of the
delicate, neate, and pretty kind of
dogges called the spaniel gentle, or the
comforter. . . . These are little and
prettie, proper and fine, and sought out
far and neere to satisfie the nice
delicacie of daintie dames; instruments
of follie to plaie and dallie withal in
trifling away the treasure of time . . .
meete playfellowes for mincing
mistresses.' The warmth of these
'comforters' when held close to the
body was supposed to reduce aches and
pains but they also attracted the fleas
that plagued their noble owners. Both
in Europe and the Far East, toy dogs
were used as hot water bottles,
warming the extremities of owners
whose living conditions tended towards
icy splendour.

The earliest pictures of these Toy
Spaniels show them to have been
miniature replicas of the larger
sporting spaniel. They were probably
introduced into England by Henrietta
of Orleans when she married Charles I.
Charles II was particularly fond of
the breed and his statesmen observed
somewhat sourly that he spent more
time playing with his dogs than
attending to the business of his realm.
Because of the royal patronage these
spaniels were called King Charles.
Louis XIV was also fond of Dwarf
Spaniels, many of which were brought
from Spain and Italy to the French
court. Madame de Maintenon spoke
of having ten such spaniels in the
room as she wrote her letters. At this
stage these spaniels all had drooping
ears but a little later a dog with an
upright ear was produced which
became known as the Papillon. In
Britain the King Charles underwent a
great modification. Youatt in 1845
speaks of the new short-nosed type as
an innovation: 'The King Charles
Spaniel of the present day is materially
altered for the worse. The muzzle is
almost as short and the forehead as
ugly and prominent as the veriest

**Above: Small dogs, often white,
with shaggy coats of loose curls
have remained popular from the
time of the Ancient Greeks to the
present day. The surviving modern
breeds include the Maltese.**

perform certain tasks, and it might
therefore be assumed that keeping
dogs solely for the pleasure of their
companionship is a modern
phenomenon. This, however, is far
from the case as many of the toy
breeds have histories as long and as
well documented as the more
utilitarian varieties. Small dogs have
been valued throughout history and,
although scorned by the sportsman,
have been coveted and cosseted
throughout the civilized world.

One of the earliest of the toy breeds
is associated originally with the island
of Malta. There is a vase painting of a
young man walking with a small
long-coated dog which is labelled
Maltese and dates from the fifth
century BC, and there are terracotta
models of the same sort of dog at a
slightly later date. Aelian tells us:
'That they may become small and
remain so, they are shut up in boxes
and fed there. They are fed on the
choicest foods. . . . That they may be
born with shaggey coats their keepers
line the places where they lie with
sheepskins that they may always have
them before their eyes.' And from about
100 BC we have this charming epitaph:

Guard to Eumelus, very true and dear
was this white dog from Malta, says
the stone. We called him Noisy
here; now, far from here, Night's
quiet paths have hushed his every
tone.

Small dogs, often white, with shaggy
coats of loose curls have remained
popular from the time of the Ancient
Greeks to the present day. It seems
unwise to be too dogmatic about the

bull-dog.' This difference in skull shape was probably produced by a Pug cross, and was a great success for the older long-nosed kind became very scarce. In the 1920s an American citizen called Mr Eldridge offered extra prizes at Cruft's dog show for King Charles Spaniels of the original type. British breeders took up the challenge and in a very short space of time recreated the Longer-nosed Dwarf Spaniel which became known as the Cavalier King Charles. So successful were they that this breed is now among the most popular of toy dogs in Britain.

Nearly all the Oriental toy dogs are snub-nosed and, although it seems likely that they are connected, this relationship must be far back in time. The Japanese Chin developed solely in the courts and homes of the Japanese nobility but possibly it reached Japan originally from China, for trade was common between the two countries from the fifth to the seventh century and small dogs are mentioned as presents between the Imperial courts. Robert Fortune described the Japanese dogs in 1863: 'The lap-dogs of the country are highly prized both by natives and by foreigners. They are small–some of them not more than nine or ten inches in length. They are remarkable for snub noses and sunken eyes, and are certainly more curious than beautiful. They are carefully bred; they command high prices even amongst the Japanese; and are dwarfed, it is said, by the use of sake.' In the late nineteenth century as trade expanded between Japan and the Western hemisphere, these dogs were exported in some numbers. An observer notes at the end of the century: 'When a Japanese mail boat arrived at the Circular Quay, Sydney, I used to go aboard and see the already sold Toy Spaniels from overseas. Each dog had its neatly woven wicker cage, the delicacy of the craftsmanship appearing to suit the smallness and the sprightliness of the pet it contained.'

The Japanese, however, never achieved the popularity of the Pekingese, which took America and England by storm. Research reveals that in AD 100 the Chinese were breeding 'pai' dogs, described as short-legged, short-mouthed dogs which belonged under the table. At that time Chinese tables were low and people sat round them on the ground. By the time of Kublai Khan, small golden-coated dogs resembling lions were being bred in Peking. The cult of the lap-dog reached its height in China about 1820 when sleeve dogs, i.e. those small enough to be carried in the wide sleeves of the owner's gowns, were very fashionable. In 1860, French and English troops sacked the Peking Palace and among the loot took five Pekingese, the first to reach the Western world. Another brace were smuggled out from China in 1896 and a few more in the early 1900s. From this handful all the western dogs are descended.

At the beginning of this century three varieties of toy dogs were being bred in the Imperial Palace of Peking. One was a very long-coated lion dog which is now known as the Shih Tzu. These had reached China from Tibet. The second was the Pekingese and the third was a smooth-coated, flat-faced dog called the Happa. When the Portuguese and the Dutch started trading with Canton in the sixteenth century they are believed to have brought some of the latter back home, where they became known as Pugs. These reached England with the court of William and Mary of Orange and became very fashionable, as numerous porcelain models testify. At this stage in their history the whole of the ear was cropped as the pain of the operation was believed to deepen the desirable wrinkles on the dog's forehead. European Pugs became cobbier and more massive than their Eastern counterparts, a fact which became apparent when Lady Brassey imported the first black Pugs from China in the 1880s. The difference in type between these colours was very marked for a number of years.

Written history tends to make the process of domestication and breed development sound a tidy and methodical progression. Nothing could be farther from the case, for many false starts and happy accidents have contributed to the breeds we know today. It is probable that an almost equal number of dog types have become extinct down the centuries, some breeds are verging on extinction now, while others, more fortunate or more adaptable, have caught the public eye and are all set for a spell in the limelight.

Right: A scene from the Bear and Boar Hunting Tapestry dating from the Middle Ages which shows the hunt setting out with the dogs on leads, after the friendly-looking bears in the background.

Hunting to Hounds

N O one really knows how long ago it was that Man first domesticated the dog, but what does seem certain is that the first purpose for which Man used dogs was to help him hunt and kill other animals.

It is likely that Man used dogs to hunt before he actually domesticated them. From early times right up to the present day, falcons have been used for hunting, but they have never been domesticated, and there have been several instances of rat-catchers using tame foxes to help them in their work. It is probable that the first dogs used by Man were orphan cubs taken from the nest and hand-reared. These would have been only too willing to hunt and kill the other animals which at that time were essential for Man's survival.

Having realized their usefulness, Man no doubt bred from these dogs, and naturally he bred selectively, from the best stock – and the best stock to him were the best hunters. As we have already seen, one cannot put an instinct there or take it away, but one can strengthen or weaken it by selective breeding. It is for this reason that all hunting breeds have a stronger hunting instinct than any wild dog. The wild dog only kills what it needs to eat, but once the hunting instinct has been aroused in the domestic dog, it will kill and go on killing, purely for its own sake. There are authentic records of terriers killing incredible numbers of rats; for example, in the early 1820s a terrier called Billy killed 100 rats in little over 5 minutes. Unfortunately there are also records of whole flocks of sheep being killed and maimed by packs of domestic dogs. In this case the hunting instinct has been stimulated by the influence of the pack instinct, and it should always be remembered that it only takes two dogs to form a pack.

One of the remarkable things about the domestic dog is the many different shapes and sizes in which it is to be found. On looking at them, it is hard to believe that all the different breeds, from the tiny Chihuahua to the giant Irish Wolfhound, are descended from an animal whose survival depended on its ability to kill. But it is easy to understand if one studies their behaviour, and many breeds which have not been bred for hunting for centuries still retain a strong hunting instinct.

The majority of those dogs which have been bred specifically to hunt and kill their prey are all the many hounds and terriers. These breeds must form at least half the world's dog population. The hounds can be divided roughly into two groups, those which hunt by scent and those which hunt by sight. The former usually hunt in packs in much the same way as wild dogs, the main difference being that the huntsman is the pack leader.

Although hounds existed in Britain before then, most of today's British and Continental hounds are believed to be descended from a pack of hounds founded by Saint Hubert in the Ardennes in the sixth century. They were brought to England during the Norman Conquest, at the same time as the Talbot Hounds and Bloodhounds, both of which were descended from the original Saint Hubert Hounds. The Saint Hubert Hound and the Talbot are now extinct, but the Bloodhound has survived practically unchanged. Originally used to hunt such animals as deer and boars, it was found that Bloodhounds also had an extraordinary ability to track human beings. There are many records of their use (usually successful) in the days of Border fighting between Scotland and England. Today the Bloodhound is used, usually singly and on a tracking line, almost exclusively to track people, although they are sometimes also hunted in packs with mounted followers. They are used by prison authorities in many parts of the world, their task being to track down escaped criminals. Contrary to common belief, Bloodhounds do not attack their quarry and indeed usually greet him like a long-lost friend, slobbering all over him. Because of this, they are usually hunted on a tracking line so that their handler can keep up with them. Once on the track, the dog must ignore all other tracks, human or animal. Here the Bloodhound has no equal, and it is not uncommon for one to pick up a track several days old and stick to it, even when it has been crossed by several fresh tracks.

Apart from its terrific scenting abilities, the Bloodhound also excels in tone of voice, another characteristic handed down from the Saint Hubert Hound. When hounds are hunting loose, it is essential that they give tongue, otherwise they would be lost from their handler as soon as they went out of sight. But to the true huntsman the Bloodhound's call means far more than that. He talks of the 'music of hounds', which excites horses just as much as it does men. And there is no music to surpass the deep melodious tones of the Bloodhound in full cry. This very asset, however, is one of the main reasons why Bloodhounds are only used to a very limited extent by the police. They want a dog which will work quietly and which will, if necessary, pursue and capture the criminal. Working trials are held for Bloodhounds and there are also classes for them at the larger shows, so their unique tracking ability is likely to be preserved.

Man has retained his natural hunting instinct just as much as the dog, and long after it was necessary for him to hunt for food he continued, and still continues, to hunt for sport, often using hounds to help him. Stag hunting with packs of hounds was for centuries the most popular sport of the nobility throughout Britain, France and most other European countries. Many breeds and strains of hounds were crossed

Left: A Foxhound pack in kennels.

Right: The Devon and Somerset Staghounds.

Overleaf: The Suffolk Foxhounds.

Right: The Peak Bloodhounds.

Opposite page: The Waveney Harriers.

in an effort to produce dogs with better and better hunting ability. At first big, strong hounds were in favour, and as they often hunted in thick forest the ability to stick to a line was more important than speed. Then, as the forests were cleared to make room for agricultural land, a lighter, faster hound gradually developed. Today there is comparatively little staghunting, mainly because there are fewer deer, not because they have been reduced by hunting but simply because Man has removed much of their natural habitat. For the modern huntsman, the stag has been replaced by the fox.

Although there are records of foxes being hunted as far back as the thirteenth century, it was not until the mid-eighteenth century that foxhunting became a popular sport. Until then the fox was regarded as vermin, to be killed in any way possible. The first Foxhounds were bred from the Staghounds in existence at the time. They became smaller, lighter and faster than the Staghounds and great detail was, and still is, paid to breeding. Some packs have records going back to the early 1700s and the Master of Foxhounds Association has kept a stud book since 1880. That does not mean there is only one correct type of Foxhound. In open country where the followers can gallop across grassland on fast horses, hounds are required to set the pace. But in wooded country where there is rarely an opportunity to gallop far in the open, hounds are needed to stick to a line (often crossed by other foxes, deer and people) and to give tongue so that the huntsman knows where they are.

Hounds from different packs are consequently often quite different in appearance, but at the same time the hounds within one pack are remarkably alike. Although new blood is continually being introduced to any pack of hounds, a great effort is made to preserve its own type. Even colour is taken into account; while some packs are all black and tan with no white markings, others are predominantly white with only very light markings.

The main type of Foxhound is the English Foxhound, which is also the type generally found in Scotland and Ireland. There is also a Welsh Foxhound, which has a rough coat. The history of this breed seems to be lost in the dim past, but it appears certain that it is older than any of the other British hounds. The Welsh Foxhound's admirers even claim that it is descended from the original hounds of Gaul. It is noted for its good voice, tenacity and general toughness.

Not surprisingly, packs of Foxhounds have been established in America, Australia, New Zealand and many other countries. These were originally formed from importations of British and French stock and closely resemble the English Foxhounds. In America, one finds English *and* American Foxhounds. The American Foxhound is really a separate strain of the English Foxhound, suited to the country in which it hunts. In England the crime of all crimes for any foxhunter is to shoot a fox, but in some parts of America the foxhunter carries a gun and uses two or three 'foxdogs' to flush the fox out of cover, rather like a spaniel flushing game.

The history of hare hunting goes back to 350 BC, long before foxhunting and possibly even before staghunting. Harriers with mounted followers are used to hunt the hare. The history of some of the English packs goes back much further than that of Foxhounds but, like Foxhounds, the breed has been evolved from a mixture of various types of hounds. Even today there are several types of Harrier. To the layman they look like small Foxhounds and, in fact, undersized hounds are sometimes drafted from Foxhound to Harrier packs and some Harriers are used to hunt the fox as well as the hare.

The origin of the Beagle is not quite clear, but Xenophon, writing in 350 BC, described hare hunting with small hounds which sound very much like the Beagle of today. The Romans probably brought some of these Greek hounds with them to Britain and it was in Britain that the breed and the sport of beagling developed. But it was not until the reign of Henry VII that we find any further writing on the subject.

The present-day Beagle in many ways resembles a small Foxhound. Beagles vary in height from about 25–40 cm (10–16 ins), but most of the hunting packs have hounds ranging from 37–38 cm (14½–15 ins). This is big enough to catch a hare, but small enough to be followed on foot. Most are smooth-coated but the Welsh Beagle, like its Foxhound counterpart, has a rough wiry coat. The Beagle has a very good nose and 'packs' well, in other words the pack will stay together without straggling.

There is much less pomp and ceremony about beagling than there is in foxhunting. To many foxhunters, much of the enjoyment lies in turning out in style on a well-groomed horse, but to a beagler the main object is to watch the hounds working. One has to be very keen – and fit – to run across bogs and moors in all sorts of weather, but many beaglers do just that.

In Canada and America the Beagle has become even more popular than in its native country, and the American Kennel Club registers more than 60,000 of the breed each year. Sometimes they hunt in packs to run down their quarry, the cottontail rabbit, but they are used more extensively in conjunction with guns, when their job is to push the rabbit out into the open. Their good voices enable the hunters to know when they pick up a trail, and whether the quarry is approaching or going away. In England small packs of Beagles are also sometimes used in the same way.

The Beagle has also become popular as a show and pet dog on both sides of the Atlantic. It is a smart-looking little dog, easy to keep clean and look after, but unfortunately not always so easy to train. Several small 'pocket' Beagles have been imported from America, but in fact these miniatures were not developed there. In the *Sportsman's Encyclopedia*, published in 1830, we find the following: 'and as to the very smallest distinguished by the name of lapdog beagle, though they are very pretty in appearance, and may occasionally kill a hare, yet ultimate satisfaction cannot be expected from their exertions'.

The Basset is a very old breed which has been popular for centuries on the Continent, particularly in France. It was originally used to hunt wild boar, deer and wolves. There are several different types,

some with quite straight legs and some with very crooked legs, some with smooth coats and some with rough. All bear a strong resemblance to the Bloodhound in shape of head, voice and scenting ability.

The first Bassets were not introduced to Britain until 1866, when the Marquis of Tourman presented a pair to Lord Galway. They quickly became popular as show dogs and among their many distinguished breeders was the late Queen Alexandra who kept both rough- and smooth-coated Basset breeds. There were many importations at that time, the smooths being of the low, crooked-legged variety (*Basset à jambes tortues*) and the roughs of the half-crooked kind (*Basset à jambes semi-tortues*). For some reason, the Basset Griffon Vendéen never became popular and most of the Bassets shown today in Britain and America are of the smooth variety.

It was not until 1884 that Bassets were first used for hunting hare in Britain and, although a few packs have been in existence since then, they have never become nearly as popular as the Beagle. This is probably because they are much more independent dogs and do not hunt so well as a pack. Nevertheless, they are terrific hunters and the music of a pack of Bassets in full cry is worth going a long way to hear. In America and in Europe the Basset is used more as a gun dog, to find and push game out of thick cover.

Bassets have great character and their appearance is often deceptive. They are not soulful, quiet or lazy dogs, indeed they are probably the toughest and most persistent of all the scenting hounds. Once a Basset gets its nose onto a line, it is oblivious to everything else and some have even been known to hunt until they dropped dead from exhaustion. They are also much bigger and more powerful dogs than people imagine. Though only 30–38 cm (12–15 ins) at the shoulder they weigh up to 22.5 kg (50 lbs), about twice the weight of a Beagle of the same height. Because of its very short legs the Basset is not very fast for its size, but this can also be deceptive, as many owners of wayward Bassets can testify! Its lack of speed is compensated for by sheer courage and determination, which make it crash its way through the thickest gorse or thorn, water or bog.

Otterhunting is a very old sport in Britain, the first known Master of Hounds being King Henry II. Queen Elizabeth I also had a pack of Otterhounds and was probably the first lady Master of Hounds. Many other members of the Royal Family hunted the otter, the last being Charles II. In appearance the Otterhound resembles a rough-coated Bloodhound and in some ways it also resembles the Welsh Foxhound. Its colour varies from black to light grey and from red to pale fawn. There are no white markings but the colours are often mixed. for example, black and tan, grey and fawn. and so on.

Otters of up to 16 kg (35 lbs) have been recorded, and even when much smaller than this the animal is a very formidable enemy. As well as its razor-sharp slashing teeth, it has powerful claws which can inflict very severe injuries. Otters are very agile on land, and even more agile in the water, so an Otterhound must be tough, really tough. It may have to swim for hours on end and it may have to stand shivering on the riverbank for equally long periods. And when the hound does come to grips with the otter, it will not be able to kill it with one snap like it would a fox or a hare. Like the badger, the otter has a tough skin and will fight to the bitter end, often inflicting severe injuries on its adversary. Otters have sadly become very scarce in Britain, as a result of which very few packs of Otterhounds remain. Those which do seldom consist entirely of Otterhounds, being mixed with drafted Foxhounds, Staghounds and crosses between all three.

Now we come to the hounds which hunt by sight – the Gazehounds, as they are sometimes called. These dogs were bred to hunt a wide variety of quarry in open country where it could easily be seen. Instead of following the trail by scent. they could see their quarry and simply streaked after it. Speed and determination consequently became the number one priority. Stamina was also necessary, but obviously the very fast dog which could catch a hare in 500 m (550 yds) needed a lot less stamina than a slower dog which had to pursue it for 1,000 m (1,100 yds).

Above: The Taw Vale Beagles.

Right: Many more Beagles are now kept as pets than for their original role as hunters.

The history of the Greyhound goes back much further than that of the hounds which hunt by scent, and it is much more authentic. This is not so much because these hounds have been used by Man for a longer period, but simply because they originated in the East where history itself goes back much further. Several types of Greyhound were in existence thousands of years ago, the only real differences being in the coat and the shape of the ears. Otherwise the physical structures were almost identical, which is not so surprising when one considers that they were all bred for the same purpose – speed. Egyptian monuments show hunting scenes over 4,000 years ago, in the days of the Pharaohs, with hounds exactly as we find them today. The very first treatise on any breed of dog was written by Arrian at the beginning of the Christian era. Not only does he describe the dogs then as being very similar to the Greyhounds we know today, he also describes coursing which sounds almost identical to that practised right up to the present time. In particular, he stressed the point that the killing of the hare was unimportant; the object was to test the speed and skill of one dog against another.

In Britain the Greyhound has been written about and mentioned in the Laws of the Land since the days of Canute. In 1610 there was a law stating that 'No meane person may keep any Greyhounds', and before Magna Carta the punishment for killing a Greyhound was the same as for murdering a man. Until quite recent times the keeping of a Greyhound was a very important status symbol. A government proclamation made at Sydney, Australia, in 1804 ordered the destruction of all dogs 'except greyhounds and sheepdogs'.

Elizabeth I was very keen on coursing and in 1776 the first public coursing match was held at Swaffham in Norfolk. In 1836 the first Waterloo Cup Meeting was held at Altcar near Liverpool, and this is still regarded in the same esteem as the Derby in horse racing. In 1858 the National Greyhound Coursing Club was founded in Britain and drew up strict rules for the sport. The Greyhound Stud Book was started in 1882 and all Greyhounds have to be registered in it if they are to compete at recognized coursing matches in Britain. During the nineteenth century attempts were made to popularize coursing in enclosed grounds. The hare was released at one end of a long enclosure, which had an

Above: A Bassett Griffon Vendéen.

**Left: The Dumfriesshire Otterhounds,
one of the few packs consisting
entirely of the old type of rough-
coated hound.**

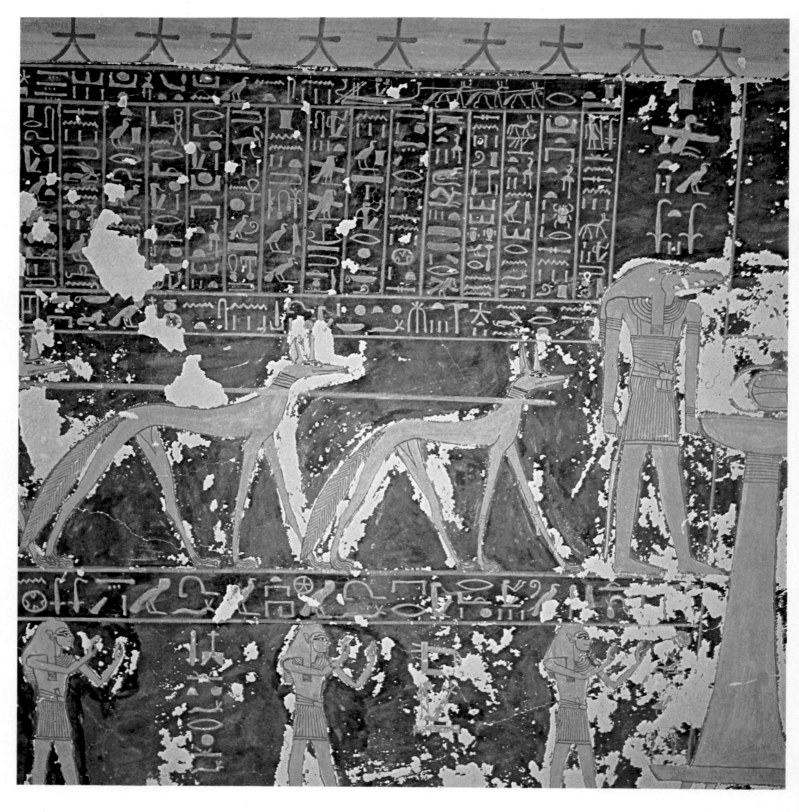

Above: A wall painting from the tomb of Ramasses VI in the Valley of Kings in Egypt, showing hunting dogs built on very similar lines to the present-day Greyhound.

Opposite page: A racing Greyhound in action on the track at Wembley Stadium.

escape hole at the other end. This was simply a test of speed, as the dogs either caught the hare before it reached the hole or it escaped. If they turned the hare before it reached the hole, it would be completely lost with no chance of escape. This method never became popular in England, although it is still used in Ireland, and is now against the rules of the National Coursing Club. It is also illegal in Britain to offer any captive wild animal to dogs for them to chase and/or kill.

Coursing in Britain, Spain, Australia and other Commonwealth countries is conducted on very similar lines, with two dogs competing against each other in heats. Each brace is put into 'slips', which are two collars attached to each other by a long lead with a special mechanical device incorporated. When a handle is pulled, both

dogs are released simultaneously and the collars fall to the ground. The 'slipper', a highly skilled expert, takes the two competing dogs and walks with them slightly ahead of the 'field' (spectators), which stretches out in a straight line on either side of him. When a hare gets up, the slipper hangs on to the dogs (by now going mad with excitement) until the hare has had sufficient 'lay', or start. The hare needs about 75 m (82 yds) start to give it time to get into its stride before the dogs are released. It is here that the slipper's expertise comes in; two young dogs would never catch up with a strong hare if it had that much start, but on the other hand two experienced dogs would kill a weaker hare without any chance to test their real ability. The judge follows behind the dogs mounted on horseback.

The first recorded Greyhound race using an artificial hare was held in Britain in 1867, in a field at Hendon, north of London. Surprisingly enough, it did not catch on, although the inaugural meeting appears to have been popular and well-attended. In 1890 the Americans made another attempt to popularize the idea, on the horse-race track at Miami. Again it failed to receive support and it was not until 1909 that the first successful track opened at Tucson, Arizona. In 1926 an American, Charles Mann, successfully introduced the new sport to Britain and the first track was opened at Belle Vue, Manchester. In 1928 the British National Greyhound Racing Club was formed and in America there is the National Coursing Association. Greyhound racing has since become one of the most popular sports in Britain, America,

Australia and many other countries. It is often described as the 'working man's racing', but it is also patronized by the rich and the aristocracy, though perhaps not to such a great extent as coursing.

In evolving the Greyhound, Man has bred for performance and performance only. Although individual breeders had preferences for different colours and types, the dog that was used for breeding was primarily the one with the greatest speed and agility. It was left to Nature to decide what the dog should look like, and fortunately the result is aesthetically pleasing as well as fast. No breed of dog is more beautifully balanced or more symmetrical than a Greyhound. Streamlined from the tip of its nose to the tip of its tail, it is as superb a racing machine as the racehorse which has been bred on the same lines – for performance rather than appearance. A Greyhound travelling somewhere in the region of 50 km/h (31 mph) can pick up a hare without stopping or losing balance. With the aid of its long sinuous neck and strong jaws, it will break the back of its quarry and kill it more quickly than any man-made device. The old adage about a good horse never being a bad colour is also true of the Greyhound, which can be found in practically every canine colour from pure white to pure black. We find reds, fawns and blues, either whole-coloured or with white markings and brindles.

This beautiful animal has found many admirers who want to show it, and classes at the leading dog shows are quite well filled. But the standard is what Man thinks the perfect specimen should look like, and we have never heard of a winner in the showring which was also successful in the coursing field. As a pet and companion, the Greyhound can be very good or very bad. In the home it is very affectionate, intelligent and quite easy to train. Its short coat carries little mud, and in spite of its size it can curl up in a remarkably small space. But out of the house it can become an entirely different animal. Its highly developed – often over-developed – hunting instinct completely overrules any training the dog has had, and many cats and small dogs have been killed by Greyhounds.

It is easy to obtain adult Grehounds from race tracks which are either too old or too slow for racing. There are a number of societies constantly trying to find homes for these dogs. Some of them have been reared on farms where, as puppies, they were familiarized with and taught not to chase poultry, cats and so on. Provided they are treated sensibly and given sufficient exercise, these dogs will usually settle down and make delightful pets. But some have never had any individual attention and the only instinct that really mattered to them was the hunting instinct. Suddenly taken out of its familiar environment, such a dog will often chase and kill anything that moves.

Another coursing breed which looks very much like a small Greyhound is the Whippet. A hundred years or so ago the breed was hardly known outside the north of England and the Midlands. There the miners used them as rabbiting dogs and later started to race them to 'the rag', usually over a course of 200 yds (183 m) which the dogs frequently covered in 12 seconds. Today they are still coursed and raced, but they are also very popular as pet dogs and in the show ring.

A fit Whippet is a beautifully balanced little dog, combining elegance and grace with muscular power and strength, and moving over the ground like a Thoroughbred. Its short, easily cared-for coat, gentle nature and adaptable temperament make it an ideal companion in either town or country, but remember this is a dog which really needs to stretch its legs and a daily run is a must if you want a fit, mentally alert pet.

There seems to be no authentic history as to when the Deerhound first reached Scotland or where it came from, and it is often very difficult to differentiate between legend and history. The English historian Holinshed tells how certain Pictish nobles went hunting with Crainlint, King of the Scots, and found that his hounds were much better than their own. The King duly presented some of his hounds to them, but he was careful to keep his best hound, the one the Picts really wanted. So they stole it and a bloody battle ensued, resulting in the death of 'sixty Scott gentlemen' and over a hundred Picts. Another famous story about the breed tells of the hounds Help and Hold, which belonged to Sir William St Clare in the days of King Robert the Bruce. Apparently Sir William was given to boasting about the abilities of these hounds, while the King had no hounds worth boasting about. So the King issued a challenge that they should pull down a 'white faunch deer' on Pentland Moor, not far from Edinburgh. 'Pentland Moor is yours if your hounds hold her and your head is off if they lose her' was the ultimatum. There must have been considerable excitement all round and some misgivings in the mind of Sir William when the stag jumped into the march burn, the stream forming the boundary of the moor. But Help and Hold plunged into the water and pulled the stag down before it reached the other side. Thus Sir William kept his head and gained the whole of Pentland Moor as well.

The old writers refer to the Deerhound as the Scottish Greyhound or Highland Greyhound and it is more than likely that they were originally the same breed but that a strain of big, strong, hairy dogs was developed to hunt the deer and a smooth, smaller strain to hunt the hare. Not surprisingly, the one developed in Scotland where deer were plentiful and the other in England where hares were plentiful.

At one time great deer drives took place, with Highland chieftains killing enormous numbers of deer. These hunts decreased with the reduction in the number of deer and the advent of sheepfarming, and ended altogether with the introduction of the rifle. When stalking first started, Deerhounds were used regularly to pursue wounded deer, but this practice has largely died out and very few, if any, are kept for that purpose today. Although they have been used in many parts of the world to

Above left: An Ibizan Hound on its native island.

Above: A stalker in Sutherland with his Deerhound.

Opposite page, left: Salukis playing on a sandy beach. They seem unable to resist the urge to gallop at full speed on sand.

Opposite page, right: A pair of long-limbed Whippets.

hunt boar, wolves and many other animals, the breed has never become very strong numerically. It was one of Queen Victoria's favourite breeds and this helped to revive it at a time when its numbers had become very low. It gained popularity not so much as a hunting dog, but as a companion and a status symbol. Because of its size, the breed does not fit very well into modern city life and is unlikely ever to become very popular today, but for anyone who wants a handsome dog and has the room to keep it the Deerhound makes a staunch, devoted companion.

Hare coursing matches are held for Deerhounds in Scotland and England. It is interesting to note that nearly all competitors are also breeders and that nearly all the winning hounds are also winners in the show ring, in marked contrast to the show Greyhound.

The history of the Saluki goes back further and with more authenticity than that of any other breed of dog. Carvings and paintings have been found in Egyptian tombs dating back to 5–6000 BC, depicting animals exactly like the present-day Saluki. Quite a number of mummified bodies have been found in the tombs of kings, showing not only its ancient lineage but also the high esteem in which it was held.

To the Arab all dogs are unclean, but to him the Saluki is not a dog. Like his horse it is his most treasured possession, sharing his tent, his food and in fact his whole life. Even today an Arab sheik visiting a Western country and meeting a Saluki will often bow to the hound before shaking hands with the owner. Neither the dogs nor the bitches are ever allowed to mate with any other breed, and there have been instances of bitches refusing to allow any dogs near them except other Salukis. Like Arab horses, the ancestry of some of them can be traced back over thousands of years.

The Saluki has been used to course the swift gazelle since before the days of the Pharaohs, and still is used for that purpose. The sheik and his retinue rode on Arab stallions and the servants walked with the hounds. Falcons were often used to locate the gazelle, although they could not kill it. When the falcon could be seen hovering above its quarry, the Salukis would be released. Even today's Salukis, generations removed from desert stock, will spot a bird (or a plane) in the sky long before it is visible to human eyes.

Salukis were never sold, only given as presents to special friends, which is perhaps why they took so long to reach the West. In 1895 a brace of puppies was given to Lady Florence Amhurst, but it was not until 1920, when Major-General Lance and Mr Vereker-Cowley imported several from Egypt and Mesopotamia, that the breed began to establish itself in England. It was officially recognized by the British Kennel Club in 1923.

Built on the same lines as the Greyhound and for the same purpose, the Saluki is adorned with beautiful silky feathering on its legs, ears and tail. This breaks up the hard, clean utility lines of the Greyhound and to most people presents a much more beautiful animal. If the Greyhound is the utility model, the Saluki must be the de luxe.

To own a Saluki is different from owning any other dog. Just to see it walk across the room so lightly that it hardly seems to touch the ground is quite fascinating. It resents strangers, but in an aloof and gentlemanly way. It is very intelligent, but often uses this intelligence to do what it wants, rather than what its owner wants.

An excellent guard, the haughty Saluki is much tougher than its looks imply, and it can withstand wet weather and extremes of hot and cold much better than the Greyhound.

The big weakness of the Saluki as a pet is its strong hunting instinct, developed over thousands of years. It is usually very little trouble with cats, chickens and other domestic animals, but if it sees a small object in the distance which might be a hare or rabbit, it's off! The farther away it is, the more fascinating it seems to be. To see one of these beautiful animals galloping at full speed across a wide open space is a very thrilling experience, but not always convenient at the time, even though you can be sure that if you stay in the same place, it will always return.

Some people regard the Sloughi (pronounced 'Sloogi') as a smooth variety of Saluki, and it is probable that some of the desert tribes (particularly in North Africa) favoured this type and developed it separately. Although it has only recently been recognized in England and is still unrecognized in America, the breed was recognized in Holland in 1898 and is popular as a show dog in the Low Countries and Scandinavia. The English imports have come from Holland and Sweden.

The Afghan Hound also bears a strong resemblance to the Saluki, which could indicate that at one time Salukis were taken from Egypt to Afghanistan, or it could simply mean that two breeds bred for similar purposes have developed similar characteristics. Dogs very like the Afghans of today are to be found on rock carvings in the caverns of Balkh in north-east Afghanistan, dating back to 2000 BC. Folklore claims that this is the breed which Noah took with him in the Ark and, whether or not this is so, it is obviously a very old and pure breed. Found all along the borders of northern India, the Afghan is a hunting dog suited to the very difficult terrain of this area. It has been used to hunt leopards, wolves, boars, antelopes, mountain goats, and so on, and it is doubtful if any other breed of dog could leap from boulder to boulder and scramble up sheer rock faces like an Afghan. It can jump like a cat and, although not quite as fast as a Greyhound, has a remarkable turn of speed on the flat. The long shaggy coat (never as long in working dogs as in show ones) protects the Afghan from intense cold, thorny bushes, rocks and sometimes from its quarry.

The Afghan is one of the few hounds still kept primarily to hunt, and it is also used as a guard dog. In their native country, Afghans are left out at night to guard the flocks, and they have also been used as guard dogs at military border posts.

It seems strange that a dog with such a background should end up adorning a plush flat in London or New York, or to be used as an accoutrement to the dress of some elegant fashion model. Most Afghans seem to accept this mode of life with quiet disdain, but there are some which show their resentment in no uncertain manner.

A pair of 'Afghan Barukzy Hounds' were exhibited in London in 1895, but it was not until Captain John Barff imported Zerdin from Afghanistan in 1907 that the breed started to make headway in England. In 1926 it received official recognition from the British Kennel Club and has gained in popularity ever since both as a show dog and a companion.

There is something quite fascinating about the Afghan, and it is not really surprising that many people buy one who do not really have the facilities to keep it properly. As one would expect from its background, the Afghan is really a very tough dog. A great character and very intelligent, it can be trained to a very high standard, but it is also very dominant – a leader rather than a follower – and only certain people possess the necessary willpower and determination to train it, let alone the time and energy needed to keep its exotic coat well-groomed or to give it sufficient exercise.

Two very similar hounds which have recently become known in the show ring are the Pharaoh Hound and the Ibizan Hound. Both belong to the ancient Greyhound breed, and drawings of dogs very like the Pharaoh Hounds are to be found in Egyptian temples dating back to 4000 BC.

The Ibizan Hound comes from the island of Ibiza in the Balearics, and is also to be found on the other Balearic islands. It is a useful, medium-sized hound, very active and intelligent, and hunts by scent as much as by sight. In their native islands Ibizan Hounds are used to hunt partridge, hare and rabbit as well as larger game. They retrieve and point and are sometimes hunted in packs as well as singly. Although usually thought of as smooth-coated, these hounds can be wire- or long-coated, the long coat being really a rough coat.

Both these breeds have rather long, lean heads with erect ears. The Ibizan can be red and white, tawny or whole-coloured. The Pharaoh is chestnut and white or tan and white, preferably with a white tip to the tail. Both are friendly, attractive dogs and make good companions for anyone wanting a day's rabbiting in the country.

Another breed which may seem oddly classified as a hound is the Dachshund, but not if we remember that it belongs to the Teckel group which is popular throughout

Overleaf: Hound trailing is a sport confined to the Lake District in the north-west of England. It is nevertheless extremely popular and indeed could be described as an obsession with many of its followers. The hounds used are of pure Foxhound descent and have been bred exclusively for tracking for many generations. The trail is laid by dragging along it a piece of sacking soaked in a mixture of aniseed and paraffin. This provides a powerful enough smell for the dogs to follow the trail for up to 10 miles (16 km) racing flat out.

Germany and Austria as a hunting dog. There are several different types of Teckel, some quite small and others as large as a Basset, to which breed they were probably related in the past.

There are six varieties of Dachshund – long-haired, smooth-haired and wire-haired in standard sizes, and the same varieties in miniature. The ideal weight of the Miniature Dachshund is under 4.5 kg (10 lbs). Queen Victoria's husband, Prince Albert, brought several of the breed from Germany when he came to England. They very quickly caught on in England and soon afterwards in America.

In German, Dachshund means 'badger dog' and all Dachshunds are essentially sporting dogs, with excellent scenting powers and plenty of courage. Long and low, with a bold carriage, intelligent expression and lively character, they are now very popular as pets and in the show ring, but are not used to any great extent as workers outside their native country, which is rather a pity. Most Dachshunds are very determined little characters and, whilst by no means unintelligent, are not always too willing to co-operate. They come in a great variety of colours. The smooth-coated ones tend to feel the cold and will appreciate a warm jacket on a cold winter's day.

Last but definitely not least among the hounds is the Irish Wolfhound, the tallest dog in the world. At one time the breed nearly became extinct, but it is now numerically quite strong. Legend has it that the Irish hero Fionn mae Cumwell had an aunt who was turned into a hound by her enemy. Fionn managed to get her restored to human form but was not successful with her twin children, born when she was a hound. These two, Bran and Sceolaun, became his devoted companions – and the first Irish Wolfhounds. At one time they were used to hunt and kill wolves, which were so prevalent in Ireland in the 1650s that Oliver Cromwell forbade the export of Wolfhounds. Today there are no more wolves to hunt and, standing about 90 cm (35 ins) high and weighing over 45 kg (100 lbs), Wolfhounds are not the fastest of hounds after hare. For someone who can spare the room to house them, the money to feed them and the time and space to exercise them, they make devoted, gentle companions. And, although far from aggressive, they make excellent guards, their majestic size and dark eyes peering out from shaggy brows being enough to put off any intruder.

Left: A Borzoi on the track of game.

Opposite page, centre: Dachshunds rarely lose their sporting instincts, even when they have been kept as pets for several generations. They relish any opportunity to go to ground – or partly to ground.

Opposite page, bottom: This laughing Dachshund has obviously enjoyed its digging.

Below: An Irish Wolfhound on the shores of its native country.

Gun Dogs

MAN has used the dog's hunting instinct yet again by developing gun dogs for use in the shooting field. When a wild dog catches its prey, it very often picks it up and carries it back to its den or some other place of safety. This behaviour forms the basis of the retrieving instinct, which has persisted in a lesser or greater degree in the majority of dogs right up to the present day.

The hunting instinct enables a dog to hunt for game in cover often inaccessible to Man, who in any case does not have any 'nose'. But the gun dog must not catch or even pursue its quarry; instead it must stop dead in its tracks and watch its master shoot the prize. This requires a great deal of self-control in the dog, which has to be developed by careful training. Unlike the Greyhound, which is completely out of its handler's control the moment the slips are released, the gun dog must hunt with enthusiasm but still be under restraint, and this is only possible when the submissive instinct is strong enough to balance the hunting instinct.

Gun dogs can be divided into various kinds, used for different jobs in the shooting field. Some flush out the game, some point or set, and others retrieve the shot game. Some modern breeds, noticeably the European gun dogs, have been specially bred as 'pointer/retrievers' and will tackle most jobs involved in the course of shooting.

Gun dogs, as such, have only been in use since the invention of guns and gunpowder. One of the earliest books to describe them was *An Essay on Shooting*, published in 1789. In a chapter on 'Instructions for Training Pointers', the writer (anonymous) says 'there are three species of dog capable of receiving proper instructions and of being trained. These are the Smooth Pointer, the Spaniel and the Rough Pointer. The last is a dog with long curled hair and seems to be a mixed breed of the water dog and the spaniel, but in general is proper only for open country.' Another early gun dog book, Blaine's *Encyclopedia of Rural Sports* published in 1840, tells us that 'the spaniel group includes the Setter, the Common Spaniel, the Newfoundland dog and the Retriever; the whole of which there is much reason to

Right: A Wire-haired Pointing Griffon retrieving. This dual-purpose breed both points and retrieves the game.

believe are derived from the eastern hunting dogs of scent.'

Depending on what the shooting man of today needs, there is a wide range of gun dogs to choose from. For one or two sportsmen engaged in rough shooting, the best choice is probably a spaniel, such as the large versatile English Springer. But members of a syndicate, where beaters are employed to drive the game, might well have retrievers which wait quietly until given the order to retrieve the shot or wounded birds. Pointers and setters need plenty of open space where they can range out and find the game, indicating its position by coming up on 'point'.

It is often said that the spaniel originated from Spain, but this is by no means certain. There is, however, a nice legend as to how it got its name. When the Carthaginians landed in Spain, the first thing they saw were hundreds of rabbits scurrying from bush to bush. So the soldiers all shouted '*span, span*' which in their language meant 'rabbit'. The country was consequently named Hispania, or Rabbitland, and the dogs used for hunting the rabbits were called spaniels. By the beginning of the nineteenth century, four varieties of spaniel were known, the large and small Water Spaniel and the large and small Land Spaniel. The large Land Spaniel probably became the Field Spaniel and the small one the Cocker Spaniel. In the early

1800s, Lord Rivers spoke of having a well-known strain of black and white 'Cocking Spaniel', the Duke of Norfolk had a larger strain which made 'very good Springers' and the Duke of Newcastle owned a Clumber Spaniel.

At the early dog shows, the spaniel classes were considerably confused and it was not until 1901 that the British Kennel Club began to sort them out into various types. Usually when anyone thinks of a spaniel, it is the little Cocker that springs to mind. Its job in the shooting field is to flush the game from thick cover. It is usually a fast, willing worker, with a very good nose, and can often be taught to retrieve as well. But few Cockers are big enough to lift a large hare and many shooting men prefer the larger Springer. As a companion, if not allowed to indulge its healthy appetites or become lazy, the Cocker is a happy, cheerful little chap, always ready to go for a walk or play games. Most are usually very good guards, and some can even be a bit too keen if not kept in check. One drawback of the Cocker as a housedog is its coat, which does bring in mud and dirt and needs a lot of attention if it is not to become matted. But if you are prepared to spend some time and trouble, you will be rewarded with a smart as well as cheerful pet, and you can take your choice of colours as Cockers come in nearly as many colours as the rainbow.

The American Cocker varies in several respects from the English Cocker. Both types are shown in both countries and the American Cocker is now making great headway in Britain. The American dog is smaller than the English, has a shorter muzzle and comes in almost as many colours as the English Cocker. It is distinguished by a long, profuse coat which usually touches the ground. These Cockers seem to be very friendly, active little dogs. but not over-renowned for their prowess in the shooting field, where their heavy coat is hardly an asset. It is quite an art to present them well in the show ring and even the pet dog will need a good deal of knowledgeable grooming.

There are also two types of Springer Spaniel, the English and the Welsh. The English has the reputation of being the ideal rough shooter's dog and a good all-rounder. Most are natural retrievers and hunters, like the water, and are tough dogs which take a lot of tiring. They are larger than the Cocker, weighing up to 22 kg (50 lbs), which tends to make them slightly slower in the field. They can be liver and white, liver, tan and white, or black and white, and being fairly high in the leg with not overlong ears do not carry too much

Left: Two alert Brittany Spaniels.

Below: A Welsh Springer Spaniel, trimmed more for show than for work.

mud around with them. They are still docked, but the working strains usually have more tail left on than the show dogs, the gun dog owner liking to see a bit of 'flag' waving when his dog is working in the field.

The Welsh Springer differs quite a lot from its English cousin. Always a rich red and white, it is smaller and its ears are not so long. It is a strong, active dog, and a very keen worker, although some tend to get rather over-excited. In spite of this, Welsh Springers are very good game-finders with plenty of stamina.

The Clumber Spaniel is rather unlike the other spaniels, more so today than it was 100 years ago. Unfortunately the modern show dogs have become very heavy and big-boned, apt to tire easily when working in rough country. Never a fast worker, the Clumber was at one time very popular in the shooting field; it had a reputation for being very easy to train and for being a good, steady, reliable worker. Before the First World War, these dogs were often trained to work as a team, doing the work that human beaters usually do nowadays. Two of the team would be trained to retrieve, so that when a bird was shot the two chosen would go out on command and fetch back the shot birds, the rest of the team remaining behind. Present-day Clumbers weigh up to 31·5 kg (70 lbs) with massive heads. They are seldom seen working, which in view of their history is rather a shame. Clumbers have never been very popular as pets, probably because of their rather heavy appearance. Their colouring is white, with occasional lemon markings.

Above: The Irish Water Spaniel is not seen much today, but it is a tough, hard-working dog, especially in the water.

Opposite page, top: The Sussex Spaniel, one of the more rare spaniel breeds today.

Opposite page, bottom: These two Cocker Spaniels seem great friends.

Although popular in the early part of this century, both Sussex and Field Spaniels are now relatively rare. In 1946 only two Sussex Spaniels were registered with the British Kennel Club but their numbers have since picked up again. The Sussex is a unique golden liver colour, a strong, low dog on short sturdy legs. It is a persistent worker and will go into the most formidable cover after game. It would be a pity if this breed should die out, but there are very few in England and even fewer in America.

Field Spaniels are still in favour with some gun dog men as workers, but it is now very difficult to acquire them. Like the Sussex, they are larger spaniels than the Cocker, with a moderately long body and always self-coloured. They lack the panache of the Cocker, especially in the show ring.

The Irish Water Spaniel is rather an odd man out in the spaniel group and not many are seen today, although the breed has a long history as a gun dog. Perhaps more of a retriever than a spaniel, this dog makes an excellent wildfowling dog and comes into its own on the marshes where its oily, curly coat resists the water. This same coat can be rather a hindrance if it is worked in thick cover as it picks up leaves, brambles and other debris. They are known as rather 'hard' dogs and need competent handlers to get the best out of them.

A very attractive spaniel from France which has recently become more popular is the Brittany Spaniel. It is known as a 'pointing spaniel' because it ranges out and then points the sitting birds in the same way as a pointer or setter. Most are orange and white in colour, lightly built with a dense coat and not overmuch feathering. They are moderate-sized, active dogs which make very good companions as well as working dogs.

The retrievers are well known to every sportsman and are equally successful in many other spheres of canine activity. The Labrador and the Golden Retriever are often, for example, used for guiding the blind. A cross between the two breeds is also used and the rejection percentage is low. Both these breeds have made their mark in obedience classes and working trials, and Labradors are frequently used by the police and Customs for drug detection work.

The Labrador is one of the most popular dogs in the shooting field; it responds well, is a good game-finder, a first-rate water dog and a fast and stylish worker. Its short water-resistant coat has many advantages for the pet owner and many Labradors often make good guard dogs. The Labrador came to Britain in the mid-nineteenth century, arriving on the Newfoundland fishing boats bringing cod to Poole harbour. In 1840, in his book *The Moor and the Loch*, John Colquhoun tells of a retriever which would go back a great distance to pick up its master's whip if it had been accidentally dropped, and on another occasion picked up a shawl which had fallen from an open carriage and tenderly brought it back. So apparently retrievers were just as versatile then as they are today.

Opposite page: Although the Clumber Spaniel naturally looks sad, most are tenacious workers.

Left: The Labrador Retriever has been used for many other jobs besides retrieving. Police forces throughout the world use them as 'sniffer dogs' to detect drugs and explosives.

Below: A Labrador employed at its traditional work of retrieving game.

The Golden Retriever is popular both as a working and a show dog, and many prize-winners work with enthusiasm in the shooting field. Golden Retrievers were first exhibited in 1908, but their origin is uncertain. They are handsome dogs, with good noses, kind temperaments and a ready acceptance of training. The Golden Retriever carries more coat than the Labrador, with feathering on legs and tail, but most owners feel that the satisfaction of owning such an attractive and sensible companion is well worth any extra time spent caring for it.

The Curly-coated and the Flat-coated Retrievers are not so well known, although the Flat-coat was used extensively at the large shoots held in the early part of this century. First shown in 1870, Flat-coats were then called Wavy-coats, but the wave was discouraged and they are now universally known as Flat-coats. At one stage a Borzoi cross was introduced into the breed, resulting in completely foreign heads, but by careful breeding this has now almost been eliminated. The Flat-coats are medium-sized, very active dogs, black or liver in colour, and easy to train and handle.

Although kept by many gamekeepers of 50 years ago, not many Curly-coated Retrievers are seen today. They are tough dogs, not among the easiest to train and not averse to having a go at a poacher as well as retrieving shot game! Good dogs in the water, some tend to be scatterbrained but they make up for this with a tremendous amount of courage. Like the Flat-coat, they can be black or liver-coloured and their coat should be a mass of crisp curls all over.

The Chesapeake Bay Retriever is an American breed which originated in 1807 when two puppies, said to be from Newfoundland, were shipwrecked off the coast of Maryland. Both proved to be first-class water dogs and were mated with local gun dogs to start the Chesapeake strain. Although not very popular with dog show enthusiasts, the Chesapeake is a regular participator in American field trials. Not many are seen in Britain, perhaps because the native retriever breeds have proved more than adequate for the work required of them.

Last of the gun dogs are the setters and pointers, which are required to range out over open country, find the game and then 'point' or 'set' to indicate its position to the following guns. In America pointers and setters are also expected to retrieve the shot game, but in Britain they are usually restricted to their original work of pointing, as it is felt that it tends to make them unsteady if they are taught to retrieve as well. The show and working types of setters are very different.

The handsome English Setter, the flashy Red Irish Setter and the workman-like black-and-tan Gordon Setter from Scotland were all originally 'setting spaniels' until gradually, by selective breeding, the different types emerged.

The English Setter is a beautiful animal with a soft, silky coat, feathered tail and attractive colouring. Slightly smaller than the other setters, it makes a decorative and easily trainable companion. In America, where they are very popular as working dogs, a small strain has been developed solely for trials.

With its rich red coat and handsome good looks, it is not surprising that the Irish Setter classes at the dog shows are well filled and that it is also a popular family dog. It should nevertheless be remembered that these are dogs bred for ranging over open country and that they do not take kindly to being kept on a leash in town. The Irish Setter has a reputation for being rather headstrong, so if you should decide to own one bear this in mind and be prepared to spend time on training and exercise. When worked in field trials, it usually has a good nose and a wide range but it can be a little unpredictable.

The Gordon is the largest of the setters, a big, handsome fellow, jet black with bright chestnut markings. Believed to have been bred by the Duke of Richmond and Gordon in 1827, both Bloodhound and Collie crosses are rumoured to have been included in its genealogy. Gordons first reached the show ring in 1859. They are very strong, well-built dogs, not quite as fast as the other two setters but good stayers and persistent workers. They are usually very trainable and make good companions and family dogs.

The classic image of a pointer is of a dog standing still as a statue, head and nose lifted on outstretched neck, one foreleg lifted, tail stiff and straight, the whole animal the epitome of concentration. Largely because of changing times and the encroachment of towns into the countryside, not so many pointers are now used in the shooting field in Britain, although the show classes are very well filled. Many years ago the Spanish Pointer was imported to Britain and today's pointers are probably bred from this stock. They are normally highly strung, like most bird dogs, but at the same time stylish workers and fascinating to watch.

More recently, several other pointers have been introduced to Britain, America and Australia. The Vizsla hails from Hungary, and the Weimaraner, the German Short-haired and the German Wire-haired Pointers from Germany. The German Wire-haired is not so well known outside its

Opposite page: Irish Setters always catch the eye with their beautiful bright chestnut coats.

Above: A working-type English Setter, not as glamorous as the show type but an attractive working dog.

native country but is becoming increasingly recognized in Canada and America. These breeds are all-purpose gun dogs, being expected to find the game, point it and then retrieve it when shot. A tall order for one dog but many manage very well, even if they do not have the style and expertise of the specialists.

The Vizsla was specially bred for the shooting field in Hungary, even down to its sandy yellow coat which fits in so well with the Hungarian countryside. It is a strongly built, smooth-coated dog, perhaps a trifle self-willed but nevertheless a good sporting dog.

The Weimaraner is sometimes confused with the Vizsla, although it is always a silver grey colour, earning it the nickname of the 'grey ghost'. Used originally for tracking game, it was later trained for pointing and retrieving and quickly adapted to its new role. These dogs have been used by police forces and are sometimes also seen in obedience and working trials where they give a very good account of themselves.

Dating back to the early nineteenth century, the German Short-Haired Pointer is now well known the world over as a dual-purpose gun dog. It is believed to have both Spanish and English Pointer blood in its veins. These are clean-cut, smooth-coated dogs, popular with both sportsman and exhibitor alike. A number of show-winners work in the shooting field, and to become a full champion in England a dog must also win certain qualifications in field trials.

The German Wire-haired Pointer is very like the short-haired version to look at, except that instead of a smooth coat it has a harsh, wiry coat.

Below: A Weimaraner, a dual-purpose German gun dog, making light work of carrying a rabbit.

Right: A Golden Retriever retrieving a pheasant.

Middle right: A German Wire-haired Pointer is an excellent companion in the field.

Bottom right: A German Short-haired Pointer in a classic pose 'on point'.

Training and Obedience

Although house training may well be number one priority to most owners, coming when called is equally important to the owner, to other members of the community and to the dog itself. Many dogs are killed or injured and many accidents caused simply because so many owners do not take the trouble to teach their dog to come when called.

Start by calling the puppy in a friendly persuasive voice–never use a harsh corrective tone. If you stand upright he is likely to stand back staring at the tall figure towering above him, but if you squat down he should come up to you even if you do not ask him. A timid puppy will move away every time you move towards him, but is almost certain to come nearer if you move away. An outstretched hand with moving fingers will attract almost any puppy and most adult dogs, while the same hand with fist clenched will be ignored. There is a common belief that one should always present the back of the hand to a strange dog but I usually find that this puts the dog off completely.

Perhaps the most common mistake people make in approaching a strange dog (and that includes a new puppy) is to stare at it. The only animal which likes its friends to look it 'straight in the eye' is the human being. Other animals do this only if they are afraid of each other or about to attack. Watch two dogs meeting each other. If they look straight at each other you can expect a fight, but if they approach shoulder to shoulder and walk stiffly round and round the odds are they will end up on friendly terms.

Imagine that you are out in the garden with your new puppy and you want him to come when you call him. He is probably sniffing around the gatepost or digging up the flower bed. Do not call him–for the simple and obvious reason that he will not come anyway! An untrained puppy will do the thing which provides, or is likely to provide, the greatest pleasure at the particular time. Anyone who thinks

that his voice is more attractive to a puppy than a hole in the ground has completely the wrong idea of a puppy's priorities. Wait until the puppy appears to have nothing important to do and then call him. The best time is usually when he happens to be coming to you anyhow. Crouch down, hand extended, and call the puppy in a friendly persuasive tone. When he reaches you make a great fuss of him, fondle him and possibly offer a reward in the form of food. Do this several times when the puppy is sure to come and he will soon associate the sound of his name with the reward of food and/or petting. He will then have this association of ideas to strengthen his natural inclination to go to a friendly voice or hand. In most cases this combination will soon be strong enough to induce the puppy to leave the hole he is digging or the smell he is sniffing.

The mistake most people make is never to call the puppy unless he is doing something they don't want him to do–which is usually something he *does* want to do. Every time you call a puppy and he obeys you (even if he happens to be coming anyhow) you have taken a step forward. Every time you call him and he disobeys, you have taken a step back. If you persist in calling him when he is certain to disobey, you will actually teach him not to come when called. Whatever you do, never under any circumstances scold or correct a dog in any way when it comes to you–no matter how much you may feel like murdering it!

Soon we have a puppy which comes in response to reward alone. But he will only do so if the reward is preferred to the alternative–and a dog's life, like our own, is made up of alternatives. A puppy will probably find food and petting more rewarding than aimlessly digging a hole or sniffing a gatepost. If, however, the hole leads to a stinking old bone buried deep down or, when the dog is a bit older, a bitch in season has been round the gatepost, a cooing voice, outstretched hand or even a pocketful

Opposite page: English Springer Spaniels eagerly awaiting the command to go into action.

of titbits will prove to be no more than a poor alternative. We must then resort to correction as well as reward to build up the association required. Correction must however be employed only when reward has failed.

Our puppy is back in the same hole and you call him as before. But this is a very interesting hole and, if the puppy responds at all, it is merely to look up as if to say 'Hang on a minute I'm busy'. Here we have a situation where it is easy to correct the puppy as he is doing the wrong thing and you should always take advantage of such opportunities. You have *asked* the puppy to come by calling his name in a friendly tone and he has refused. Call his name again, this time *telling* him to come, in a very firm tone. It is possible that the puppy will respond to this change of tone. If so, change your tone of voice and your whole attitude completely and reward him with enthusiasm. If, however, he does not respond, pick up a handful of earth or small gravel and call him again more harshly. If he still does not respond, throw the earth or gravel at him. As this 'hail' descends on him seemingly from heaven, he will almost certainly take fright and look round for his 'protector'–that's you! Call him to you, make a great fuss of him and do all you can to console him in his misfortune. The object is to get him to associate the harsh tone of voice with something nasty happening out of the blue. He must not know that you threw it and, if you do it properly, it is almost certain that next time he hears that harsh tone he will anticipate another 'hailstorm' and rush to you for protection–which you must always provide.

Never allow a puppy to run loose in a strange place until he will come to you every time you call him in the house or garden. Even then, you may find that when he sees another dog he will rush off. I cannot over emphasize the importance of nipping this habit in the bud. This can be done in several ways but the best way for the novice is probably by the use of a check cord– about 9m (30 ft) of light cord attached to the dog's collar at one end with the other end in your hand. Let the puppy rush off and, as he nears the end of the cord, call his name in a harsh tone. This time instead of the handful of earth the jerk on the check cord will provide the correction. He will probably do a somersault but do not worry–this method has been used by generations of gun dog trainers and I

have never heard of a dog hurting himself. As he recovers from the jerk, call him in a friendly tone and when he reaches you, reward him well. Never drag him to you. The line should be used as a means of correction when the dog tries to run away, but always encourage him to you by reward.

This method of training should naturally never be carried out until the dog is accustomed to a collar and lead. It is unlikely, however, that a puppy will run after other dogs until he is about six months old. He will have to learn to go on a collar and lead before you take him out in public. The place to teach him is not on the street or in the park but in his own garden or even indoors. Remember that a lead should never be regarded as a means of making a dog go with you but merely to prevent him going too far away. Never put a lead on a puppy until he will follow you without one.

Opinions differ as to the best type of collar. Generally, an ordinary buckled leather collar is adequate for a puppy at the outset. He can be allowed to wear this and to become familiar with it before the lead is put on. Start with a light, long lead and use it only to stop the puppy. Encourage him to come with you by rewarding him in the ways already described. Provided that he will follow you without a lead (even if you do have a pocketful of biscuits) he should soon follow you with one. It is more a question of familiarization than training.

A common problem is not how to get a puppy to walk on a lead but how to stop him pulling once he has become used to it. Here again this should be stopped before it becomes a habit. When the puppy pulls you must not pull against him. Correct him with a sharp jerk on the lead and when he comes back to you in response, praise him well. When training a lead should be three or four feet long, pliable (nylon web leads are now used almost exclusively) and with a strong clip. If the puppy pulls release the lead suddenly and, before he has regained his balance, give a sharp jerk. With a young puppy quite a small jerk will suffice, but it requires a considerable amount of skill and strength to cure an adult dog of pulling. There is little pleasure in taking out a dog which constantly pulls, so that for your own sake as well as that of the dog do not let this habit develop.

If, in spite of your efforts, the puppy is pulling by the time he is six months old I would suggest taking him to the

local training class. I have mixed feelings about training classes where one often finds the blind leading the blind–and not very successfully. I receive many cries for help from owners and almost always their dogs have already attended training classes. Some of the advice given by self-styled experts is frightening. I have met many sensitive dogs with temperaments completely ruined by classes.

On the other hand I know many dogs and their owners who have benefited beyond belief. Like many other successful trainers I started by going to classes. It depends largely on the instructor who often gives his services free. Unfortunately free advice is often worth just what it costs. My advice is to go along to a training class without your dog, and see whether dogs which have been attending for some time behave in the way you want your dog to behave.

You now have a puppy which is clean in the house, comes when you call (and stays with you) and walks on a loose lead. Another important exercise to make him a pleasure rather than a nuisance is designed to ensure that he stays where he is told without bringing complaints from neighbours. Here we must go right back to the start with the puppy play pen. If, when you leave him, he cries to get out and you take him out, you will be rewarding him for crying. It is incredible how quickly a small puppy will learn that whenever he wants attention all he has to do is to howl. The longer you stay with the puppy cuddling and consoling him the longer he will howl or whine when you leave him. If you just go away and leave him alone he will probably howl for a while and then settle down and go to sleep. A puppy accustomed from the start to being left alone in his play pen is unlikely to be a nuisance when later you have to leave him in a car or any other strange place.

If he does persist in howling or barking when left alone, put him in his pen or shut him in a room and go away –but just for a short distance. Wait for the noise to start. When it does, go back quietly. The puppy will not hear you when he is making a noise, so if he stops you must wait until he starts again. The aim is to get right to the door while he is actually howling, then to open it suddenly (which will certainly surprise him) grab hold of him and scold him sternly. Now start all over again and if he makes a noise repeat the whole process. It is unlikely that this time he will make a noise. Wait a few moments (don't tempt Providence by waiting too long) and go back to him. Make a great fuss to reward him for being quiet.

Often people make the unintentional mistake of rewarding the dog for making a noise. They say 'Now, now, be a good boy, don't make a noise' or 'It's all right, Mummy's here, no need to cry', and they say it all in the most soothing and rewarding tone possible. Having been rewarded by tone of voice (probably by gentle stroking too) for barking or whining, the dog naturally does it again and again and yet again for as long as he is rewarded. Bad tempered owners never have problems of this sort. They don't bother about reading books on the subject. The dog annoys them by making a noise and as it is actually barking, it is told in no uncertain terms to 'Shut up'. If it does not, it probably gets a clout on the ear so that next time it hears 'Shut up' it does just that! That is not how I train dogs or believe that dogs should be trained, but it is effective.

Your pup should now be clean in the house, come when called (at any time and in any place) and be quiet when left on his own. That is more than can be said for many dogs working in national obedience championships. If you do aspire to more advanced training, and I hope that some of you will, there are several books on the subject and many people willing to offer advice.

Tricks

All training should be made as enjoyable as possible for both dog and handler. So whether you want to produce an obedience champion or just a well behaved companion dog, teach him a few tricks—just for the fun of it. Most dogs enjoy showing off and some of the easiest tricks making use of the dog's basic instincts will give a lot of pleasure to you both.

One such trick is 'shaking hands'. Tiny puppies instinctively knead at the bitch to stimulate the milk supply so that kneading becomes an action associated with pleasure. As they grow up pups often suck when the bitch is standing up. If they try to reach up and knead they topple over so that they usually sit down and reach up with one paw. This is why so many dogs appear to teach themselves to 'shake hands'.

To teach a dog to shake hands on command, first place him in a sitting position and stand or kneel in front of him. Give the command 'Shake hands'

If your dog has already learned to ignore his name you will have to resort to correction. One way of doing this is with a check cord. It enables you to provide correction when the dog is close to you and prevents the dog running away. When it is removed you cannot correct the dog but you can still reward him, so the object is to get him to respond for reward rather than because of the correction.

and at the same time press against his right shoulder with your left hand. This will make him move his paw off the ground, and as it comes up take it in your other hand and praise him well. Gradually ease the pressure, merely giving the command and holding out your other hand. Once he has grasped the idea, repeat the process with the other paw, saying 'Now the other one'.

Another favourite trick is 'begging'. Do not try to teach this too soon as it can easily strain a puppy's back, especially if he is of a large, leggy breed. Start by putting a collar and lead on the dog and sitting him in the corner of a room. When he sits up, the walls will then give him some support and a feeling of security. Give him the command 'Beg', lift up both front paws and gently keep him in this position with the aid of the lead. Try to encourage him to balance himself. Take plenty of time or he may panic. Once he is sitting up without any help from you, try him again away from the supporting walls. Hold a titbit above his head and be ready to steady him at first if he starts to wobble. Short-legged, stocky dogs, such as Pugs and Sealyhams, usually find this trick very easy and can often be started away from any wall.

To play 'dead' or 'die for your country' is a little more difficult. Assuming that you have taught your dog to lie down on command, the next step is to teach him to lie on his side. Do this by giving a command such as 'On your side', gently push him into position and hold him there. Once he is doing this on his own and remaining steady, you are ready for the next stage. Give the command 'Dead' in a harsh tone of voice which will tend to make him 'freeze'. Try to keep him quite still even if only for a few seconds at the start. When he understands the command and responds to it, try to speed up the action until he will go straight into the 'dead dog' position from standing. Start by giving the command and pulling him down with the lead or pushing him with your hand. Although he will need a lot of praise, make sure you do not praise him too soon or you will tend to make him move from his position.

As well as being fun it can be very useful to teach a dog to catch on command. A dog taught this trick is always easy to photograph. He will be watching your hand in anticipation of something being thrown, so that he will be looking really alert. Some dogs, like some small boys, appear to be

All dogs show the ability to modify their behaviour through training. Most dogs learn to beg without difficulty. Some will beg almost instinctively and others will pick up the idea if you hold a titbit just out of their reach, but not so high that they feel encouraged to jump for it. Naturally, a dog tends to repeat the actions which it finds pleasant and to refrain from doing the things it finds unpleasant. Training for any task consists of establishing an association between a certain signal, the desired act, and a reinforcement, such as praise from the handler.

'naturals' but others seem to miss every time at first. Place the dog, on a lead, standing or sitting in front of you. Have a pocketful of small biscuits and show him the food in your hand. When he is watching it, give the command 'Catch'. At first throw it gently towards him from a very short distance. Should he miss, check him with the lead, pick it up yourself and try again. If you are lucky and he catches a piece fairly soon, praise him and leave off until the next day. If he appears to be getting nowhere, try to finish by dropping a piece into his mouth, tell him how clever he is and try again later. It may take time, but with patience most dogs get the idea sooner or later—and some much sooner.

Later you can teach him to catch a ball. Be sure, however, that it is soft and never throw it far or fast as it might hurt or even choke him.

Obedience Competitions and Working Trials
Obedience training for dogs, like dressage for horses, originated in the field of battle. The Germans were experimenting with dogs for military purposes as far back as 1870, and at the outbreak of hostilities in 1914 were able to mobilize about 20,000 dogs for active service. Dogs were also used by almost all of the European countries, but it was December 1916 before any were employed by the British Army and even later by the Americans. Many British and American servicemen saw for the first time what dogs could be trained to do and they returned with ideas (and sometimes also dogs) for running trials for dogs which were not catered for in either gundog or sheepdog trials. Between the wars, trials and obedience competitions steadily grew in popularity on both sides of the Atlantic.

Strangely enough the British Government abandoned its Army Dog School after World War I and in 1939 found itself in exactly the same position as in 1914. Nor were police forces making use of dogs.

It was during and since World War II that the value of the dog has become fully appreciated for both military and police work. It is now used extensively throughout the world for these purposes. It is also since the last war that the popularity of competitive obedience training has gone ahead by leaps and bounds.

Having studied the rules and regulations for trials and competitions

in the U.S. and compared them with those existing in Britain it is clear that it would require a whole book to explain all the differences—most of these are in any event of a minor character. Good advice to the would-be obedience competitor is to go along to a competition, try to understand what is going on and if he cannot understand (which is quite likely) ask a competitor. Most of these are invariably helpful and my experience is that obedience enthusiasts are much more friendly than those showing dogs in beauty or conformation classes. Indeed many take up the pastime in response to the social, rather than the competitive spirit.

Generally speaking trials and competitions can be divided into two categories. First, there are obedience classes and competitions which are usually, but not always, held at general dog shows, in a ring similar to that used for the breed classes. These tests of obedience are no guide at all to a dog's intelligence or to his ability as a worker. (No one would claim that the smartest man on the barrack square is invariably the best soldier.)

Working trials, on the other hand, are held out of doors and here the dog has to prove his ability to work. In these trials the dog has to track a human being, search for hidden articles, negotiate obstacles and, in some cases, to arrest and 'hold' a 'criminal'. Of course, the dog must be obedient but that is not the most important factor. Indeed, some dogs which have been most successful in obedience classes have proved useless in working trials, chiefly because their training—overtraining in some cases— has inhibited their natural working ability. Some dogs do take part in both obedience classes and working trials but it is rare indeed to find an animal excelling at both.

The majority of people who attend training classes have little or no ambition to win in obedience competitions. All they want is a well-behaved companion. But the standard exercises used in competitions have proved to be as effective as any for making a dog responsive and obedient and, of course, this is the reason why they became standard exercises in the first place. The most important exercises are those used in the novice classes—the foundation exercises—and many people never go beyond this stage. Those who do so have, by then, acquired sufficient knowledge to enable them to study the subject much more deeply than can be dealt with here.

The following are the standard exercises for the novice class laid down by the American Kennel Club:

(1) Temperament test.
    To take place immediately before heel on lead. Dog to be on lead in stand position. Handler to stand by dog. Judge to approach from front and run his hand gently down dog's back. Judge may talk quietly to dog to reassure it. Any undue resentment, cringing or growling to be penalized.
(2) Heel on lead.
(3) Heel free.
(4) Recall from sit or down position at handler's choice. Dog to be recalled to handler when stationary and facing dog, sit in front, go to heel – all on command of judge to handler. Distance at discretion of judge. Test commences when handler leaves dog.
(5) Sit one minute, handler in sight.
(6) Down three minutes, handler in sight.

In the U.K. the exercises are the same except that the down (No (6) above) is for two minutes and there is an additional exercise of retrieving a dumb-bell (which may be the handler's own).

Of course, many dogs can carry out all these exercises and indeed all dogs should be able to do so. That does not mean, however, that they would win in competition. The exercises have to be carried out with a precision well beyond the capabilities of the average dog owner.

Training should be unnecessary for the first exercise. Any dog should allow a person to handle it provided that the owner agrees. Those who have followed the advice on choosing a puppy should have no trouble in this direction.

'Heel on lead' does not merely mean that the dog walks on a lead. It must keep close to the left leg of the handler, neither ahead of him nor lagging behind, with the lead hanging slack at all times. The judge or steward will command the handler to take left turns, right turns, about turns and halts, in almost military fashion. Throughout all this the dog must keep his place by the handler's left leg and must sit smartly every time the handler halts. Many handlers when they are beginners lose points because their own drill is not quite what it should be!

'Heel free' is the same as 'heel on lead' except that the lead has been removed. It is often asked why obedience dogs are always taught to walk on the left. This is derived from military origins where this type of training started. Like the cavalryman who rides with his reins in his left hand, the dog handler leaves his right or weapon hand free. Dogs can be taught to walk on either side (people do break their left arms on occasion) but it would be difficult to conduct a training class unless the dogs were all on one side.

If you have taught your dog to come when called as described in the beginning of this chapter all that is left is to teach him the sit, the down and the finish. It is no use if he comes gambolling up and leaps all over you. The faster he comes the more he will please the judge, but he must halt, sit smartly in front of you and wait until you tell him to go to heel.

The same applies to the retrieve in British trials. Many dogs making what is regarded as a perfect delivery in the shooting field, will lose points in obedience tests. The dog must pick up the dumb-bell and return with it quickly, straight to the handler without mouthing or playing with it. He must then sit in front of the handler, holding the dumb-bell until he is told to drop it. The handler must not give the order until told to do so by the judge. Having delivered the dumb-bell the dog must wait until told to go to heel, and again the handler must wait until told by the judge.

For practical purposes it is sufficient for the dog to stay where he is told but this is not so for competition work. If he lies down during the sit or sits up on the down he will lose points, even if he does not move from the spot. He may not lose as many points as he will if he gets up and walks away, but they will certainly be sufficient to make it important that he should learn to stay in the correct position.

Field Trials
Field trials for gundog breeds are held in both the U.S. and Britain. In addition the U.S. has a number of trials for other breeds. These include Beagles, Dachshunds and Bassets which compete by trailing cottontail rabbits. The hounds must be fast and tough, neither running mute, nor behaving as 'babblers' (giving tongue for no good reason). Needless to say a good nose is essential. American Foxhounds also have their own trials, usually run at night. These Foxhounds need tremendous stamina and very good noses as they may have to trail a fox for as many as 12 hours.

1

2

3

Coonhound trials are only for the hardy – both hounds and handlers. Mostly run at night, the hounds work in swampy country where they have to find and 'tree' a racoon. Judges take a lot of notice of their 'voices' and when they give tongue their owners identify their own hound by its individual voice. As well as night trials there are Coonhound races in the daytime, when hounds have to swim wide and fast rivers and 'tree' a racoon on the other side.

In Britain there are trials for retrievers, spaniels, pointers and setters. There are also those run by specialist clubs for dual purpose breeds such as German Short-haired Pointers and Vizslas. Conducted under strict Kennel Club rules, the trials are run to resemble a normal, organized day's shooting.

As the dog does work similar to that of an ordinary day's shooting, anyone with an obedient, tender-mouthed, sensible dog has a chance of competing successfully. But the handler should take a good look at himself – a nervous handler makes a nervous dog. Some otherwise good dogs have had their chances spoilt by bad handling, for example, too much whistling, a confusion of commands and a lack of trust in the dog. If you have a good dog and he is working well, resist the temptation to think you know better than he does!

In retriever trials the dog must walk to heel or wait with his handler in the butts. He must remain quiet at all times and will be penalized if he makes a noise. When a bird is shot he must go out on command and retrieve it. If the bird is a runner, he must seek out the line and bring it back quickly

and tenderly. He will probably be told to cross a river to retrieve a fallen bird from the other bank and must accept directions from his handler if needed. Before this stage is reached long hours of work will have been spent to accustom him to gunfire, learning to drop on command, not to run in, not to riot on hares or rabbits and to use his nose to the best of his ability.

In spaniel trials the dog is expected to hunt for game as well as to retrieve it. He must be taught to quest out hunting for game, but to stay within gunshot, to respond to directions and to enter any cover, however thick, such as gorse, bramble or thorn bushes. Most spaniels from good working strains have a strong instinct to hunt and it is the handler's job to train them to make the best use of it. When game is found the dog must remain quite steady until he is either instructed to hunt again or sent to retrieve. The spaniel, who is usually a merry worker, has a lot to do in the shooting field and his training should be geared to having him completely under control while still keeping him working stylishly and enthusiastically.

Pointer and setter (bird dog) trials are somewhat different as they are often held in the spring when birds are not shot. This makes no difference to the dogs, as their sole task is to quarter the ground ahead of the guns and when game is found to come to a 'point' to indicate its whereabouts. The bird dog has to learn to turn or stop in response to whistles or vocal commands. It must be steady to gunfire and free from chase. After coming to a point the dog is usually sent slowly ahead to flush the birds for the following guns. He must drop immediately the birds rise

1. The correct position when giving the command 'Heel'. The lead is looped over the thumb in the handler's right hand, hanging slack enough to reach the dog's chest.

2. When training for the 'Sit', the handler should stand on the dog's right. The command is given and at the same time the handler pulls back on the collar and pushes down on the rump.

3. Kneel in this position when training for the 'Down'. Give the command and at the same time push on the withers with the left hand and pull the forelegs forward with the right hand.

4. Having taught your dog to sit and lie down, put him in either position with his lead on. Give the command 'Stay' and move away in front of him, holding the lead in one hand.

5. Teaching your dog to come when called is one of the first lessons he should learn. Call him by name in a friendly tone.

6. It is important that the dog's owner should do the training. Never punish your dog for not obeying a command. Always praise him when he has done well.

4

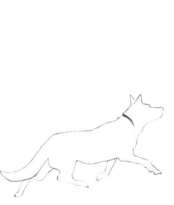

5

6

and remain steady until sent out again. Trials are for single dogs and braces. With the latter the second dog must support the first when it comes on point, and is penalized if it interferes in any way. Bird dogs should work with their heads held high, seeking for the body scent of sitting birds, whereas the spaniel hunts out game with his nose to the ground.

Sheepdog Trials

Sheepdog trials have steadily increased in popularity since they first started over 100 years ago. At the start they were popular with men who worked sheepdogs, providing an outlet for the competitive spirit, an excuse for a social gathering and an opportunity to see the results of specialized breeding and training. Today the sheepdog trial has become a popular spectator sport attended by thousands of people who are unlikely ever to work a dog of any sort. Indeed the vast majority have little or no idea of what the dog is supposed to be doing and it is largely for their benefit that the following explanation is given.

It is very difficult to run trials of any sort which are not to some extent artificial. One reason is the need to give spectators an opportunity to see the dogs at work as well as giving the competitors a chance to show what their dogs can do. Sheepdogs are used

for many purposes, some of which are quite imcompatible with trial work. A well trained Border Collie working on the sheep ranges of the U.S.A., Australia or New Zealand or on a hill farm in Britain should be able to go to a trial and give a good account of itself. On the other hánd a dog used to working sheep kept under intensive conditions would probably be useless in a trial although still a good working sheepdog.

In the New World, where sheep are herded in much larger numbers than in Britain, trials have been modified to suit the prevailing conditions but they are all based on the rules laid down by the International Sheepdog Society. And these have changed very little since they were first written.

In Britain where trials of varying standards are held throughout the year, courses differ according to the circumstances. Large international trials are also held in places such as London's Hyde Park, usually sponsored by one of the national newspapers. These are nearly always invitation events with dogs invited from many different countries, and the main object is to entertain the vast crowds which attend.

The important trials for sheepdog breeders and trainers in the British Isles are the four national events where the dogs qualify to run in the

Above: A retriever must learn to pick up a bird and carry it without doing it any damage. He may often have to cross a river to retrieve a fallen bird from the opposite bank. It must be held gently in the mouth, carried right up to the handler and given up as soon as the sportsman bends to take it from his mouth, but not so quickly that the game falls to the ground. A dog who learns to hold the game tenderly is said to have a 'soft' mouth.

Right: This diagram shows the course for the national sheepdog trials and the qualifying trials at the international.

international, the top event in sheepdog circles. The best 12 dogs from Scotland, England, Wales and Ireland qualify for the international where they must first take part in the qualifying trials. From these the best 12 dogs, irrespective of country, qualify to run in the supreme championship.

The course for the national trials is the same as that for the qualifying trial at the international, but the championship course is much more difficult. These courses have been practically unchanged from the start, although some modifications have been adopted over the years. They are also adjusted to suit the different locations, but the accompanying diagrams are always used as a basis.

In the national and qualifying trials the handler starts by walking out to a post from which he must not move more than a specified distance. Five sheep are then released from a pen and manoeuvred to a point some 366 m (400 yds) away. When the sheep have settled in a good position the judge instructs the handler to send his dog to 'gather' which he may do either to

right or left at his discretion. The dog should go out in a circle, not too wide, not too close, and 'lift' his sheep quietly. He will then 'fetch' or 'wear' the sheep straight to the handler, passing between two hurdles on the way. The dog should then take the sheep close round the handler, drive them away through two hurdles then across and through another pair and bring them back to the handler. The latter then moves with the dog into the shedding ring which is marked with sawdust. In the national, two of the five sheep are marked and the object is to shed any two of the unmarked sheep, without going outside the ring. When the dog has kept the two sheep away from the others to the satisfaction of the judge it runs them together again and the handler moves to the pen. Here he takes hold of the rope attached to the gate, which he must keep hold of throughout the penning. The dog brings the sheep to the pen and the handler may assist so long as he maintains hold of the rope (which is six feet in length). Once the sheep are inside the pen the handler closes the gate. He then lets out the sheep,

closes and fastens the gate of the pen and again goes to the shedding ring. Here the dog must shed one of the two marked sheep and keep it away from the others until the judges are satisfied. As sheep have such a strong instinct to stay together this is a difficult task, sometimes made more so when time is fast running out. If he exceeds the time allowed he is disqualified.

For the international championship 20 sheep are used and released in two groups of 10, nearly ¾ km (½ mile) away and where the dog cannot see them. Sometimes the handler himself cannot see them and has to rely entirely on the dog until they come into view, a common occurrence in everyday work. The dog is sent to gather one group of ten and fetch them at an angle through two hurdles. He must then leave them at a spot marked by a pole, go back for the other ten sheep and bring them through the same two hurdles. If he is lucky the first group will have remained near the spot where he left them and running the two groups together will be easy. If he is not so lucky, the first group will have gone

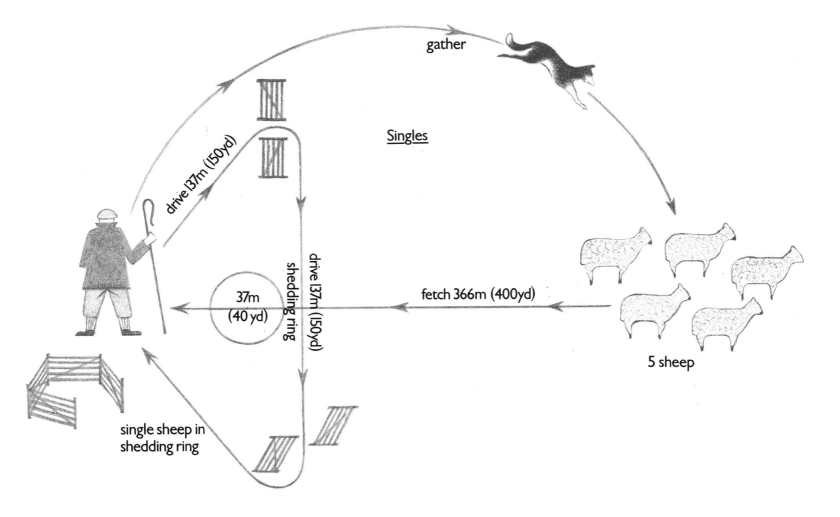

73

and will have to be brought back to join the others. All 20 sheep are then driven round a similar course to the first, ending up in the shedding ring. Here 5 marked sheep are shed from the 20 and the trial ends when these are penned.

To many spectators the most exciting trials are the 'doubles' where two dogs work together. This requires a very high degree of training by two dogs compatible in their work. In sheepdog breeding and training circles, however, a win in the 'singles' is a far greater honour than in the 'doubles'.

Some people are under the impression that the main object of a sheepdog trial is to get the sheep through all the obstacles in the shortest possible time. If the sheep miss a hurdle there are often sighs of disappointment from the crowd, whereas if they are completely out of control and, by a stroke of luck, gallop between the hurdles, the crowd will applaud. But the object of a trial is to test the ability of the dog to control the sheep. If he is unlucky enough to miss an obstacle he will lose marks but not nearly as many as the dog whose sheep career madly round

the field, even if they go through all the obstacles on route. Incidentally many remarks are heard that the dogs are 'almost human'. If you have any such ideas try to drive five wild sheep round a national course on your own! This will teach you how ludicrous it is to compare canine and human ability.

Training a dog for trial work is no different from training it for any other type of work with sheep. As with all competitive work it is necessary to apply much more 'polish' than for everyday work, but the basis of training is no different. The first essential is the right dog. In most training it can be said that the finished product depends perhaps 50% on the dog and 50% on the training. For a trial sheepdog, however, at least 75% depends on the dog. A dog can be taught to lie down, get up and move to left or right but he cannot be taught how to do it. And it is how he does it – called 'style' in sheepdog circles – which wins or loses top awards.

Only five basic commands are necessary to train a sheepdog and these are used in varying tones. Some

This diagram shows the more difficult international championship course, which is much longer than the national and qualifying trials and involves 20 sheep.

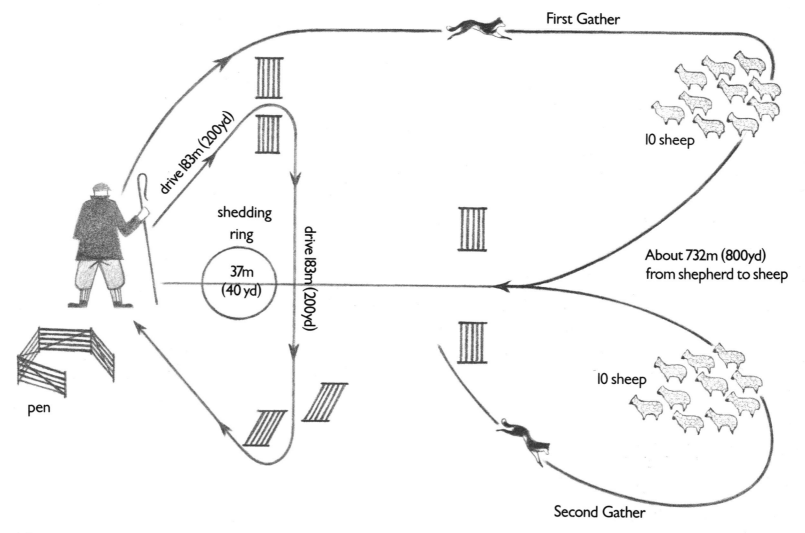

First Gather

drive 183m (200yd)

shedding ring

37m (40 yd)

drive 183m (200yd)

pen

10 sheep

About 732m (800yd) from shepherd to sheep

10 sheep

Second Gather

handlers work with whistles and some by words of command but the majority use a combination of the two. A whistle carries better when working at a distance while most people find it easier to use their voice and alter its tone when the dog is close at hand. There are exceptions to this and some handlers, particularly those from Wales, can virtually talk to a dog by whistling. As has been said elsewhere in this book, a dog understands sounds only, not words, so that to him it makes no difference whether whistles or words are used. The important point is that the dog understands what each command means. Although often used in everyday work, hand signals are not favoured in trials as they make the dog take his eye off the sheep.

The most important of the five basic commands is to stop. This is usually the only command taught to a young dog before it is introduced to sheep. It is taught to lie down flat in response to a long shrill whistle or command such as 'Down' or 'Lie down'. The commands to go left or right refer to the left or right side of the dog. It should keep moving round its sheep in a clockwise direction in response to the one and in an anti-clockwise direction for the other. One command is used for the dog to move towards his sheep irrespective of his position. The same command is used whether he is at the other side of the sheep coming towards his handler or between the sheep and the handler and therefore going away. The fifth command, to leave the sheep and come back to the handler, is next in importance to the command to stop.

Hound Trailing

Hound trailing, which is really a form of racing, is a sport confined to the Lake District in the North of England, where it has been the leading sport for generations of local countrymen. There are strict rules and regulations not only as to how the trail should be run, but also concerning the breeding of hounds. Although bred as pure Trail Hounds for many generations they were originally evolved from Foxhounds and evidence of other blood is strictly taboo.

The exact details of size of the drag and the mixture in which it is to be saturated are laid down in the rules for the trail. A mixture of aniseed, paraffin, turpentine and whale oil is most commonly used and a piece of woollen material is soaked in it. When this is dragged along the ground it leaves behind a very potent smell. This hangs in the air, even on a hot day, so enabling hounds to follow at speed without having to check to pick up the scent.

The route of the trail is governed by the prevailing conditions, but it is usually laid in the shape of a horseshoe with start and finish close together. Two people lay the trail, one from the start and the other from the finish. The route normally goes up the fells so that the hounds can be seen all the way from start to finish. The standard distance is ten miles for adults and five for puppies from one to two years old. The time taken to cover the 10 miles is usually around 30 minutes–a very fast time considering that such obstacles as rocks, rivers and stone walls have to be negotiated. Hounds which do not finish in 40 minutes are disqualified. So, too, are those which complete the course in under 25 minutes. This is because it is assumed that a hound which takes less than that time must have cut a corner somewhere. A clever hound will learn to do this but it does not make him popular with the punters! This is a common problem with older hounds on a trail which they have run before. During the run they suddenly remember where the finish is–and the waiting food–and go straight to it.

Trail Hounds are reared and trained as individuals by their owners who are often their breeders as well. Their early training includes familiarization with sheep which are always plentiful on the ground where trails are run. They are taught to follow a trail more or less as a police dog is taught to track a man. Food is used as bait and the young hound is usually started by letting it see a piece of meat placed some distance away. A woollen rag soaked in the trail mixture is dragged from the meat to where the pup is being held, and it is then released to pick up the meat. Next, the meat is hidden and the process repeated until the pup knows that if it follows this particular smell it will find a piece of meat. Gradually the distance is increased until the pup will follow a trail of five miles or more on its own.

Once a Trail Hound learns to follow an aniseed trail it becomes almost addicted to the smell. It is probably this which has given rise to the belief that aniseed has magic powers over dogs. Tests have shown, however, that most dogs dislike the smell and it is only after they have been accustomed to associate it with food that trail hounds become enthusiastic about it.

The hound trailing season starts on March 1 and ends on October 30. Although confined to a small area it is rapidly becoming popular as a spectator sport with the many holiday makers and tourists who frequent the Lake District. Sponsorship makes good prize money available and the sport is likely to attain much greater popularity.

Drag Hunting

Drag hunting is an alternative to fox hunting and most packs consist of draught fox hounds and stag hounds. Because of changing farming methods and urbanization of such a large part of the country, fox hunting becomes increasingly difficult in England and hence the increasing popularity of drag hunting. Some packs are now breeding their own hounds for the express purpose of hunting a drag.

As it is not a competitive sport, no rules are laid down as to what scent should be used on the drag. Most huntsmen have their own ideas–and very secretive some of them are too! The general practice is to use animal scents which hounds will track naturally. Aniseed, turpentine and their like are now never employed, although they may have been used in the past. Urine forms the basis of most drags but it is not always easy to find out what particular sort is used. Fox urine would be the obvious choice for ex-foxhounds, but at least one pack is known to use wolf urine with good results.

The drag hunt is usually about eight to ten miles in length and laid in three sections by a person on foot. After each section there is a short break which allows the horses–not to mention the riders–to get back their wind. As there are usually some 40 jumps to negotiate, these short breaks are often necessary to allow the field to get together again.

Drag hunting is not for the faint-hearted. This is probably one reason why these packs have always been associated with universities and military establishments. Because the scent is laid for them, hounds run much faster than they would if hunting a fox, although with nothing like the speed of Trail Hounds. As the drag is more often than not laid over what is known as 'good galloping country', the whole exercise tends to become something like a glorified steeplechase –except that some of the jumps are bigger and tougher.

Most drag hounds have previously

been trained as foxhounds and the training now concentrates on hunting a drag instead of a fox. This is not difficult as long as there are no foxes around for, as with most dogs, they find the natural much more exciting than the artificial. On the other hand, it is easier to teach a hound to follow an artificial track simply because one knows where it is and therefore has a certain amount of control. Even if a hound finds the drag less interesting than a live fox, it will soon learn that if it follows the scent it will be rewarded with food – strong encouragement to the average hound.

Those drag hounds which have not previously been trained in a pack must be taught discipline before they are taken out. Like foxhounds they must learn their names, go to the huntsman when he calls them and, perhaps most important of all, must not chase livestock (see the chapter on training foxhounds).

Most people regard drag hunting as a poor substitute for fox hunting. Hounds do not have to work a drag as they do the line of a fox, and to many people the chief pleasure in hunting is to see hounds work. Many other people, however, find a gallop on a good horse far more exciting than watching hounds at work. But the anti-hunting brigade has not yet thought of a reason to protest about drag hunting and it may well be that the future of drag hunting is brighter than that of fox hunting.

Sledge Dog Racing
Only a few years ago a number of people were concerned about the future

of the sledge dog. At one time the only means of transport in the Arctic regions, its role has now been taken over by specially built mechanical vehicles. Sledge dog racing has, however, become so popular in Canada and the northern states of the U.S. that the future of the dog is assured.

One reason for the tremendous surge in popularity of this winter sport is that the whole family can take part and have fun. Most clubs meet at weekends, when training sessions and club races are held. Children can drive small teams of 3 or 4 dogs, while keener competitors will handle a team of 10 or 12. At these club events drivers can acquire the skill to handle a large team before competing in the more important events.

For success in the big events the dogs will need to be fast, fit, well trained and behave as a team. Starting in the summer, the driver will have to spend a lot of time in selecting and training his team. Great importance must be paid to the selection of the leader. He must have a strong enough personality to command the respect of his team mates, but at the same time be easily controlled by and responsive to his driver. He must be fit and fast, for this is the dog which sets the pace which the whole team must be capable of maintaining. A chain is only as strong as its weakest link and a dog team is only as fast as the slowest dog.

During their early training in the summer, the dogs will pull a cart on wheels instead of on runners. The harness, usually made of nylon or soft leather, will be carefully fitted and the dogs accustomed to wearing it

Foxhounds have probably been bred with more care and thought over the centuries than most other animals and the result is a compact, powerful animal of tremendous stamina and scenting power.

comfortably. They will be taught different words of command such as 'Haw' to turn left and 'Gee' to turn right. As in driving horses the voice is of great importance and drivers can often be heard 'talking' their teams through difficult places.

The team will gradually be built up to peak fitness until shortly before the race season starts they are having three to five working sessions a week.

The dog most often seen in competitive racing is the Alaskan Husky. Although not recognized by the Canadian Kennel Club, this dog breeds very true to type. Most often seen at club weekends is the slightly smaller Siberian Husky, usually an even-tempered dog with a strong instinct to pull. Drivers are, however, always on the lookout for better and faster racing dogs and crosses with other breeds are common. Coonhounds, collies and setters have all been used for this purpose and teams of these breeds have also been raced successfully. Children often start out with the family pet hitched to a home-made cart. It might be a mongrel, spaniel or a giant Newfoundland but the children—and the dogs—seem to derive a lot of fun out of it. Many well known and successful adult competitors will tell you that this is how they themselves first started.

Mountain Rescue Dogs

In recent years more and more dogs have been trained to become important members of mountain rescue teams. They are now widely used in such countries as Switzerland, Scandinavia and Scotland.

Although several breeds have been used, German Shepherd Dogs (Alsatians) predominate. The training is long and arduous. Many dogs and handlers apply for initial training but by no means all are accepted.

Firstly, the dog must be fit and strong enough to cope with the harsh conditions encountered in this type of work. It must be mentally well adjusted and able to accept general obedience training before going on to specialized 'nose work'. Obviously it is essential for it to have what is known as a 'good nose' and to be trained to use this to the best advantage. The dog must also be completely safe with livestock and not distracted by any kind of game which it might encounter on the mountain.

If accepted for training, both dog and handler first undergo an initial period of training similar to that given to police dogs. This is followed by more intensive training in nose work until the dog can locate people buried under drifting snow or an avalanche. A novice dog usually has a probationary period before being tested to qualify as a fully trained member of a team. Even then it is re-tested regularly to ensure that a very high standard of work is maintained.

Apart from being able to work just as well in the dark as in daylight, these dogs have the great advantage of speed, a vital factor in mountain rescue. In a recent demonstration a 'casualty' buried in snow in an area 23 metres square (25 yards square) was located by a trained dog in 30 seconds, while a team of men with the usual probing rods took 28 minutes.

Training Foxhounds

Foxhound puppies are usually reared 'at walk'. This means that when they are about eight weeks old they are sent singly or in pairs to a number of people, often farmers, who are prepared to rear them until they are old enough to return and enter the pack.

Once the hunting season has ended in March or April, the huntsman collects the pups from their various walks and starts to train them for the next hunting season. These pups vary in age from about 9–15 months and are a motley crew. The huntsman's task can be compared to that of the sergeant major faced with a new bunch of recruits. Some have been well reared and educated and some have just run wild. Some are willing, even anxious to learn, and some are entirely the opposite. The huntsman must try to teach every one of them to behave properly both as an individual and as a member of the pack.

First, he has to gain the confidence of these young hounds. No training is ever successful unless the animal trusts its trainer. Some of these youngsters will have been reared on isolated farms where they may have seen very few strangers. In the unfamiliar surroundings of the hunt kennel they are likely at first to be shy and bewildered. This may be made worse by the fact that some of the bolder hounds will be bullies until they are put in their place. Most Foxhounds, however, are greedy by nature and a pocketful of titbits can be a huntsman's best ally. Many of the young entry will know their names but others will have no idea. He will concentrate on the latter by calling their names individually and offering food as a reward. Soon each one will respond when it hears its own name.

Foxhounds are fed in long troughs. The general practice is to put out the food in one yard and let the hounds through from an adjoining yard to feed. But they must not be allowed through in a great stampede. Each animal should come only when his name is called—and not beforehand. Not only does this help the huntsman to maintain discipline but it enables him to allow the slow feeders to have longer at the feed trough than the greedy members of the pack.

Once the young hounds know their names and are on friendly terms with the huntsman, they are taken out for exercise with him and his whipper in on foot. To help them to learn 'pack discipline' young hounds are often coupled to older ones. As the older hounds respond to the commands of both the huntsman and the whipper in, the youngsters have little option but to conform. Very soon these young hounds will pick up the commands for themselves.

At this stage the young hounds are familiarized with the crack of the whip. Whip shyness is a serious fault in a Foxhound. This may surprise those readers who think that whips are used only to harm unfortunate animals. A whip crack is the equivalent of a blast on a whistle to a gundog or a harsh 'No' to a pet dog. It simply means 'Don't do that' and it is surprising how quickly hounds learn to ignore it when it does not apply to them. The whip is also used as an extension of the arm to administer a sharp flick on the behind of an inattentive or disobedient hound, but it is used as a means of punishment only to break up a fight or to stop a 'riot' i.e. chasing something which they should not.

Soon the older hounds are relieved of their irksome task and the youngsters are coupled together. Care is taken to match them as nearly as possible for size and temperament. Now the whole pack can start exercising with a view to building up peak physical fitness as well as instilling obedience. Most huntsmen use bicycles for this purpose as it is usually easier to concentrate on hounds when riding a bicycle than when on a fresh horse. Every opportunity is taken to introduce hounds to cattle, sheep, poultry, dogs and cats, in order to impress on them the important rule that under no circumstances must they chase any farm stock or domestic animal.

By midsummer the pack should be running nicely together and some of the young hounds will be uncoupled. Prevention, however, is better than cure and many huntsmen continue to couple any likely troublemakers until well into the hunting season. It is now time to start exercising the hunt horses so that they will be reasonably fit when cub hunting starts in the autumn. The huntsman rides in front and the whipper in behind, with the pack between them. They are now able to go across fields and along rough tracks which were impassable on bicycles. The whippers in (there are usually two of them) will also be able to go after any hound breaking away and turn it back to the huntsman. Gradually the amount of exercise is increased until 32 km (20 miles) or more will be covered in a day with the hounds showing no signs of fatigue even when the weather is very hot.

Cub hunting usually starts when the harvest has been gathered in, probably in late midsummer. By now a great deal of time, skill and effort has been expended in educating the young hounds. But no one yet knows which of them will be good workers and which will be useless. It is rather like obedience training which gives no clue to a dog's intelligence or working ability. All the huntsman knows is that the pack is physically fit (an animal that is physically fit is also mentally alert) and that the young entry has been bred to hunt. Now he waits in anticipation to find out if they will hunt and, if so, how they will hunt.

The main purposes of cub hunting are to educate the young hounds and to disperse the litters of cubs, which by now are nearly full grown and beginning to go their separate ways. Because the sun destroys scent, meets are held soon after dawn, which at this time of the year is very early in the morning. The huntsman has no problems with large 'fields' of followers, and those who do turn up are keen to see hounds working. In hunting proper the object is to push the fox out of the covert into the open in the hope that he will provide a good run. Any follower who, however inadvertently, turns a fox back into cover usually has the mistake pointed out in the most colourful hunting language! In cubbing, however, followers make every effort to turn foxes back into cover in order to encourage young hounds to use their noses and to hunt for themselves, rather than to rush off in a headlong

gallop after the older hounds.

Many huntsmen start by taking the pack on foot into covert to put themselves in a better position to encourage the young entry to go forward. The pack instinct now plays a big part. Elsewhere in this book it is said that dogs rarely learn anything from an older dog which one wants them to learn. But then we seldom want them to hunt. The pack instinct certainly strengthens the hunting instinct and it is unlikely that a young hound will not hunt. Some youngsters, however, will merely follow the older hounds and the huntsman may have trouble encouraging them to hunt for themselves. Some huntsmen take out young hounds a couple at a time, without older hounds to lead them, in order to make them use their own initiative. Any young hound which is obviously not going to make the grade is discarded before the end of the cubbing season, but a doubtful case may be run on in the hope that it will improve. Some excellent hounds have indeed been very mediocre in their first season.

By the time hunting starts in mid Autumn the young entry, although still lacking in experience, will be able to contribute to the success of the pack. There are many different views about fox hunting but one thing is certain, few dogs—certainly very few pet dogs —lead a life half as enjoyable as that of a foxhound.

Police Dogs

Police dogs are a familiar sight in many parts of the world. Several breeds are used including the Doberman Pinscher, Rottweiler, Labrador and Giant Schnauzer, but many forces still prefer the German Shepherd Dog (Alsatian). A good German Shepherd Dog is bold, alert and intelligent and has a weather resisting coat so that it does not feel the cold and wet as much as, say, a Doberman Pinscher. Another advantage of this breed is that many wrong doers seem to have an inborn fear of German Shepherd Dogs. Police dogs must be physically sound with plenty of stamina and have a good nose and a steady temperament. Contrary to general belief they are not vicious animals. All dogs *can* bite. Police dogs are taught *when* to bite and, just as important, when *not* to bite. Like policemen their job is to protect and help the public. No shy or nervous dog would be considered for training. A police dog may be dashing after a dangerous criminal one day and on the

next day be searching for a lost baby.

Some police forces breed their own dogs, some are bought from suitable strains but many are gifts from the public. These last often include 'difficult' dogs which have proved too clever for their owners. Given the right sort of training, however, properly housed and fed, and with no chance to get bored, they can turn into excellent working dogs. Those between 12 and 18 months may be considered for training as this is the age at which they usually start their police dog course.

Police dogs usually live at home with their handler, and in the case of a home-bred puppy it will go straight to the handler's home after weaning. Great care is taken to see that the whole family will provide the right environment for the puppy to grow up. In the U.S., police dog handlers have to obtain written permission from their wives before taking a dog home!

Dogs and handlers together attend an initial police dog training course for about three months. Later on there are more advanced courses and refresher courses. The prospective handler needs to be physically fit, cheerful, persevering and fair. He must learn, as it were, to get inside the mind of his dog and to 'read' it correctly.

Obviously police dogs must be obedient and under control. The first lessons relate to simple obedience, such as walking to heel on and off the lead, coming when called, standing, sitting or lying down and remaining in any of these positions. Then comes the retrieve, a very important exercise. The dog must learn to retrieve correctly and reliably before it can go on to more advanced nose work such as looking for lost articles or persons, tracking and searching. It must also learn to speak on command—easy with some dogs but very difficult with others. The handler must seize every opportunity to encourage the dog to speak when it does so of its own accord. There will be many uses for this exercise—barking at a criminal, or when it has found a suspect, or when it has discovered an object too heavy for it to lift.

The dog has to learn to jump over or scale high walls and is taught long jumping in order to negotiate obstacles such as ditches. Later in the course the dog is taught to swim, and handlers themselves sometimes have to enter the water to encourage a reluctant starter. A dog is tested for its reaction to gun fire and loud noises—no gun-shy dog would be of any use as a police dog.

When the dog has proved satisfactory during the initial training he is introduced to tracking and criminal work. This is where the need for a good grounding in general obedience will be appreciated. The dog is taught to apprehend a wrong doer and, if necessary, to chase and catch him, holding him until either he stands still or the policeman arrives to take control. Unnecessary biting and aggression are firmly dealt with as an over-sharp dog would be a liability on patrol duty. Dog and handler are carefully taught by a qualified instructor and efforts are made to ensure that the dog does not regard every person who runs as a criminal. An important part of the training team is the 'criminal', who can make all the difference to the dog's final work.

Back at his unit the police dog will have many jobs to do – and many of them it will do far better than any human. It will travel round with his handler in a radio van and, in addition to routine checks on buildings, it may be called to a break in. It will probably be sent in to see if the suspect is still in the building and if he has made a get away it will be needed to track him. It might be used for riot control, to find a lost child or search for missing objects. A lot of the work will be at night when men are handicapped by the dark but when a dog can use its keen senses to the fullest advantage.

Drug Detection Dogs

In recent years the dog handlers of many police forces have given specialist training in drug detection to selected Labradors. These dogs are not ordinary police dogs and receive no police dog training. Indeed they receive only the minimum of obedience training, as they must in no way be inhibited from working freely and using their initiative. Labradors used for this job are not home bred but are purchased from strains of keen, working gundogs. First and foremost the dog must possess a good nose and a strong retrieving instinct. It must have persistence and an ability and willingness to keep on searching, even in difficult circumstances.

Training will start when the dog is about a year old. During the first eight weeks it is carefully studied and trained by experts, and an assessment made of its potential as a drug detector dog. If it shows an ability to search and retrieve after this preliminary training it goes on to a further eight

weeks with its future handler.

The dog and handler are then trained together. It is essential that they learn to work as a team with complete confidence in each other. Once fully trained these 'sniffer' dogs may be called out by any police force, customs officer or other authorized officials, if hidden drugs are suspected.

Dogs may be used to carry out searches in dockyards, private houses, custom sheds, vehicles and in fact in any place where drugs are suspected.

In Britain during 1975 drug detector dogs were called out 748 times and drugs were found on 405 occasions. No less than 928 persons were arrested as a result of their work. There is no doubt whatsoever that the 'sniffer dog' has more than proved its worth.

Guide Dogs For The Blind

There is a saying that 'Braille makes the blind man literate – the guide dog makes him mobile.' There is no doubt that thousands of happy guide dog owners would agree.

There are training centres for guide dogs in America, Britain, Australia, South Africa, Germany, Holland, Israel, Italy, Belgium, Sweden and Norway. Britain has five such centres as well as a breeding and puppy walking centre. About 80% of guide dogs are Labradors, the remainder are mostly German Shepherd Dogs (Alsatians) and Golden Retrievers with some cross-breds. Guide dogs must be a minimum height of 49 cm (19 ins) for anything less would not maintain the balance between dog and owner.

The value of the German Shepherd Dog (Alsatian) as a deterrent is one of its greatest assets. Not only are they an added protection to the patrolman, but the threat of sending in the dogs has caused many a suspect to surrender. The handler must have complete control over his dog and the first lessons of simple obedience are very important. Training the dog to come when called and to remain in position are essential exercises.

The blind person and the guide dog have to be carefully matched for compatibility and the relationship between them becomes very close. Through her harness the dog can guide a blind person's steps and indicate obstructions, when to stop for traffic and when it is safe to proceed. She will guide them around all obstacles and must learn to allow for the height of her charge and ensure that there is space for them both to pass. A guide dog will give a blind person enormously increased mobility and independence.

Some puppies of suitable breeding are bought in, together with a few adult bitches. Bitches make up 80% of working guide dogs and the rest are castrated males. Bitches are spayed after their first season. The Guide Dogs for the Blind Association (G.D.B.A.) in Britain has about 100 brood bitches and since the introduction of the selective breeding policy the rejection rate has dropped to 35%. German Shepherd Dogs are all home bred.

Puppies leave the breeding centre around 7 weeks old and go to live with a 'puppy walker' where they stay for the next 10–12 months. Puppy walkers have a very responsible job. They usually live in or near towns, often have a family and probably another pet, perhaps a cat. The puppy will be house trained, taken to meet the children from school, travel by bus and car, taken to railway stations, into shops, in lifts, over bridges and generally familiarized with all the hazards of twentieth century life. The puppy walker will teach it some basic obedience such as the sit, the down and the re-call. When out on the lead it will be encouraged to walk on the left side, slightly in front of the handler and in the centre of the pavement–the position it will take up when working. It will also be taught to walk quietly past other dogs and cats and not to sniff at lamposts or street corners. During its stay with the puppy walker there will be frequent visits from a supervisor to see that the puppy is developing along the right lines, and to deal with any problems which might arise. As German Shepherd pups tend to get very attached to a particular person, they are always returned to the kennels for a short period before they are five months old. This loosens the ties with the puppy walking family and makes it easier for the dog when it finally goes back for training. The age at which they return varies–Labrador bitches return at 10 months, Labrador dogs at 1 year, German Shepherds at about 15 months and Golden Retrievers at 17 months.

The potential guide dog needs many special requirements. It must be physically sound, free from any nervousness or aggression, intelligent, responsive and willing to please. Body sensitivity is also very important. A dog with high body sensitivity might react violently to a sudden bang or jolt and so cause an accident, or an insensitive dog might bump into obstacles not bothering whether it, or its handler, were crushed or bruised.

On arrival at the training centre the dogs are given time to settle down. Then the basic obedience imparted by the puppy walker is developed until the dog is completely reliable on sits, downs, re-calls, is sitting properly at kerbs and walking happily in its harness. It learns that when the harness is on and the handle taken up it is working, but that when the harness is removed, or the handle lowered onto the dog's back, it is off duty.

More advanced training follows. The dog is taught the meaning of 'Forward', 'Right', 'Left' and 'Back', and obstacle training and traffic work are also started. The trainer has to teach the dog to regard the handler as an extension of itself. At the start a dog passing under a ladder or walking round a hole in the ground will not leave enough room for its handler to pass safely. But an intelligent dog, with confidence in its trainer, will soon learn by correction and reward that he must consider his handler as well as himself.

Having been taught to sit automatically at the kerb and not to cross until given the order, the dog now has to learn to ignore this command if a car is approaching. Another member of the training staff will drive the car, or several cars may be used. By constant repetition the handler will teach the dog that a moving car is dangerous and that it must wait until the road is clear before proceeding.

Training takes from five to eight months. The dog spends the final four weeks with the blind student so that the pair learn to work as a team. Great care is taken to match students with suitable dogs. The students learn to groom, feed and exercise their dogs as well as how to work them. The trainer has the difficult task of transferring the dog's affection to its new master, and of teaching the student how to handle the highly trained dog without damaging its confidence.

Once the dog goes home with its new master the trainer pays frequent visits to see that all is going well and to help with any problems which may arise. All owners are encouraged to give their dog plenty of free running exercise. The dog wears a collar, with a small bell attached to help the owner to locate him. The average working life of a guide dog is about eight or nine years and it is a sad day for the blind owner when they have to part.

Herding Dogs

BY the time Man started to domesticate animals such as the horse, cow and sheep, the dog must have been well established as an aid to hunting and probably as a guard dog. But the hunting dog would have been of little use to the farmer who kept sheep or cattle, and indeed it might well have killed them. On the other hand, a dog which would help round up other domestic animals without attacking them would have been a great asset. And so the herding breeds were developed from the dogs which were already there – the hunting breeds.

The herding instinct is only a slight variation of the hunting instinct and it was probably not very difficult to develop one from the other. In any hunting pack there are dogs which will run round the quarry and turn it back into the pack. By breeding from these dogs, one could produce dogs with a natural instinct to run round other animals. It was also vital that these dogs should not kill their quarry. Working sheepdogs still retain their instinct to hunt and kill and the reason they do not do so when working is because they are trained, and they can only be trained provided the submissive instinct is strong enough to counter-balance the very strong hunting instinct. In developing the herding breeds, Man has therefore bred for a strong submissive instinct. Generally speaking, dogs from the herding breeds are more easily trained than those from the hound and terrier groups.

Some breeds classified as sheepdogs are not, in fact, herding breeds at all. They are really guard dogs and are only called sheepdogs because they have been used to guard sheep. They usually originated in parts of the world where flocks needed to be protected against predators such as wolves and bears, even humans. There are also sheepdog breeds which have been used as guard dogs without any particular association with sheep.

In some countries, particularly on the Continent, sheepdogs have been produced which both herd and guard the flocks. It is the practice to 'fold' sheep in enclosures of hurdles or netting, which are moved on to fresh ground each day. For this type of work, the dog has to be 'close-run' and noisy – a driver rather than a true herder. The British shepherd, unlike his European counterpart, has not needed to keep dogs which could tackle a wolf for several centuries and he does not need to bring his sheep into enclosed areas every night for protection. The sheep are simply left to roam the hills day and night. But when he does want to gather them in, he requires a very different sort of dog from that needed in most other parts of the world. He needs a true herding dog and it was in Britain that this type of dog originated, and from Britain spread to most countries in the New World.

At one time, practically all sheep in the south of England were kept in folds. This was not for protection, but because more sheep could be kept by cultivating crops like turnips and kale and grazing them with sheep in a controlled manner. The shepherd's dog was very like the Old English Sheepdog, and it was also the drover's dog and the cow dog on the dairy farm. On top of these duties, it was also expected to be a good guard dog. It has always been the custom to dock this breed very short and the Old English Sheepdog is often referred to as the Bobtail. In winter the Bobtail spent most of its time working in mud, when one would expect its enormous coat to be a hindrance, but it should be remembered that working dogs never develop the heavy coats of the show dogs. It was also the general practice to shear the dogs at the same time as the sheep, and even to dip them.

As folded sheep were replaced by grassland sheep, so the Old English Sheepdog declined as a worker. It was, however, crossed with the Border Collie which came from Scotland, and we find local strains like the Dorset Blue Shag and the Smithfield Dog of East Anglia. The latter was a favourite with drovers in the days when sheep and cattle were driven to London's Smithfield Market.

Left: A small Hungarian cattle dog demonstrating the herding dog's capacity to 'heel'.

Left: A windswept group of Bearded Collies. The colour of the 'odd man out' is permitted in the standard.

Below: The Old English Sheepdog has a lot in common with the Beardies above, but it is larger and heavier-coated.

As the Old English Sheepdog's use as a working dog declined, its popularity as a pet and show dog increased. This breed has become particularly popular in America and in many other countries where dog shows are common. It is an intelligent, active dog, very trainable and an excellent guard. But it should also be remembered that it is really quite big and boisterous, especially when young, and it has an enormous coat, now cultivated to such an extent that it looks almost more like a sheep than a sheepdog.

Scotland also has a shaggy sheepdog, the Bearded Collie, and superficially its appearance is similar to the Bobtail. It has the same heavy coat, though not so long, but the tail is left on, giving the dog a somewhat different outline. Like the Bobtail, the Beardie is a 'close-run' dog and

a very noisy worker favoured by drovers and farmers, but it was never very popular with shepherds because its coat 'balled' in the snow. The half-Beardie – a mixture of Border Collie and Beardie – is also very popular in some areas. Several attempts were made to popularize the Bearded Collie as a show dog, but it was not until 1948 that the breed was recognized by the British Kennel Club. Since then it has become quite numerous on the Continent and in Scandinavia. As a worker it is much in favour in New Zealand and there are far more Bearded Collies working there today than in Scotland.

As a companion, the Beardie is similar in many ways to the Bobtail. It is intelligent, affectionate, very active in both mind and body, and requires plenty of exercise. Like most of the herding breeds,

Below: If you like Collies but not the long coat, the Smooth Collie has the same shape but a less troublesome coat to look after.

the Beardie can be easily trained and is normally a good guard dog. Though long, its coat is not curly or woolly and therefore does not carry as much mud as one might expect. It is much easier to groom than the dense coats of the Bobtail or Poodle.

Another breed of shaggy sheepdog native to Britain is the little-heard-of Old Welsh Grey. This is very similar in appearance and style of working to the Bearded Collie, and it is possible that these two breeds and the Old English Sheepdog have common ancestry, although history does not tell us nearly as much about the herding breeds as it does about the hunting dogs.

The Collie is believed to have existed in its present form since very early times; it has been said that the rough-coated ones were bred in the Highlands of Scotland where they needed their coats as a protection against the cold, and that the smooth-coats were used by drovers in the Scottish Lowlands. But working dogs are bred for working ability rather than type, and Nature has been left to develop the type best suited to the purpose. The result is that there are many different types of Collie, which nevertheless are all pure-bred Collies.

One of the first breeds of dog to achieve fame as a show dog was a Collie. In 1860 Queen Victoria bought a very handsome dog when on a visit to Balmoral, and it subsequently became one of her favourite breeds. Royal patronage almost invariably draws public attention to a breed and the Collie quickly became popular both as a companion and a show dog. It was first shown in 1861 as a 'Scotch sheep dog' and in

1881 the Collie Club was formed. To say the breed became popular is something of an understatement, as in the 1880s several dogs were sold for prices varying from £500 to £1,500 and in those days one could buy a fair-sized farm for that amount. This breed is now officially known as the Rough Collie, but also unofficially as the Show Collie or the 'Lassie Collie' because of its association with the M.G.M. film star Lassie. Today the Rough Collie, either in its original form or its modern show type, is rarely seen as a working dog, but it is very popular as a show dog and companion. Many people regard it as one of the most handsome dogs and it is not too difficult to keep it looking well. Although heavy-coated, there is only slight feathering on the forelegs, while the hindlegs are quite smooth to the hocks. The coat is straight and harsh, so that mud does not cling to it as readily as with some other breeds.

There is also a Smooth Collie, identical to the Rough apart from its coat. Admirers of the breed claim that it is more beautiful than the Rough as one can see and admire its graceful outlines. It is a very clean dog to keep in the house, but it has never become as popular as its Rough cousin.

Many other types of Collie have been used in the hill sheepfarming areas of Scotland, England and Wales for centuries. One dog can do the work of ten men – and do it better – and the high cost of labour has made the dog more valuable today than ever before.

In recent years the breeding and training of sheepdogs has become much more scientific and sophisticated. Sheepdog trials have had much to do with this and

have resulted in a specialist dog bred for the purpose, now known generally as the Border Collie. Because the first sheepdog trial was held in Bala in North Wales in 1873, and because trials have been popular in Wales ever since, many people think the Border Collie is of Welsh origin and even refer to it as the Welsh Sheepdog. But at that very first trial it was a Scotsman with a Scottish-bred dog who won the championship, starting a big boom in the export of dogs from Scotland to Wales and, as a result, the native Welsh Sheepdog has become practically extinct.

The Border Collie derives its name from the border between Scotland and England, but it is a name only used in recent times. The International Sheepdog Society, founded in 1906, refers to it as a working sheepdog, and the stud book has sections for rough-coated, smooth-coated and beardie-coated. In Scotland it is also called the 'trial-bred dog' or 'creeper', a most apt name for describing its style of working. It is the style of working, rather than its appearance, which makes this dog different from all other breeds and types of sheepdog. The Border Collie has what is known as 'strong eye', enabling it to 'hold' a single sheep with its 'eye'. What it does, in fact, is to creep steadily and stealthily towards its 'prey', never for an instant relaxing its menacing stare. The sheep becomes almost mesmerized and either stands still or moves backwards. The 'eye' is so strong that it even affects people.

Dogs cannot be taught to work in this way, they must be bred to do it. The 'strong eye' is merely an exaggeration of the wild dog's natural instinct to stalk its prey. Until

Opposite page: Sheepdogs at work. The one on the left is a 'strong-eyed dog', showing the style of working which has made the Border Collie supreme for trial work and for some of the work on a sheep farm. The 'loose-eyed dog' standing up at the back is more of an all-rounder.

Above: The Swedish Valhund has a lot in common with the Welsh Corgi.

Right: A Pembroke Corgi playing with her puppy.

they are trained, the majority of good young dogs follow that instinct a stage further by grabbing hold of the sheep, but as their submissive instinct is also very highly developed it is not usually very difficult to teach them not to do this. The attitude adopted by the strong-eyed sheepdog is exactly the same as that adopted by pointers and setters, and a sheepdog will set at a sheep which it scents but cannot see, for example, a sheep buried in snow, just as a bird dog sets at a grouse.

'Strong eye' is by no means the only quality of the modern Border Collie. It is a wide-running, stylish worker which, when handled properly, can surpass any other type of sheepdog for certain types of work. But, because it is such a high-powered dog, it does require very delicate handling. Bred carefully, the herding instinct in the Border Collie can only be described as over-developed. It will literally work, or try to work, anything from a mouse to an elephant. Contrary to common belief, sheepdogs do not learn to work by watching other dogs or by being taught by their owners. They 'run' instinctively and it is up to the owner to teach them how, when and where to run.

The Border Collie has found its way to every country in the world where sheep are herded. Sheepdog trials are held in Australia, New Zealand, North and South America, Africa and many other countries. In recent years the breed has also become very popular and successful in obedience competitions. A dog so completely obsessed with work as the majority of Border Collies are will quickly become neurotic if denied any outlet for this instinct. When the

submissive instinct is equally strong, the dog will try to do anything its trainer asks of it, which is why the breed is so successful in the obedience ring. Without training and adequate exercise, the Border Collie is one of the most unsuitable of all dogs to keep as a pet.

At present the Border Collie is not recognized by the British Kennel Club or shown at dog shows, although it is shown in Australia. It is a difficult breed for which to set a standard of points, as there is a wide variation in size, with some smooth, some rough and some 'in-between' coats. The predominant colour is black and white, followed by black and tan and white, but one also finds dogs which are nearly all black or nearly all white, as well as chocolates, sables and blue merles.

The Welsh Corgi is another British herding breed which was made popular by royal patronage. Although known to be a very old breed, there seems to be no conclusive evidence as to where it originated. It is essentially a cattle dog and, although it will work sheep, it is much too rough and inclined to 'heel'.

There are two types of Corgi: the Pembroke and the Cardigan. The most obvious difference between the two is that the former has a short tail and the latter a long tail. The 'Cardi' is altogether a bigger dog, in a wider variety of colours. It has a less 'foxy' head and its forelegs are slightly bowed. The Corgi was first recognized by the Kennel Club in 1925 but it was not until 1934 that the two breeds were separated. Until then docking was prohibited and, although most Pembrokes were born with short tails, they varied in length from half

tails to no tails at all, presenting rather an untidy spectacle in the show ring. Since docking has been allowed, their appearance has become more uniform, but the percentage of natural short tails has decreased until it is quite unusual to find a natural bob-tailed puppy.

In 1934 the already popular Corgis were given a great boost when the Duke of York bought a Pembroke Corgi puppy for Princess Elizabeth, now Queen Elizabeth II. From then on the Pembroke Corgi quickly rose in popularity and for several years it was one of the top registered dogs in Britain. The Cardigan Corgi has never become as popular, either because it never had the good fortune to be patronized by royalty or because most people prefer the rather smarter, smaller Pembroke Corgi. Corgis also became popular overseas and were exported to America, Canada, New Zealand, Australia, South Africa and most European countries. Though not quite so much in favour today, the breed still ranks as one of the most popular show dog breeds in the world. In comparison with many other breeds, the show Corgi is hardly any different to its working cousin, and the shape of the head in particular has not changed at all.

As a pet the Corgi has many virtues and quite a few faults. It is a very game and gay little dog, with characteristics falling somewhere between the sheepdogs and the terriers. It is very intelligent but not always anxious to please, and its worst fault is a tendency to be over-excitable and noisy. The old heeling instinct very often comes to the surface and the human Achilles tendon seems to make a very good substitute for a cow's heel! Fortunately the show strains of today have much less inclination to do this than the original Corgis which came from the Welsh hills fifty years ago. It is one of those instincts which should be nipped in the bud very quickly. Generally speaking, the Cardigan has a steadier, less excitable temperament than the Pembroke.

A couple of other breeds bear a remarkable resemblance to the Corgi: the Lancashire Heeler of Britain, a very localized breed rarely seen outside its native county, and the Swedish Valhund, so closely resembling a Pembroke Corgi that one feels sure they must have common ancestry. Some say the Vikings stole the Corgis from Wales and took them back to Scandinavia, and some say that the Corgi came to Wales with the Vikings. The Welsh believe that Corgis have always existed in Wales and many legends surround the breed.

As its name implies, the Shetland Sheepdog is native to the group of islands off the north coast of Scotland. There seems to be little information on the history of the breed. It has been said that the reason why Shetland ponies, cattle sheep and dogs are small is because larger animals could not live under the rigorous conditions on the Islands, but while this is probably true of the herbivores it would not apply to dogs which do not live directly off the land. Small sheepdogs have existed in the Shetlands for as long as anyone can remember, and when tourists started going there they brought these pretty little dogs back with them. At Crufts Dog Show in 1906 several were exhibited and the breed was recognized by the British Kennel Club in 1909, although there was much dispute as to which was the correct type. The native Shetland Sheepdogs were not much like the ones seen in the ring today; they looked more like miniature Border Collies and are still to be found working in the Islands today. They had broad heads, well-defined stops, bold friendly eyes and were smaller than the average show ring specimen. Some breeders agreed, quite reasonably, that as this was the type to be found in the Shetlands it was the type which should be maintained, but others argued that the breed should resemble as closely as possible a miniature show ring Rough Collie. The latter opinion won the day and the Shetland Sheepdog of today looks very much like a miniature Rough Collie.

The breed is popular in most countries both as a show and pet dog. It is very pretty, easy to keep looking well and of course eats less than the larger sheepdogs. It is very intelligent and easy to train but it is a sensitive breed and some are very nervous. But if you take care to choose one with a good temperament, the Sheltie is a charming little dog to own.

With the Border Collie, the Kelpie is one of the two most important breeds of working sheepdog in the world today. But unlike its British ancestor, the Kelpie seems to have stayed in its native Australia where it has proved its value on the great sheep stations. It is estimated that some 80,000 of the breed are currently working in Australia.

Not surprisingly, Australia's first sheepdogs came from Scotland. In 1870 a pair of Scottish sheepdogs produced a puppy called Gleeson's Kelpie which, mated to Caesar, also bred from imported stock, produced King's Kelpie which won Australia's first sheepdog trial in 1872. It is believed that all Kelpies are descended from that one bitch, but there is some difference of opinion as to what other ingredients went into the creation of the breed. Some people say that Dingo blood was introduced, pointing to the Kelpie's prick ears and smooth coat as evidence. But there always have been, and still are, sheepdogs in Scotland and Wales which have prick ears and smooth coats. The most likely answer is that the Australian ingredients went into the creation of the stock to evolve their own sheepdog to work under their own conditions. They needed a dog which could work sheep in thousands rather than hundreds, as in Britain, and they ended up with a tough, independent working dog, very wide-running and showing as much 'eye' as a good Border Collie.

There are classes for the breed at Australian dog shows and some are kept as pets, but it will always be on the huge sheep stations that the breed really comes into its own, doing the work it was bred for and at which it excels.

The Australian Cattle Dog came into existence at about the same time as the Kelpie and no doubt with much of the same ancestry. In this case, however, it seems to be generally agreed that Dingo blood *was* used to add toughness to the already tough Scottish stock. Dogs had worked cattle in Britain long before Australia was discovered, but 100 head of cattle was considered quite a big drove and there were hedges and ditches round the fields and

Right: A large number of Alsatians, or German Shepherd Dogs, are trained for obedience work.

Opposite page: An Australian Kelpie 'backing' sheep in a truck. If there is no room for the dog to get round the side of the sheep to bring them out of a truck or sheep pen, then it must go over their backs.

along the old drove roads. In New South Wales and Victoria a 'mob' of cattle can be over 1,000 head, while the 'paddocks' can run into thousands of acres. The cattle are controlled by dogs working alongside mounted 'jackaroos', or cowboys. Weaklings have no place in this type of farming and, just to be able to survive, dogs need to be really tough. Explicit commands cannot be given in the same way as they are with a dog working at a sheepdog trial or on a quiet hillside in Wales or Scotland, so the Cattle Dog has to be able to think for itself and use its own initiative. The result is an extremely intelligent animal with exceptional agility of both mind and body.

The breed is remarkably true to type, with a head very similar to that of the Welsh Corgi. It has been popular in Australia as a show dog since about 1936, but does not seem to have attracted much attention outside its native country.

Perhaps the best known of all the herding breeds is the Alsatian or German Shepherd Dog, but today it is far better known as a police dog, guard dog, guide dog for the blind or family pet than as a sheepdog. The Alsatian, however, is essentially a sheepdog breed and trials are held for it in its native country. Sheep are kept under the folding system on the Continent, so the trials are very different and the German Shepherd would stand little chance in a British-style sheepdog trial, just as the Border Collie would be pretty hopeless in a trial run under German rules.

The Alsatian is a very old breed and has been used to herd and guard flocks for as long as anyone seems to remember. In a country where wolves are not unknown, even today, it was necessary to have a larger, stronger dog than the sheepdogs of Britain. The breed first attracted attention during World War I when Alsatians were used extensively by the German Army as messenger dogs, patrol dogs, Red Cross dogs, and so on. At the beginning of hostilities in 1914, when the British authorities had never thought of using dogs in war, the Germans had 60,000 dogs already trained. Most of these were German Shepherds, a breed physically as well as mentally suited for the job. During the War, soldiers from many countries came in contact with the breed, realized its abilities and took the dogs home with them. A puppy from a litter found in a dug-out in France was taken to America and became Rin-tin-tin, the first great canine film star.

Because of the War, the name German Shepherd Dog was not very popular in Britain and so the breed was renamed the Alsatian Wolfdog, Alsatian because the dogs which were brought to Britain came from Alsace. Wolfdog was subsequently dropped from the name and the breed became officially known first as the Alsatian and then as the Alsatian (German Shepherd Dog).

By 1926 the breed had the highest number of registrations in both Britain and America, but many dogs unfortunately got into the wrong hands and earned themselves a bad reputation. Many of the breed do have a nervous trait in their make-up and a nervous dog the size of a German Shepherd is a dangerous dog. It is essentially a working dog and can become very frustrated if given nothing to do. As a result, there have been many tragic cases of

children being badly mauled or even killed by dogs not under proper control. This is very unfortunate as, given correct handling, a good German Shepherd is a very good dog indeed. No dog breed has ever suffered so much from adverse publicity and the numbers dropped rapidly. Australia put a complete ban on imports of Alsatians on the grounds that they worried sheep, and this ban has only now been partially lifted. But in spite of all that was said against it, the breed retained a strong band of staunch supporters and has today come back into favour again, though more quietly.

During World War II, the breed again served with armies on both sides, not only as a guard and patrol dog but also as a mine detector and First Aid dog. One of its tasks as a First Aid dog was to go out looking for wounded soldiers in the battle zones, carrying with it medical equipment. Members of the breed have proved most successful as guide dogs for the blind and, of course, everyone knows how successful they have been as police dogs. What must be remembered is that the dog which arrests an armed criminal today may be searching for a lost infant tomorrow, and in most civilized countries the first essential of a police dog is that it does not bite unnecessarily.

No other breed can equal the German Shepherd Dog for versatility and one reason for this is its convenient size. It is a big dog, but not too big, with a close, weather-resistant coat which requires the minimum of attention. The German Shepherd does not shiver like a Boxer or a Doberman when out on a wet, cold night with a policeman on the beat.

Quite a few members of the breed have long coats, but these are regarded as a fault in the show ring and there is no separate recognition for long-coated specimens as there is with Rough and Smooth Collies.

In Holland and Belgium there are sheepdogs with a strong likeness to the German Shepherd and it would appear that at one time they all had common ancestors. One example is the Dutch Herder which is very popular in its native country, but has never become very well known outside Holland. It is divided into three breeds: rough-coated, long-coated and smooth-coated. It is still used as a sheepdog, cattle dog and guard dog and appears to be a good all-rounder. The predominant colour is grey, in various shades from very light to nearly black.

Belgian sheepdogs are similar in type to the Dutch Herder and have become quite well known outside Belgium, particularly in America. Best known is the long-haired, black variety established from old working stock by a M. Rose of Groenendael in 1880 and consequently named the Groenendael. In Belgium it was recognized as a breed in 1891 and soon became popular in both France and Holland. The breed first came to Britain from France in 1931 but was little heard of before the Second World War. After the War it became steadily better known and the Belgian Shepherd Dog Association of Great Britain was formed in 1965.

Slightly lighter in build than the German Shepherd Dog, the Groenendael is used in Europe as a police, sheep and cattle dog as well as for many other purposes. In America and Britain it has proved equally

Opposite page, above: A German Shepherd Dog (Alsatian) with its police handler in Florida.

Opposite page, below: A police German Shepherd Dog being worked on a long lead so that it will not be confused by the scent of its handler.

Above: Samoyeds are popular members of the Spitz family.

popular as a worker, companion and in the show ring. Given the opportunity, this Belgian Sheepdog could be expected to carry out any of the tasks usually allotted to the German Shepherd.

The Belgian Tervuren was established by breeders near the Tervuren and is to all intents and purposes a fawn-coloured Groenendael. Indeed the first Tervuren champion in 1907 was by the black Piccard D'Uccle, the foundation sire of the Groenendael. In many countries the two breeds are still shown in the same classes as Belgian Sheepdogs. Tervurens have only recently come to Britain where they are still shown under the classification of a Rare Breed. As a worker and companion. the Tervuren is no different from the Groenendael and one day it may well catch up with its black brother in popularity.

A popular French sheepdog is the Briard, one of the many herding breeds which have also been used for a long time as guard dogs. The Briard is a very well-established breed dating back to the twelfth century, and it is believed that Emperor Charlemagne gave pairs of Briards as gifts to his friends. The breed was also a favourite with Napoleon, who took them on his expedition to Egypt and had several with him in exile in Corsica.

There is so much similarity between the Briard, the Old English Sheepdog and the Bearded Collie, both in appearance and behaviour, that it seems likely that there is a connection between the three breeds. The Briard is larger than either of the other two and is used in its native country as a police dog as well as for working with sheep and cattle. It was also used successfully by the French Army in both World Wars. Apart from the usual duties of patrol dog, messenger dog and so on, the breed was found to be strong enough to carry ammunition and equipment on a specially made pack saddle.

The Briard has been popular in Canada and America since the 1920s but has only recently become known in Britain, although its popularity is increasing rapidly. It is a very active breed, both physically and mentally, and has a surprising turn of speed. It is a natural guard and is often suspicious of strangers. Some, unfortunately, are actually afraid of strangers and if you are considering buying one, you should be careful to select a puppy from stock which is not nervous. Apart from this, it is a most affectionate dog, responsive and easy to train. For some unknown reason, the breed standard insists on double dew claws behind and these can cause trouble if not kept well trimmed and can even grow right back into the leg, causing a very painful sore. The long, slightly wavy coat needs daily attention if it is to look as beautiful as it should. If it is not kept well groomed, mats can form, causing a lot of unnecessary discomfort to the dog when you do have to remove them and, if left for too long, eventually ruining the coat.

Another European breed only recently imported to Britain is the Bouvier de Flandres. 'Bouvier' means cowherd or drover, and although there are a number of cattle dogs in the Low Countries the Bouvier de Flandres has always been very popular with cattle men. However, since modern farming methods took over and cattle have been transported by road and rail, rather than driven along the roads, this breed has been less in demand as a working dog. But this has been remedied to a certain extent by the fact that it has become quite well known as a show dog, especially in Canada and America. It is also often trained for working trials and police work. Rather like a Giant Schnauzer in appearance, this is a tough, rugged-looking dog, muscular and cobby, with a rough wiry coat. Kept under proper control, it is a determined guard dog.

Further south, and found on both the French and Spanish sides of the Pyrenees, is the home of the Pyrenean Mountain Dog, known as Great Pyrenees in America. This impressive dog, massive in size with a thick, warm white or nearly white jacket, was specially bred centuries ago to guard the flocks from wolves and bears. It needed to be able to work day and night 1,500 m (5,000 ft) up in the mountains and is consequently extremely hardy. It is doubtful if Pyrenean Mountain Dogs ever worked the flocks as sheepdogs, their main duty being to guard them. The smaller Pyrenean Sheepdog, with a shorter coat and more agile, was used alongside them for the actual herding.

Not surprisingly, this handsome, dignified dog has become popular all over the world as a show dog and companion. If you intend to own one, remember the thick coat needs a lot of attention and tends to leave white hairs on the carpets. This breed also needs plenty of space and plenty of food – many of them weigh over 45 kg (100 lbs). The Pyrenean Mountain Dog is very independent and a superb guard, often a little too keen for the conditions under which we expect it to live today. We knew of one massive dog which travelled on the back seat of the car when out with its attractive young female owner. All was well if her passenger was another girl. But let her dare to take a boyfriend with her, and sooner or later a huge paw was thrust between them and the poor chap felt heavy breathing down his neck and heard a warning growl in his ear. Only doing what it considered its duty, the poor dog had to find another home as its owner got a little tired of finding new boyfriends!

From Hungary comes another handsome all-white dog, possibly an ancestor of the Pyrenean. The Kuvasz has been known for some time in the American show ring but has only recently been seen at British dog shows. Its name comes from the Turkish word 'kawasw', meaning 'guardian of nobles', and it has been used for well over 1,000 years to guard the flocks of sheep and cattle herded on the great Hungarian steppes. Today it is now used mainly in its native country as a guard dog on farms and estates. The Kuvasz is a very keen, ardent guard and at one time it was common to see it with heavy logs attached to its collar as a precaution to keep it within the boundaries of the farm. Strangers stood little chance of escaping unharmed if one of these dogs was on patrol.

Two more Hungarian herding breeds are the Komondor and the Puli, both of which are also very ancient breeds. A legend about the Komondor tells how a tenth-century Serb shepherd found a litter of wolf cubs. He killed those which sipped, wolf-fashion, but gave those which lapped, dog-fashion, to the village women to bring up. In due course they were crossed with

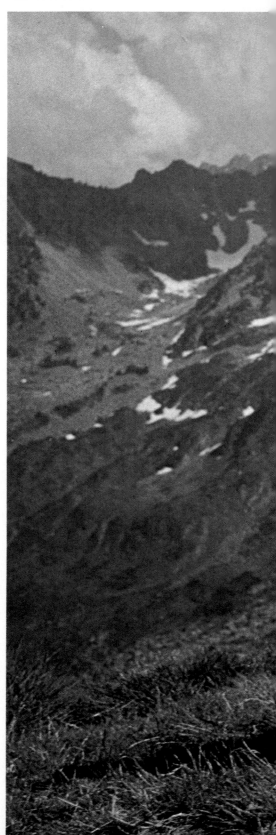

Right: The Briard, an attractive old French sheepdog breed, can still be seen working in France, although not in England.

Below: A Pyrenean Mountain Dog in its home setting. Compared with the show dogs on page 174 this dog has an altogether more workmanlike appearance.

local dogs and the result was the Komondor. The Hungarian sheep live semi-wild out on the bleak Hungarian steppes for four or five months of the year and the Komondor has no equal at herding these timid sheep quietly and competently.

Both the Komondor and the Puli have extraordinary coats. Long and extremely dense, their coats form into cords – in working conditions, felty mats – making them ideal for the constant exposure to harsh weather conditions they have to withstand when they are out with the sheep. Show dogs, of course, do not have the mats but the cords are carefully cultivated and the dogs can be washed without disturbing them. The Komondor is always white, but the smaller Puli is usually reddish-black or grey. Pulis have traditionally worked nearer the villages and

consequently seem to have adapted to town life quite happily, making good companions and house guards.

Another large, mainly white sheep dog, obviously a close relation of both the Pyrenean and the Kuvasz, is the Maremma from the central plains of Italy. Slightly smaller and lighter in build than the Pyrenean, this breed has never become very popular in other countries although a few are seen in England and at the larger dog shows. The Maremma is a tough, hardy breed, as would be expected from its history; used for guarding the flocks against wolves, bears and human thieves, the dogs would stay out day and night in all weather, their food consisting mainly of curds and whey and a sort of mealy porridge. They make excellent, and decorative, guards on large estates for they have a strong territorial

instinct. We have known several which
when first let out in the morning would do
a complete tour of the whole property
completely on their own. Being satisfied
that all was well, they would then come
back and lie calmy, but watchfully, by the
gate.

Portugal has several rather attractive
herding breeds, most of which are dual-
purpose dogs, inasmuch as that they are
also used as guard dogs. As a rule, cattle
dogs are rather on the small side, but in
countries where they were required to
defend the flocks from wolves and bears
they were usually larger. Two of the better-
known Portuguese breeds are the Estrella
Mountain Dog, formerly known as the
Portuguese Mountain Dog, and the
Portuguese Sheepdog. Both are exhibited in
their own country and are gradually

becoming known elsewhere. The first
Estrella Mountain Dogs came to Britain in
1974. They are heavily built dogs, weighing
up to 45 kg (100 lbs), with a soft, medium-
length coat in a variety of colours, and a
sensible broad head with a well-defined
stop. The Estrella is a hardy, independent
breed which still retains its keen guarding
instinct, and in Portugal was often used
rather like a small horse to draw carts
carrying wine or cork.

The Portuguese Sheepdogs are bright,
lively dogs, not as large as the Mountain
Dogs but originally used for the same
purpose. They have fairly long hair with
whiskers and eyebrows and come in a
variety of colours from fawn to black; there
is also a smooth variety. They are now
quite rare even in their own country and
they are not yet shown outside Portugal.

Opposite page: The Puli is not to
everyone's taste, but if you can cope
with the unusual coat these dogs have
a lot of character.

Above: Like the Puli, the Komondor is
a working dog from Hungary. Its coat
is a mass of weather-resistant cords
which hang down over its body.

Apart from the German Shepherd Dog, Germany has produced several other well-known breeds of what could be termed 'general utility dogs' – dogs that will help with the cattle, make good companions or equally good police dogs. Some are of ancient lineage, others of more recent 'manufacture'.

The Rottweiler is one of the more ancient breeds, taking its name from the town of Rottweil in southern Germany. Many years ago it was called the Rottweiler Metzgerhund – the butcher's dog of Rottweil. There are many legends surrounding the breed. One says they came into Germany with the Roman legions, who used them as guard dogs and also to drive the herds of cattle needed to supply food for their advancing armies. Yet another suggests that they are descended from the strong, powerful boar-hunting dogs of the Swabian Knights. These dogs were put out to 'walk' as puppies, which is still done with Foxhound puppies in England. Severe penalties were inflicted on the 'puppy walkers' if the dogs were not returned in good condition, and it became the custom for the farmers to take them out with their own dogs when they were herding the cattle, so that they could keep an eye on them. As boarhunting decreased, fewer dogs were bred by the nobility and several were left on the farms. The farmers used them as guards and herders, and when the butchers came to buy their beasts often sold them the dogs to drive the cattle back to town.

The Rottweiler was imported from Germany to Britain in the 1930s and has increased in numbers ever since. Large powerful, thick-set dogs, they have smart black, smooth coats with tan markings and

Opposite page, top: Two attractive Maremma sheepdogs, from Italy.

Opposite page, bottom: Strong sensible guards, these two Rottweilers give the impression that they would soon see off any unwanted intruders.

Below: The Kuvasz is another newcomer to Britain and a relative of the Maremma and Pyrenean sheepdogs. It is a large dog and a keen guard which needs a sensible, capable owner.

intelligent brown eyes. They can still give a hand driving cattle if required, but nowadays Rottweilers are more likely to be seen giving a good account of themselves in working trials or on active duty with police forces.

The Giant Schnauzer, or the Riesenschnauzer as it is known in Germany, is another very old breed of herding dog which worked the cattle on the farms of southern Bavaria many years ago. Rather like the old-fashioned Kerry Blue from Ireland, the Schnauzer was expected to turn its hand to any job on the farm that a dog could do. It has plenty of initiative – too much for some owners – and can still do its original herding work, but today it is more often seen guarding docks and warehouses. Schnauzers have never really become very popular, although quite a few have spread

to Scandinavia. There is at least one working with the British police force, and making a good name for itself.

Schnauzers are large dogs, standing about 60 cm (2 ft), usually black or pepper and salt, and look what they are – tough, workmanlike dogs ready and willing to 'have a go', be it catching a criminal or bringing home the cattle.

Guard Dogs

ALTHOUGH the majority of present-day police and guard dogs come from the herding and allied breeds, there are a number which have always been bred as guard dogs. Most important of these are the various types of Mastiff, originally used as ferocious and fearsome war dogs.

Bas reliefs from Ancient Babylon, dated around 2000 BC, show dogs of Mastiff type going into battle with Hammurabi's armies. There are many other references to this type of dog being used by fighting armies right through the ages. Suits of armour worn by war dogs are to be seen in several European museums and there is one in the Tower of London.

History concentrates on two types of Mastiff: the Tibetan Mastiff and the Old English Mastiff. The Tibetan Mastiff has been described as the most savage dog in the world, but it has never established itself outside its native country and is now very rare even there. It is a huge, thick-coated dog, of similar type to several mountain dogs like the Pyrenean, Bernese and St Bernard.

The Old English Mastiff is much better known and its history is well documented for the past 2,000 years or so. When the Romans came to Britain, they were very impressed by these huge dogs which appear to have been quite numerous. An officer called the Procurator Cynegii was appointed the task of collecting and exporting Mastiffs to fight in the Roman arenas, where they were pitted against bears, lions and bulls, not to mention human beings. Later in its history, the Old English Mastiff was used in Britain as a guard dog to protect farms, castles and other property against human adversaries, and also to protect livestock from the attacks of wolves. Mastiffs were mentioned in the Forest Laws of King

Opposite page: It is easy to see why the Dalmatian got his nickname of 'Plum Pudding Dog'.

Right: Not many people can afford to feed the large St Bernard today, or to keep one properly in modern towns and cities.

Canute, and in Norman times they were the only breed, apart from the hounds belonging to the nobility, allowed in the forests, as long as they had their front claws cut off so that they could not hurt game.

The breed fought in the Battle of Agincourt and other wars of that period and was also used for the fashionable sports of bull- and bear-baiting. A Master of the King's Bears, Bulls and Mastiffs was created in the reign of Henry VIII, and in Elizabethan times plays were not allowed on Thursdays as that was the day reserved for bear-baiting. It was not until the early nineteenth century that animal baiting was banned in England and there immediately followed a great decline in the Mastiff population. Whether one agrees with a court ruling that baiting was a 'sweet and comfortable recreation for the solace and comforts of peaceable people', or with Samuel Pepys who described it as 'a very rude and nasty pleasure', it is sad to think that such a courageous animal, which held a unique position in the history of England for some 2,000 years, should suddenly become redundant.

There is no reason to suppose, because the Mastiff was used so much in the pursuit of a 'nasty pleasure', that it must be a nasty animal. On the contrary, dogs which are bold or even ferocious in the face of an adversary are usually most reliable with people, particularly children. Unlike the timid dog, they are not afraid of being hurt themselves and it is the nervous dog which is dangerous. Even in the days when the Mastiff was still being used in the bear pit and the bull ring, its virtues outside them appear to have been appreciated. At the beginning of the nineteenth century, Sydenham Edwards wrote in his *Cynographia Britannica*: 'What the lion is to the cat the Mastiff is to the dog, the noblest of the family; he stands alone and all others sink before him. His courage does not exceed his temper and generosity, and in attachment he equals the kindest of his race . . . In a family he will permit the children to play with him, and suffer all their little pranks without offence . . .'

In spite of their virtues, by 1908 only 35 Mastiffs were registered with the British Kennel Club. A few enthusiasts tried to preserve the breed, but keeping such a large dog going through two world wars was not easy. Only three litters were born in Britain between 1939 and 1945, and at the end of World War II only twenty Mastiffs remained in their native country,

most of them too old for breeding. Fortunately quite a number had been exported to America and the Old English Mastiff Club in Britain was able to buy some of these and take them back to England. This ensured the survival of the the breed on both sides of the Atlantic, although lack of fresh blood has proved quite a problem. Numerically the breed is still much stronger in America than in Britain and it is unlikely that it will ever rank amongst the top breeds in either country. On the other hand, the risk of extinction is now gone – for good, we hope – and British breeders are now exporting Mastiffs to many parts of the world.

Only one breed of dog has been specifically created in Britain as a guard dog, and that is the Bull Mastiff. It is very much a British product, being the result of crossing two of the oldest and purest of British breeds – the Bulldog and the Mastiff, remembering that the nineteenth-century Bulldog bore more resemblance to the Boxer of today than to the Bulldog, which would not survive in a bullring for more than a few minutes. The Bull Mastiff is one of the newest breeds and was not recognized by the British Kennel Club until 1924. But these dogs were used long before that by gamekeepers, who referred to them as 'night dogs' and used them to apprehend poachers. They were reputed to be trained to attack a man and throw him to the ground every time he tried to get to his feet, without ever using their teeth. There are records of contests and wagers over the ability of these dogs, one of which was reported in *The Field* of August 20, 1901:

'Mr Burton of Thorneywood Kennels brought to the show one night dog (not for competition) and offered any person one pound who could escape from it while securely muzzled. One of the spectators who had had experience with dogs volunteered and amused a large assembly of sportsmen and keepers who had gathered there. The man was given a long start and the muzzled dog slipped after him. The animal caught him immediately and knocked him down with the first spring. The latter bravely tried to hold his own, but was floored every time he got to his feet, ultimately being kept to the ground until the owner of the dog released him. The man had three rounds with the powerful canine but was beaten each time and was unable to escape.'

The Bull Mastiff is still used by gamekeepers in Britain, and is one of the steadiest and most reliable of modern breeds. It makes a good, natural guard but is very reluctant to bite unless trained to do so. The very appearance of this dog, standing four square and staring a stranger straight in the eye, is enough to deter most people. Bull Mastiffs make quiet, stolid family dogs, reliable with children.

Although today not usually thought of as a guard dog, the Dalmatian has a long tradition in this field and was at one time also used as a war dog. There are various different theories about its origin, but it is known that years ago a dog very like the Dalmatian existed in Dalmatia on the eastern shores of the Gulf of Venice. These Dalmatian dogs did sentinel duty on the borders between Dalmatia and Croatia, to give warning against the inroads of invading Turks. Old engravings show Dalmatians standing by chariots, and it appears that they have always had the strange affinity with horses for which they are so well known.

An American writer in 1901 said of the Dalmatian that 'now he is a dog of wheels and more connected with roads than inroads'. The breed has only fairly recently been upgraded to show dog and house pet, and for many years its place was in the stable yard, where it acted as a guard dog when not out with the carriages. Dalmatians were bred for stamina, and a newspaper report of 1851 tells of one dog which used to run with the Brighton to London coach – a distance of 116 km

(72 miles). In the early part of the nineteenth century Dalmatians used to precede the carriages, but later they took up their station behind, the rear of the vehicle being quite unguarded.

Today Dalmatians are only usually seen out with carriages at horse shows. Apart from being very decorative, they make capable guards when left to look after an unattended vehicle.

As house pets, they are clean, short-haired dogs, not too large but with a tendency to shed white hairs. They need a lot of exercise and if left idle tend to get fat and bored. The pups are born white and the spots, liver or black, develop later.

The Great Dane, often known by many other names, has been around for centuries but the modern animal is essentially a fairly recent German product. The late Lord Rank called the breed 'gentlemanly, alert, courageous and elegant', an assessment many Great Dane owners would agree with.

The Great Dane looks, and is, an excellent guard dog. Its awe-inspiring appearance and deep-throated bark, almost a bay, should scare away all but the very bold or foolhardy.

Danes are not cheap to buy, rear or keep, but if you can afford one and have the facilities to keep it properly you will have a devoted companion and guardian. One problem that sometimes arises is its long tapered tail which can get in the way

Left: The Old English Mastiff.

Above: Not a pretty sight today, bear-baiting was a popular sport of the past.

Left: This Chow shows a very typical Oriental expression and also the black tongue. This is the only breed of dog which has the colour of its tongue mentioned in the breed standard.

Below: Strong, active and alert, this Doberman Pinscher looks capable of doing the job for which it was originally bred. The cropped ears would bar this dog from the show ring in Britain.

indoors, knocking over furniture or people, and if confined for long the dog can do its tail a lot of damage.

The origin of the Boxer is not very clear, but it has only been known in its present form since the end of the nineteenth century. Quite likely it is a descendant of the old Bullenbeiser, which was once used in Germany for bull-baiting. When this cruel sport died out in Germany, the breed declined in numbers, but towards the end of the nineteenth century it received a boost of English Bulldog blood and finally emerged in 1895 at Munich as the Boxer. Since then the breed has never looked back and is well up in the popularity charts of most countries as a companion and guard dog.

Boxers are compact, short-coated, medium-sized dogs which soon caught the eye of the German police and were put into use with the Customs men and for general police duties. They are extremely boisterous dogs which take a long time to 'grow up', but they are ideal dogs for energetic owners.

The Doberman is a comparative newcomer and was created in the 1890s by Herr Doberman of Apolda. He used Rottweilers, German Pinschers, some varieties of Vorsthunde and maybe a dash

of Weimaraner, the result being an elegant, streamlined dog, only too eager to go into action. Not surprisingly, the new breed inherited many of the tough working qualities of its ancestors and it was said of the earlier dogs that they feared nothing and that it took a brave man to own one. Their nature has softened in recent years but they still make formidable enemies, as many would-be criminals have discovered.

Dobermans are popular in the show ring and with police forces and armies all over the world, and Herr Doberman would be delighted to know that his skill and hard work have paid off so handsomely. The breed is well adapted to work in hot climates and is used with considerable success in the Middle East. In America many are used to guard stores and office blocks. They are well to the front in working trials and obedience classes and make exceptionally good tracking dogs. Kept as pets and companions they need careful handling and firm discipline, without bullying. A well-trained Doberman can make an excellent guard and companion; an untrained one can be a bit like carrying around a loaded gun – it may go off with disastrous results.

The term 'guard dog' tends to conjure up visions of large Alsatians chasing after desperate criminals or Dobermans ferociously guarding security vans, but many small breeds have served as guards for centuries and have done the job very well indeed.

The small, black, tailless Schipperke is one such guard dog. According to the archives of some Flemish towns, it was in use on the canal barges to repel boarders at least 150 years ago. Schipperkes were often to be seen riding on the tradesmen's vans, which they were left to guard while the vanmen made their deliveries. They are active, bustling, vigilant little dogs, and their shrill piercing bark gives obvious warning of strangers. Quite a number are shown in Britain, but not many are seen as pets. This is perhaps no bad thing as these active little dogs are not really suited to an idle life.

A larger breed, but still quite small compared with most guard dogs, is the Keeshond from Holland. At the beginning of the nineteenth century, most farms and barges had a Keeshond as a guard dog and they were used as such until about 1925 when they reached the show ring in several countries. Keeshonds make cheerful, adaptable companions and alert, sensible guards. They are medium-sized, do not eat a great deal nor take up a lot of room. Their grey, offstanding, thick coats look as though they would need a lot of grooming, but in fact water runs off the outer coat and mats seldom form. These dogs have plenty of personality and make good family dogs, usually only too happy to oblige the children with a game.

From the East comes the Lhasa Apso, usually associated with the monasteries where they were bred, although they were also owned by the ordinary people of Tibet. They are believed to be bringers of good luck and it is considered a great honour in Tibet to be given one as a present. Happy little dogs with thick coats, necessary in the Tibetan climate, they seem to have adapted to the Western world very well. They make courageous little guards and are quick to give warning.

Also from Tibet comes the Lhasa Apso's larger cousin, the Tibetan Terrier, resembling a small Old English Sheepdog and in colours ranging from black to white. These dogs were often to be seen around the nomads' camps where they were expected to guard their master's property, including his children and livestock. Like the Lhasa Apso, they were also considered as a sort of talisman and good luck token. Another job they were expected to do was to retrieve objects which fell into awkward rocky places, which means that most of them have what is known as a good 'nose'. In summer they were often clipped with the sheep. and their thick hair was then mixed with Yak hair and woven into soft cloth. Quite a number are now shown and kept as companions. Most are charming little dogs. and they make discriminating guards.

Above: Head study of a Bulldog.

Above: The Keeshond is a medium-sized spitz breed from the Netherlands. A happy, sensible dog, but it does need to be kept well groomed.

Opposite page: This little Shih Tzu will have a lot more coat when it gets older.

Below: The Lhasa Apso is another breed that needs plenty of grooming.

Terriers

AFTER the hounds, the terriers are probably the best known of the hunting dogs. They come in a tremendous variety of shapes, colours, sizes and coat textures and have been native to the British Isles for centuries.

In the fifteenth century, Dame Juliana Berners, Prioress of Sopwell Nunnery, wrote, rather surprisingly, a book on field sports, in which she classified 'Teroures' as a breed used in field sports. In 1576 John Caius, physician to Queen Elizabeth, wrote a treatise on English dogs where he also mentions 'Terrarius or Terrars' as 'dogges serving y pastime of hunting beasts'. He described how their work caused them to creep underground in pursuit of foxes and badgers. So the twentieth-century terriers that bolt foxes and rabbits and kill rats are doing the same work as their ancestors of over 400 years ago.

Most people's idea of a 'Terour' is the well-known Fox Terrier. Very popular as a show dog and companion in the 1920s and 30s, it is still seen in well-filled classes at shows but not so often as a family pet. For some unknown reason, the Wire Fox Terrier has always been more popular than the Smooth. The Smooth is very easy to keep clean and tidy, although when it is casting it leaves large quantities of short white hairs all over the carpet, but the Wire needs professional trimming to be presented in the show ring and expensive visits to the beauty salon to remain a smart pet dog.

Although Dame Juliana's treatise mentioned both Smooth and Rough Terriers, it is difficult to trace their ancestry. For centuries packs of hounds have kept hunt terriers but only a few have kept records of their breeding. It is from the terriers of these packs that the modern Fox Terrier is descended. From the mid-1850s to the 1870s many of these working terriers appeared at early dog shows.

Someone once said of the old Bull Terrier that 'To own a fighting dog you must be a fighting man' and to own a terrier and appreciate it you must be 'a terrier man'. And the Reverend Dr Rosslyn Bruce described them thus: 'Of all God's creatures, animals are easily the highest; of all animals terriers are undoubtedly the most useful; of all terriers Fox Terriers are probably the most desirable; a Smooth Fox Terrier is the most heavenly thing on earth.' The modern show Fox Terrier has changed a great deal from those early days and not many show champions would be allowed to have a go at bolting foxes or killing rats even if they wanted to. Many terriers, however, still retain their sporting instincts and make merry, happy companions.

Opposite page: Terrier racing, using traps similar to those used on Greyhound tracks.

Left: A Wire Fox Terrier trimmed and ready for the show ring.

Below: Maybe not as smart as his cousin above, this Fox Terrier shows more in common with his hunting ancestors.

A terrier, like a hound, needs a good voice so that it can keep in touch with the huntsmen when it is working. Once a terrier has marked its quarry underground, it should keep on barking to let the men on the surface know its whereabouts. They can then dig down and come to grips with the fox or badger. A silent dog can easily be lost or injured underground and never heard of again. The tendency of many of the smaller terriers to enjoy the sound of their own voices is, however, not always appreciated by owners today, who no longer want to work them.

Although so well known, the Fox Terrier cannot claim pride of place in the terrier group. This must surely go to the 'king of terriers', the large Airedale from Yorkshire. It is generally accepted that the breed originated in the locality of the River Aire near Bradford in Yorkshire, and that it was a mixture of Otterhound and various

local terriers. Known originally as the 'Waterside Terrier', it excelled at water work such as catching water voles. But it was soon discovered that this large terrier, weighing about 22½ kg (50 lbs) was the ideal all-round sportsman. The only thing it could not do was go to ground, but it would have a go at anything else. It could catch rabbits, kill rats, swim like an otter, mark game, retrieve, work on the farm, act as nursemaid to the children, and was a very reliable family guard. Small wonder then that it became so popular in many countries. In 1884 the breed was classified by the British Kennel Club and exported all over the world. Apart from becoming a popular show dog in America, an Airedale won the first police dog trials held in Madison Square Gardens. In Africa Airedales hunted water buck and bush buck, in France they hunted wild boar, and they became well known as police dogs in Britain and Germany. They even acted as war dogs during World War I. It seems sad that this game, intelligent, good-looking dog should now be low down in the popularity stakes, and that they are now only used as police dogs in Germany. But fashions keep changing in the dog world as everywhere else, and it is to be hoped that the Airedale will once again resume its rightful position as the king of terriers.

Two other large terriers which are not used for going to ground are the Kerry Blue and the Soft-Coated Wheaten, both Irishmen. The latter is said to be the oldest and the Kerry is believed to be descended from it, but both breeds can be traced back 200 years or more. Medium-sized dogs of around 15 kg (35 lbs), they have a number of similarities. The coat in both breeds should

be soft, wavy and silky, any shade of blue in the Kerry and a light clear wheaten in the Soft-Coated Wheaten. For the show ring the Kerry is trimmed and clipped to a specific pattern. Its soft coat is not stripped like a number of other terrier breeds but clipped, more like a Poodle coat. If you don't want your pet Kerry to resemble a blue sheep, its coat will need a considerable amount of time spent on it – or money, if you have it professionally trimmed. The abundant coat of the Soft-Coated Wheaten is usually left untrimmed, which may save the cost of visits to the beauty salon but still costs a lot of time and trouble to keep it in order. If left ungroomed it quickly becomes matted, not only looking unsightly but possibly causing sores to develop under the mats.

The Kerry Blue, originally known as the Irish Blue, was first shown in Killarney in Ireland in 1915 and at Crufts in 1922, but the Wheaten was not recognized in Britain until 1939. In Ireland the Kerry was, and in some cases still is, used to herd cattle, catch rats, play with the children, guard the farm, as well as being expected to do any other job that came along. It has a reputation for 'playfulness', which not all owners would appreciate. Both dogs show plenty of terrier character and need firm handling, but in the right hands they make excellent guards and loyal companions. Neither, however, is a breed for anyone who does not want to spend time and trouble on grooming and training.

Another Irishman is the smaller Irish Terrier. Weighing about 10–13 kg (24–29 lbs) with a harsh red or red wheaten coat, it fully justifies its title of 'Daredevil' and will

not be put upon by lesser dogs. The Irish Terrier is a smart-looking dog, and should be trimmed for show in a similar pattern to the Fox Terrier. Built on more racy lines than most terriers, it is usually an excellent ratter and has been known to work quite well in the shooting field. It is a merry, affectionate dog but, like most other terriers, will soon get into mischief if left with nothing to do. Its rather reckless pluck can be more of a liability than an asset at times.

Scotland also has its quota of terriers which have been known there for many centuries. It was not until the late nineteenth century, however, that the various types became separated and known by names such as the Aberdeen (now the Scottish Terrier), Dandie Dinmont, West Highland White, Skye and Cairn.

Rather like the wild Irish Terrier, the Scottie seems to have acquired some of the characteristics of its native countrymen. A Scotsman once wrote of it: 'Jock should be a thinker, a philosopher and a seer; his soul is oppressed by the crass stupidity of all things created, and he shows it on his countenance. A Scottish terrier should look like a Kirk Elder the morning after a glorious fuddle – remorse, for hard-earned money squandered and time wasted.' For all that, this dour wee terrier has a number of devoted followers. Although commonly thought of as black, the Scottish Terrier can also be wheaten and brindle. It is an independent little chap, well able to look after itself, and at times appears rather sedate. Readily adaptable to town life, its coat does not show the dirt and it is a hardy little dog which needs little fussing over.

Opposite page: Smooth Fox Terriers, similar to their wire-haired cousins but their smooth coats are less trouble to groom.

Left: A neatly trimmed Irish Terrier. Although there are differences to the expert eye, the trim is very similar to that of the Wire Fox Terrier.

Like most terriers, it is a good guard dog with a deep bark for its size.

The West Highland White has a harsh weather-resistant coat, trimmed for show but more on the lines of the Cairn and not as barbered as the Scottish Terrier. It should not carry a great deal of coat and the pet Westie will need stripping down to its undercoat about twice a year. In between times, a good daily brushing should keep it looking and feeling in order. Appealing, cheeky, self-confident small dogs, West Highland Whites are usually very adaptable and do not seem to mind living in town houses and flats. It is believed they were originally throw-outs from Cairn litters, as white Cairns were disliked.

The late Baroness Burton once said, 'Cairns have no disadvantages.' Certainly they have as many advantages today as when she wrote that over 50 years ago. A hardy, intelligent breed, they are only small, some weighing as little as 4 kg (9 lbs). Many still work with hounds and quite a number of show Cairns hold a Master of Foxhounds working certificate. Even so, they seem quite happy living in towns. Their harsh coat, with its thick undercoat, keeps out the weather and needs very little attention from the professional trimmer. Colours vary from light wheaten to nearly black. For someone wanting a small but sporting dog, the Cairn takes a lot of beating.

Although the birthplace of the Skye Terrier was the Island of Skye, it was not actually given the name until 1861. They are rather out of favour today, except as show dogs, which may be because of their long flowing coats which require a great deal of attention. But it should be remembered that the pet Skye does not carry the excessive coat of the show dogs, and it takes a great deal of time, patience and experience to develop the glistening blue or fawn curtain, carefully parted in the centre, which hangs straight down on either side of the body. It is fairly obvious that a dog with such a coat would not keep it looking that way for long after a day's rabbiting. The Skye is a stolid little dog, very loyal to its own family but not overkeen on strangers. It makes a good housedog if you can spare the time to look after its coat, which can bring in a lot of mud on wet days as it is very near to the ground.

Another terrier from Scotland with a unique character and appearance is the Dandie Dinmont. Tough little terriers were used for most kinds of sport in the Border Country between Scotland and England long before Sir Walter Scott created a fictional character called Dandie Dinmont who kept a pack of useful pepper- or mustard-coloured terriers. A bright Border farmer called James Davidson had a strain of terriers which closely resembled Scott's description and so he started calling them Dandie Dinmonts. They sold very well and soon they were being exhibited at dog shows. The Dandie is a quaint little fellow with a weasel-shaped body, short sturdy legs, a large head with dark expressive eyes and a soft silky topknot, adding up to an unusual but attractive little terrier which tends to look larger than it is. Even its deep, resonant voice gives the impression of a larger breed. The Dandie is still a game, fearless little dog and, as Sir Walter Scott wrote, 'They fear nothing that ever cam wi' a hairy skin on't.' Perhaps, though, it is really more at home in the country than the city.

A little farther south from Scotland is the home of the Border and Bedlington Terriers. The Bedlington probably shares the same ancestry as the Dandie but it is believed to have been crossed with Whippets to give it more speed to catch rabbits in the open. It arrived in the show ring in 1869 and, although quite popular in the early twentieth century, it is not seen so much nowadays. The Bedlington is quite a tall terrier, about 38–41 cm (15–16 ins), with long legs, a long neck and a long domed head crowned with a silky topknot, reminiscent of the Dandie. Its coat is what is called 'twisty', which is really a mixture of hard and soft hair. It is not the easiest of coats to keep in good trim, and a pet Bedlington will need professional attention at regular intervals. Its looks are inclined to make some people think it is a soft dog but this is mistaken. The real Bedlington is a very sporting terrier, intelligent and easier to train than some of the other, more independent breeds.

The Border Terrier has survived the transition from working terrier to show dog with little change. It is an ideal little dog for someone wanting a natural-looking terrier which needs the minimum of attention to keep it smart. Its short, hard coat is coloured red, wheaten, grizzle, tan, or blue and tan. Its head is a bit unlike the other terriers, being more otter-shaped. The Border's racy build enables it to run with hounds, and yet it is small enough to go to ground. It is a keen, plucky little dog

which will tackle anything that moves. Two Border Terriers which were exported to Canada would tackle any game including porcupine, and their owner reported that they had once done 110 km (70 miles) in the hills running with the horses. They are still used by some Foxhound packs, and they also make excellent small sporting companions.

Although classified as a toy dog, the Yorkshire Terrier is still a terrier, if a diminutive one. This tiny Yorkshireman has had a spectacular rise to popularity during the past 50 years, and there are probably few countries in the world where it is not shown and kept as a pet. Today it is a tiny dog of under 3 kg (7 lbs) in weight— many show-winners weigh less than half that – but years ago its larger predecessor could be found all over the Yorkshire moors and dales, keeping down the rats on the farms. Many of this old-fashioned sort are still seen in their native county.

To develop the glamorous, long silky coat of the show-winner, the modern Yorkshire Terrier must live a somewhat restricted life. But the pet Yorkie seldom carries as much coat and is often slightly larger than the show type, probably a bit tougher too. Its shorter coat does not need too much attention to keep it in good trim and it is a handy-sized dog to keep in a town flat. Yorkshire Terriers are loyal, active little dogs, not over-keen on unsolicited advances from strangers and not averse to telling them so with a sharp nip from their minute teeth. Like a number of terriers, they rather like the sound of their own voices, but being bright, intelligent little dogs they are usually very easily trained.

Two other very natural-looking little dogs are the Norwich and the Norfolk Terriers. Until 1965 both types, drop- and prick-eared, were called Norwich Terriers and in Britain were put in the same classes at shows; they are still classified as Norwich Terriers in America. In their native counties they worked with Foxhounds and they also became very popular in America as workers. But in 1965 it was decided to call the drop-eared type the Norfolk Terrier, while the prick-eared type remained the Norwich. So a new breed was given official recognition, when in fact it was already well established in the show ring. They are among the smaller terriers, standing about 25 cm (10 ins) high, and both breeds have hard, straight, wiry coats which need the minimum of trimming. Their

Opposite page: A West Highland White Terrier, looking very well groomed.

Top: An Airedale Terrier in Switzerland accompanies his master on a cross-country skiing expedition.

Above: The popular Scottish Terrier. This one is neatly trimmed but not over-barbered.

colour can be any shade of red, grizzle, or black and tan. They are both compact, jaunty little dogs, not usually aggressive, and they make affectionate companions which seem quite happy to live in town or country.

To most people the Lakeland Terrier looks like a coloured Fox Terrier, and at early shows in the Lake District these local dark-coloured terriers were classified as 'Coloured Working Terriers' and the rest as 'White Fox Terriers'. Lakelands were used, and still are used, to run with the packs of hounds used to hunt foxes in the rocky Fell country. These packs have foot followers, not a mounted field, as the country is too rough for horses. The Lakeland will go underground and bolt a fox, or if the fox goes into hiding in a rocky 'borran' the terrier is expected to go in after it and

either put it out for the hounds or kill it there on its own. So this is a really tough dog which prefers to have a job of work to do, preferably a hard job with plenty of action. Its hard wiry coat is trimmed for shows very much the same as the Wire Fox Terrier. There are various colours for the Lakeland, including black and tan, wheaten and grizzle. Should you decide to keep one in the town, it will not show the dirt too much and is a handy size, but remember that there is still plenty of terrier character there and it will need to be kept occupied.

A breed often confused with the Lakeland is the Welsh Terrier, one of the oldest varieties of terrier in Britain. Although it has never gained the popularity of the more flashy-coloured Wire Fox Terrier, it is still quite well known and has gained success in the American show ring.

Below: This cheerful little Cairn Terrier is an accomplished 'begger'. Never teach this trick to a puppy until its back is strong enough to take the strain.

Right: It's anyone's guess what this little Norfolk Terrier puppy is thinking.

Opposite page, bottom: A Skye Terrier on its native Isle of Skye.

Usually black and tan, Welsh Terriers are also allowed to be grizzle. It is usually admitted, even if reluctantly, that there is a cross of Wire Fox Terrier somewhere in their blood. This may have altered the original shape but it has certainly produced a very smart, modern-looking terrier. In its native Wales, the farmers often go out in parties with guns after the hill foxes and the Welsh Terriers accompany them. It is not uncommon for them to be hunted in packs, a rare occurrence with most terriers.

Another native of Wales but a comparative newcomer is the Sealyham Terrier. The breed was founded by Captain John Edwards of the Sealyham estate in about 1860. He aimed to breed a short-legged, strong-jawed, courageous little terrier with a mainly white coat, to be used for badger-digging. How he actually bred them and from what ingredients no one really knows, but the result was a very smart little dog which soon found favour in the show ring as well as in working circles. The Sealyham's courage was never in doubt, for Captain Edwards used to test the young dogs by setting them to tackle a polecat. The hard white coat served a useful purpose when the dogs were working in bramble thickets, which the soft-coated terriers usually hated. Mostly all white, some Sealyhams have lemon or badger markings on their ears. There are not so many to be seen about now, but they still have a large band of staunch supporters.

A familiar terrier today is the Bull Terrier which has many varieties, all stemming from common ancestry. There are Bull Terriers, Staffordshire Bull Terriers, Miniature Bull Terriers and the

Staffordshire Terrier. Despite its name, the Staffordshire is an all-American product, specifically bred for fighting over 150 years ago. At one time referred to as the Yankee Terrier or Pit Bull Terrier, it finally emerged as the Staffordshire Terrier when dog fighting was tabooed. A larger dog than the Staffordshire Bull, with massive cheek muscles, these tough, tenacious dogs can hold their own with almost anything. The modern descendants of the breed, however, seem no keener on fighting than any other dog and they make affectionate, reliable family guards and are usually excellent with children.

The Staffordshire Bull Terrier, from which the Staffordshire Terrier originated, was also once used for fighting. It became separated from the white terriers, later to be called Bull Terriers, in the mid-nineteenth century. This coloured version did not come to the show ring as soon as the white ones, and it was 1935 before the Kennel Club gave it recognition. By this time dog fighting had become unpopular with public and police alike and the terrier fanciers turned to showing instead. No dog is tougher than the Staffordshire Bull, and it needs careful handling and training if it is to become the asset it should be, and not a liability. If it is allowed to run free, its latent fighting instinct will doubtless be aroused and once it starts fighting nothing will put it off. But the Staffordshire Bull is nevertheless a very trainable dog, some even doing well in working trials and, if treated with respect, it is without peer as a guard of its master's property and children.

The White Bull Terrier, now known as the Bull Terrier, was crossed back to the old coloured variety in the 1920s and it is now just as common to see coloured ones as the all white. Its egg-shaped head, small deep-set eyes, tight-fitting coat and obvious strength, all set in a muscle-packed, sculptured body, make it a dog worth looking at twice. At one time there was a lot of deafness prevalent in the white ones, but this has now been practically bred out. Bull Terriers used to be very popular in

Above: Although increasingly popular as show dogs and pets, most Border Terriers are still tough, game litte dogs.

Top: Although it is not really a good idea to have a dog so near a child's face, this Boston Terrier seems sensible enough.

India, where they withstood the hot climate well. They make excellent guards and companions and are usually good with small children, but, although they are slow to anger, this is not a breed to be trifled with once aroused. The Bull's short white coat is easy to keep well groomed, though it needs very thorough brushing when the dog is casting. A good bath helps to loosen the hairs and let the new coat come through more quickly.

A small variety called the Miniature Bull Terrier is often seen at the larger dog shows. The standard is the same as for its larger cousins but it must weigh under 9 kg (20 lbs) and be under 35 cm (14 ins) high. Not a great number seem to be kept as family pets, but they are neat, loyal little dogs, easy to keep clean, and do not require too much exercise.

Although called a terrier, the Boston Terrier does not really belong to the Terrier Group. In England it is placed in the Utility Group and in America in the Non-sporting Group. An all-American product, needless to say from the region around Boston, this tough, intelligent little dog comes in three sizes – under 6.8 kg (15 lbs), 6.8–9 kg (15–20 lbs) and over 9 kg (20 lbs). They are usually brindle with white markings in a definite pattern, and are compact-bodied, short-coated active dogs with a bright, determined expression, making ideal companions. Originally bred for fighting in the pits, the modern Boston has a less aggressive temperament than its ancestors, but it is an unwise dog which dares to interfere with it, although it does not usually seek out trouble.

The Boston originated from a mixture of breeds, including a fair dose of Bulldog blood, and it is not the easiest of dogs to breed from. Many bitches require caesarian operations in order to deliver their pups safely.

A relative newcomer to the terrier clan is the Australian Terrier. Although produced in Australia and shown there from 1899, it was undoubtedly derived from British exports. Cairns, Dandies, Irish and Yorkshire Terriers were all probably used in the original mixture, and the end result was an agile, compact little dog full of terrier character and pluck, happy to take on rats, snakes or any other vermin. It is a small terrier, weighing about 5 kg (11 lbs) and standing 25 cm (10 ins) high, with a blue or silver coat and tan markings on legs and body, and a straight hard coat. The colour can also be clear sandy or red.

Below: A Lakeland Terrier head study, showing the correct way to trim the dog for show.

Left: The tough little Dandie Dinmont.

Below: A Bull Terrier, made to look even more tough by the patch over one eye.

For anyone wanting a small but sporting terrier, a good town and country dog with a coat that does not show the dirt and is not very difficult to groom, this cheeky, happy little dog has a lot to commend it.

The other native Australian terrier is the Sydney Silkie. Again a mixture of several British breeds, the most-used cross was probably the Australian Terrier and the Yorkshire Terrier. First shown in Sydney in 1907, the new breed was soon being exported to Canada and America where it rapidly became popular. The coat should be flat, glossy and quite long, reaching to the ground, and blue and tan in colour. The Silkie has erect ears, weighs under 4.5 kg (10 lbs) and is a very likable, attractive little dog. But, like the Yorkie, its coat will need a lot of attention and must be kept well groomed.

Although not a registered breed, the Jack Russell Terrier deserves a mention as it has recently become increasingly popular. Years ago a sporting parson from Devonshire had a famous pack of working terriers which became known as 'Parson Jack Russells'. Opinions vary as to what they actually looked like, the probability being that he did not breed them but bought in any terriers which appealed to him in looks and working ability. During the last few decades some owners have become disillusioned over the way fashion has changed some of the old breeds of terriers and have turned to these tough little working types instead. They come long- or short-legged, prick- or drop-eared, short- or broken-coated, usually white with black or tan markings.

Above: An Australian Silkie Terrier is difficult to tell apart from the Yorkshire Terrier, which is one of its ancestors.

Breeding Dogs

Amongst domestic animals, selective breeding has given the widest diversity of size and shape to the various breeds of dog. However, although the proportion and relative relationship of the bones differ between breeds, the basic skeletal structure remains the same whether we are considering a 2-lb Chihuahua or a 150-lb St Bernard. A knowledge of the structure is important to dog breeders as well as veterinary surgeons as it is only by appreciating the function of various parts of the dog's anatomy that breed faults can be understood and an attempt made to eliminate them.

The skull is basically a bony box (the cranium) which houses the brain, and from which two joined tubes (the nasal chambers) protrude. The lower jaw is hinged to the cranium through the cheek bones (the zygomatic arch). Many dogs have skulls which differ little from their wild ancestors. However, in the short-faced breeds (brachycephalic) the jaws are considerably shortened and the curvature of the cheekbones is increased, giving the appearance of a greater width of skull. In some of these breeds, such as the Bulldog, the lower jaw is slightly longer than the upper causing the lower teeth to meet outside the upper set, a condition known as 'undershot'. The shortening of the nasal passages can lead to breathing difficulties. Such shortened jaws also lead to overcrowding, misplacement and loss of teeth. These hazards are increased by miniaturization and the smaller the breed the less likely you are to find a sound mouth.

The dog has the teeth of a carnivore, the incisors and canines being used to tear pieces of flesh and the molars and pre-molars being used to grind them up. In this the dog is aided by very powerful jaw muscles. These can be seen particularly clearly in some of the fighting breeds, like the Staffordshire Bull Terrier, where the pronounced cheek muscles add to the breadth of the head. The dog gobbles and bolts its food in lumps as saliva plays little part in digestion, most of which is carried out by the strong gastric juices of the stomach. The dog has two sets of teeth in its lifetime. There are 28 milk teeth which start to appear at about four weeks old. These begin to be replaced by the adult teeth at about four months, though the time varies somewhat with large breeds teething rather earlier than toy dogs. There are 42 permanent teeth. The lower jaw has six incisors, two canines, eight pre-molars and six molars. The upper jaw has two less molars. In most breeds the upper incisors are required to fit snugly over the lower ones (scissor bite). A number of dogs have missing pre-molars, a disqualifying fault in the show rings of Continental Europe.

The neck and shoulder placement is considered very important in most show dogs. This is because the structure of the shoulder, in particular the relationship between the shoulder blade (scapula) and the upper arm (humerus), determines what kind of front movement the dog has. Many breeds require the forelegs to move straight forward parallel with each other, covering the maximum of ground with the most efficiency. To achieve this the ideal shoulder structure is considered to be when the shoulder blade is at an angle of 45 degrees to the perpendicular, with the upper arm at right angles to it. The 'straight' front required by some terrier breeds is achieved by a short upper arm which brings the elbow of the dog up above the line of the brisket. Conversely, many of the racing breeds have a very long upper arm.

One of the more remarkable variations in shape achieved by selective breeding is the very short-legged dog (achondroplastic). This has been accomplished by shortening the leg bones rather than reducing the size of the animal, so that the result is quite a large dog set very low to the ground, for example, Dachshunds and Basset Hounds. The length of back comes from the length of ribcage and loin. The excessive length required by some breeds can lead to spinal weakness.

The ribcage houses the heart and lungs and is particularly deep and roomy in the racing breeds such as the greyhound group. The heart of a racing Greyhound is measurably larger than that of a dog of similar size not subjected to so much exertion.

The pelvic girdle, as the name suggests, is a bony ring of hip bones to which the femur or thigh bone is jointed. The angle and the width of the pelvis are important for easy whelping, as each puppy has to pass through this bony ring on its way to the outside world. Breeds with very massive heads in proportion to their bodies tend to have more difficulties in giving birth.

The hind limbs provide the propulsion for a dog's forward movement. This is why many breed standards pay great attention to the ideal angulation and structure of the hind leg. Low set hocks and marked angulation at the stifle tend to give a smooth-flowing, long-striding, economical movement. By contrast, the almost straight hind legs of the Chow give the breed its unique hind movement.

There are a variable number of vertebrae in the tail, an organ which the dog uses as a rudder, a balancing mechanism, a signal and a cover for the extremities when it curls up to sleep. Despite its many functions man has decided that some breeds look better without it and cuts all or part of the tail off shortly after birth.

The bony skeleton and the muscles which activate it form a protective casing for the more delicate organs of the respiratory, digestive and urinogenital systems. The whole is packaged by the skin, a layer with a multitude of functions the main one of which is insulation. The skin helps to keep the internal environment of the body constant so that the complex process of living can be carried on in the optimum conditions.

Above: External anatomy.

Below: Skeletal anatomy.

Opposite page: Teeth – lateral view.

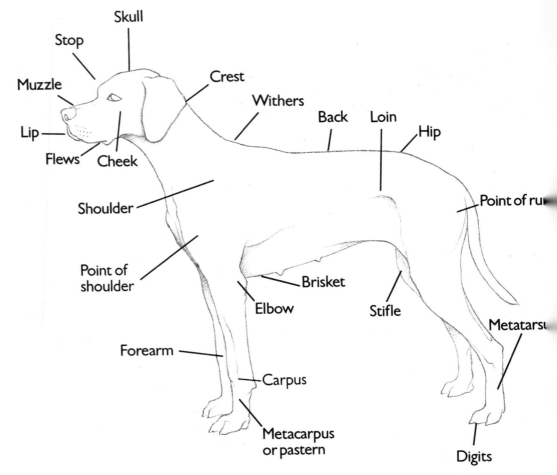

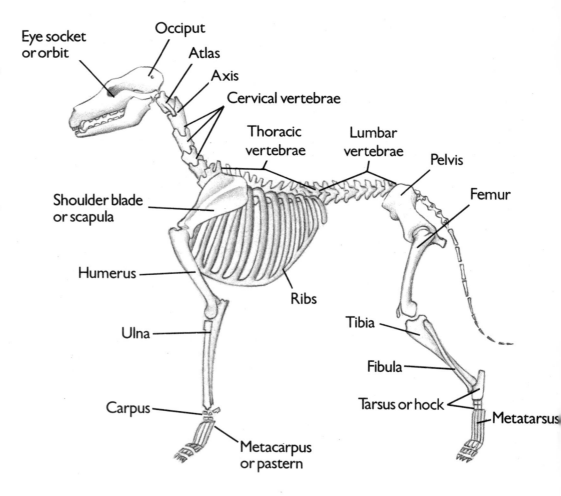

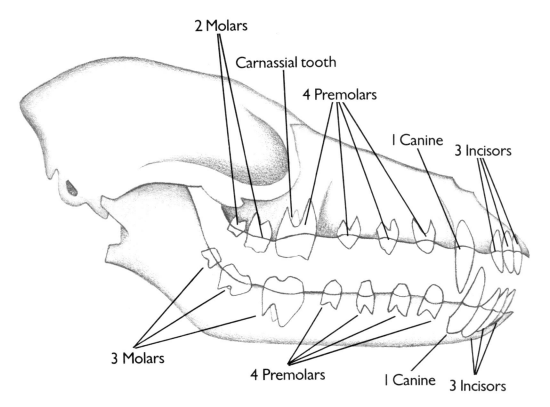

2 Molars

Carnassial tooth

4 Premolars

I Canine

3 Incisors

3 Molars

4 Premolars

I Canine

3 Incisors

In the last 50 years the whole picture of dog breeding has changed. The hobby, pastime, cottage industry – call it what you like – has attracted a new kind of interest, not always to the ultimate benefit of the dog. In the 1920s dog breeding was a specialist's business, largely an affair for country people with a background of animal lore and a natural eye for a good dog.

Countrymen would breed a litter from a bitch which performed well in the shooting field or on the grouse moor, just as the owner of the best rat-killing terrier or the fastest coursing whippet would want a pup or two to give to friends. Toy dogs were bred, too, both for pets and for pleasure. Often the actual breeding would be turned over to a groom, gamekeeper or gardener whose very job depended on producing puppies which did credit to his employer.

Family pets were mostly found from cross-bred puppies. They were easily obtainable, for dogs ran the streets and it was not unusual to see a bitch in heat pursued by a pack of dogs, of which the largest, strongest and cleverest would eventually mate her. This natural form of selection helped to perpetuate the best dog attributes.

Males were the choice for family pets. In suburbia it was considered rather daring and anti-social to own a bitch, for bitches were looked on as a nuisance which people were not prepared to tolerate. Bitch puppies were priced much lower than dogs and, even so, were largely unsaleable.

Dogs were bred by people who did not want a *lot* of pups – they wanted a few good working animals which would do them credit in the eyes of their friends. They would mate two strong animals, like to like, and rear only the healthiest of the litter. Any weak pups and most of the bitches would be discarded, thereby perpetuating a healthy strain and restricting the number of puppies on the market. Survival of the fittest was the watchword, and any pup which did not want to live was not worth keeping. There was no cossetting or handrearing. The countryman believed that the pup sickly at birth would not become a strong adult at maturity.

In the 1920s there were very few vets who specialized or who were even interested in working with dogs and pet animals. What care was afforded to pets was dispensed by unqualified animal practitioners or by animal charities, for all college-trained vets worked almost entirely with horses or farm animals. At that time there had been little study of disease problems in the dog, and not much veterinary care was offered to them, beyond sewing up cuts and cleaning ears. The sophisticated parameters of veterinary surgery which we know today, when practically any illness or injury can be treated, were unthought of 50 years ago. The idea of a vet using X-rays as a diagnostic tool was unthinkable in 1920, when the X-ray was still fairly new to the majority of human beings.

Because of the need for the dog to prove itself worthy of its place and its dinner, there was very little prospect of hereditary abnormalities being passed on. Pedigree dogs may not have been so poetically beautiful as they are today but they were fundamentally more sound.

By 1950 many changes had come about in the world. There had been a major world war, a population explosion and a new philosophy of life which maintained that every pastime and every way of life should be open to everyone. The sprawling towns stretched out into the countryside; each new house had its own garden, and each home had its fancy for a dog as its link with the fundamentals of Nature.

Owning a pedigree dog, perhaps breeding from it, became the fashionable thing to do. Dogs suddenly became big business. Everyone buying a dog in 1948 had the urge to breed a litter, and sales were so easy that there was nothing to deter them. The demand for dogs from overseas was enormous. Some purchasers were, quite rightly, disappointed with what they were sent. The new breeders did not know enough to be selective. To them all puppies were beautiful, and their kindly instincts led them to feel that every pup born had a right to live. Dogs were starting to occupy a place in the household comparable to that of small children; if they were not well, they must be nursed to better health. Poor little wailing newborn pups were bottle fed, warmed in home-made incubators, and brought along with pride of achievement until they were *almost as good as the others*. The weak puppy would eventually be sold to some other potential breeder, so that weakness was inbred by people who believed sincerely that they were doing their best for the dog.

In the early 1950s the dreaded dog disease of distemper was almost conquered when preventative vaccination for the dog became widely available. Distemper and its complications had previously carried off many thousands of dogs in their first year. This had in effect limited the dog population and also deterred people from having dogs. It was sad to see a dog die of distemper, but very difficult to avoid catching it. Within a few years of the vaccine being perfected, over half of the country's dogs were being protected by it. Distemper ceased to be a major killer.

Dog exhibiting came to be not merely

the pastime of the rich or the specialist, but a weekend hobby in which anyone could afford to participate. Beauty gained in importance over working ability, so that in many cases a dog's true purpose was almost overlooked. Cockers and Irish Setters never saw a pheasant nor heard a gun. Dashing little Westies and Yorkies did not soil their coats by ratting round a barn. Dogs had become cherished pets and status symbols, as idle as the day was long.

Lack of work or of interesting exercise to compensate for work leads to mental disturbance and neurotic frustration in dogs. It is a major cruelty to keep a dog lonely and bored, without the opportunity to exercise its natural talent for scenting, fast running, digging or hunting according to its breed. By mating deprived dogs over generations, it is easy to produce moronic animals without the brainpower of their ancestors.

Now, towards the end of the 1970s, dog breeders are recognizing a great variety of conditions of inherited disability, illness or less than satisfactory body conformation. In many cases it is not known how these disabilities are transmitted, for it is seldom as simple as a direct link from sire and dam to puppy. Every visible feature of a dog has a complicated pattern of inheritance, so that while a breeder is seeking, say, to improve the strength of the back legs, the accepted style of beauty in the head may be lost, or the coat may become harsh when softness is required. Some faults and deformities are carried invisibly for one or two generations, to emerge again unexpectedly at a seemingly well-planned mating. Dog breeding is a very complicated business when the aim is to breed for soundness and brainpower as well as for good looks.

Many factors are now combining to slow up the sales of puppies and also to make buyers more discriminating in their purchase. We are, nevertheless, uncomfortably aware that there are far too many dogs in the world and that a large number of them are unwanted.

In the U.S. recently 8,394 dead dogs were removed from the streets of Baltimore in a single year, killed by disease or by cars while running free. During the same period, 18,557 dogs and puppies, the majority under two years old, were collected by the dog pound for euthanasia or for disposal to laboratories as experimental animals, as is permitted in some states in the U.S. The total dog deaths in this one American city were one quarter of the estimated dog population. This is a convincing picture of many more dogs being born and reared than are really wanted by owners. In addition to these deaths, there are said to be large colonies of semi-wild dogs living in vacant housing and feeding from rubbish dumps and café dustbins.

In Britain the dog population which is owned has fallen by 3% in the last two years. Many people will not burden themselves with a new puppy when an old favourite dies. Dogs often run loose in the streets in the daytime, returning home when their owners get back from work at night. These 'latch key' dogs are a considerable nuisance to other people, as are barking dogs shut up alone in their homes. Of dogs taken up as strays, only one in three is ever claimed, so thousands of dogs have to be destroyed annually. Most breed societies run a rescue section to find homes for these dogs but it is sadly true that when a dog has moved home once, it is often passed from hand to hand, lacking the early training to become a successful pet.

It is evident that as good dog keeping becomes more difficult, there has to be a very good reason for breeding a litter. The three most valid reasons are to improve a line or a strain in order to obtain a better dog for exhibition or work; to produce a descendant of a well-loved dog to keep; or to give oneself the pleasure of rearing and enjoying puppies, but this will be a selfish pleasure if the future of all the pups is not assured. Bitches nearly always have too many puppies, a litter of 15 is quite common with the Irish Setter, and over 10 is nothing to a Labrador. With litters of this size an area can soon be saturated with the breed, and the frightening state can be reached when the last three or four pups are growing large and lanky, eating a great deal and needing individual training, and yet no one seems interested in buying them. The attractive age at which pups are saleable is quite short. With the larger breeds, buyers will look very critically at them after 12 weeks, feeling that they are missing out on the endearing baby stage. After four months the value of a companion puppy drops to almost nothing unless a lot of time has been spent on lead and house training, when the pup may be sold to someone who wants to be spared this part of the owner's duties. These older puppies, however, do not settle so well when introduced to a new home.

Dog breeders today are trying to return to old standards, to have at least half the litter ordered before birth by homes which they have personally approved. The rest of the litter can then be culled to a number they feel they can sell. It may seem cruel to cut off little lives when they have scarcely begun, but it is not as heartless as persuading people to take dogs they do not really want and which they will discard when the going gets rough.

Dog breeding does not make money unless done on a commercial scale in conjunction with exhibiting and a boarding business, so that each side of the enterprise feeds the others. In terms of hours of labour, worry and heartache, as well as food, veterinary bills, heating, advertising, stud fee, and the wear and tear on your home that six or more growing pups may make, there is no financial profit in having a litter. The gains you may make are in the pleasure of handling and rearing the pups, the close relationship which you will be forging with your bitch as you tend to her needs, and the enduring friendships you may make with the people to whom you sell your pups.

When you decide to breed from your bitch, you are committing to her between four and five months of your life, when the bitch herself, and later the bitch and her puppies, must be your primary consideration. The bitch carries her young for 63 days, give or take a day or two. For the week of the birth, it is essential to be available when she starts whelping, and afterwards to be on hand to resolve any problems which the dam or litter may have, especially in the first few days. After the first four weeks of pregnancy the bitch will need several small meals each day, and she will need more opportunities to be clean as the distended uterus increases pressure on her bladder. After those four weeks, it is not wise to put the bitch into boarding kennels where she may pick up some infection, or get into a fight and injure herself in some way. She may make herself miserable by pining, for bitches do seem more affectionate and vulnerable when they are pregnant. After the pups are born, there may be a few difficult days until bitch and pups are settled and feeding well and any necessary tail docking is done. Then comes an easier fortnight or so when bitch and puppies are more or less self-sufficient. At 21 days however, the pups need to socialize, to be weaned, wormed and shown to customers who

will be coming to choose. You will be really busy for the next six weeks or for as long as it takes for all the pups to go off to new homes. A litter should only be undertaken when you intend to sell each puppy into an individual home. People who care so little about the fate of their pups that they will let an agency dispose of them have no right to be bringing puppies into the world.

Having allocated your time, the next consideration will be the provision of the right accommodation. Ideally, you need three places into which the pups can move as they grow. The whelping place should be warm and secluded, a place where the bitch will not feel threatened by strangers or other animals. It should also be easy for you to attend to the pups by day or night. Many breeders sleep with the bitch in the same room for the few nights before and after the whelping time. For most families a spare bedroom or the bathroom is ideal, provided that the family is adult. A busy kitchen is definitely not suitable, garages are usually too cold at this stage and with sun porches it is difficult to keep the temperature even. At 21 days the little family will need to move to a downstairs room, within sight and sound of people, so that the pups can see and be seen. A divided corner of the kitchen, sun porch or hall is suitable, provided that temperature and light can be controlled. With a big litter, or with pups of a large breed, this accommodation will be outgrown by the time the pups are six weeks old. They will be ready for a shed or kennel, at least for daytime use, or an enclosure with shelter in the garden in good weather. Puppies running loose can do a lot of damage if allowed the freedom of a garden and it is really not practical to have them free within a room in the house. The range of accommodation needed for the medium-to large-breed pups therefore makes quite a demand on a small home. In addition you will need somewhere to interview prospective buyers.

The Bitch at Mating

Your bitch must be at the peak of condition when she is mated. She should have had her annual boosters against distemper and hepatitis so that, being fully protected herself, she can pass on the maximum amount of antibodies against disease to her pups in the colostrum or first milk. This protection will last the pups for about eight weeks, when they should begin their own vaccination programme. Any skin problems of the bitch should be cleared up and special care taken to keep her free of parasites, fleas and lice. It is worth while experimenting until you find a feeding routine which suits her well and which produces a formed motion every time. Stick to this menu throughout the pregnancy so that you do not complicate matters with bouts of stomach trouble while she is feeding the pups.

Well before the time of mating, check all the Kennel Club documents of the bitch to see that she is correctly registered and transferred so that there is no delay when registering the pups.

In planning the mating of a pet bitch, it is best to avail yourself of the knowledge of an experienced breeder who has been following the breed for a long time. Only from such a person can you get the information which will make the names on your bitch's

A bitch's milk has to supply carbohydrates, protein, fat, calcium and phosphate for her growing pups. She is able to supply these from her own tissue but it is better to make sure that she is given an adequate diet so that it will not be necessary. Increased amounts of food, supplemented by bone meal, milk and a multivitamin source should be given, the quantities being reduced as the pups begin to be weaned. Plenty of water is essential for her to produce sufficient milk.

pedigree come alive, for unless you know something of the dogs named on it, the longest and most aristocratic pedigree is just so much useless paper. Stud dog owners are usually very helpful and anxious that every litter by their dog should be a credit to his name. You have, therefore, everything to gain by making contact and taking advice long before your bitch is ready to mate.

People who keep professional stud dogs are usually well versed in the lore of their breed. They know what hereditary defects to look for and they can tell you how to go about getting your bitch examined to determine her status. They know that while both dog and bitch may to all appearances be sound, they can be carrying hidden factors capable of being transmitted to the puppies when the two are mated. Some defects, such as hip dysplasia (HD), a malformation of the joint between the pelvis and the head of the femur, can only be seen by X-ray. In breeds very badly afflicted by HD, for example Labradors, Golden Retrievers and German Shepherd Dogs (Alsatians) it is best to have your vet talk over the X-ray photographs with the stud dog owner's vet, in order to determine if the proposed mating is suitable. Relatively few dogs and bitches in these breeds have completely normal hip joints. In any case, for the beginner in dog breeding, it is sensible and reassuring to have the bitch checked by a vet before making mating plans, so that she is known to be fit and suitable. Some breeds, notably the toy breeds and the very short-faced breeds, are notoriously difficult whelpers, frequently needing a Caesarian section to produce puppies. To have to submit your bitch to a surgical operation, and make the decision that she is not going to be able to produce her puppies naturally, is a traumatic experience. You will probably not wish for such an experience unless you have very good reason for wanting to breed from a bitch which is likely to have difficulty.

In choosing a stud dog you will be influenced by its colour and physical conformation, but most of all by its soundness and temperament. An outstandingly beautiful dog which is shy or irritable may produce good-looking puppies which will be acceptable if handled by experts in the show ring, but you will more likely be selling your pups largely as companions and household pets, to people who have never previously

owned a dog. The easy-tempered, cheerful dog is the best choice as the sire of a litter of pet puppies. Stud dogs are advertised in the weekly papers of the dog fancy and in several kennel directories. The official Kennel Club in every country can also supply lists of breeders. At championship dog shows you can actually see the winning dogs of the day on their benches and in the show ring, but you cannot take your bitch with you, unless she is formally entered in the show. Do, however, take her pedigree, and perhaps also her photographs with you, for use when talking over a prospective mating.

Bitches come into oestrus (season, or heat) for the first time at about eight months old. The time can, however, vary with individuals and with breeds, up to about 15 months. If the bitch has not been in season by the latter age, it is wise to consult a vet. Failure to come into season may mean that she is of low fertility or, worse, that some disease is present. It is not usually wise to mate a bitch at her first season, at whatever age this occurs. The second season is the most usual to begin breeding, but even this is too soon if the bitch is very 'puppyish' in her attitude to life. A bitch which is still juvenile in mind sometimes refuses to settle with her puppies and treats them as toys to toss around.

If you mean to breed it is better never to give your bitch the contraceptive (progesterone) pill to retard or suppress her seasons. It is often difficult to restore a proper breeding pattern after interference in this way. Before the season at which you mean to mate the bitch, make sure that she is in first-class condition, and that her coat and ears are clean of all parasites. There is no need to worm the bitch against roundworm (*Toxicara canis*) as it is unlikely that there will be any larvae of the worm free in the intestine of the adult bitch. Any larvae she has are likely to be encysted deeply in the tissues of the liver or other organs, and no vermifuge available at present will remove them in that situation. The programme to clear the pups of the worm will begin when they are three weeks old.

When the season comes round the vulva will enlarge and swell. The bitch will show heightened sensitivity and will have been more excitable or irritable for days or weeks before the blood-stained discharge appears. It is important to discover the first day of 'showing colour'; the easiest way is to

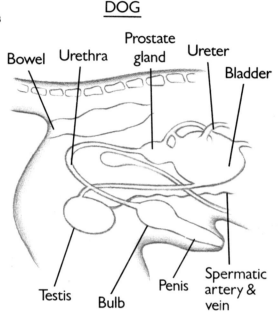

DOG

Diagram showing the reproductive organs of the dog.

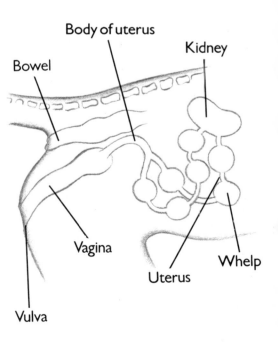

BITCH

Diagram showing the reproductory organs of the bitch.

test the bitch's vulva with a tissue swab night and morning. Some bitches will urinate more frequently when coming into season, half squatting with one hind leg slightly raised, with the intention of marking territory as males do and so carrying their message to the dog population. It is possible for a bitch to have a 'colourless' season, at which she has no bloodstained discharge but is fertile. This is not a good basis on which to start breeding, nor is any other departure from normality. Many bitches keep themselves very clean at the start of the season, when discharge is light, but it is important for your future calculations to know the very first day when blood staining is present.

You are now able to confirm the booking with the stud dog of your choice. It is important to do so at once, to give as much notice as possible, for you may want the mating as early as the seventh or as late as the fourteenth day of the bitch's season. The conventional time for mating is between the tenth and twelfth day, when the red discharge is ceasing. Some bitches, however, will stand as early as the seventh day, while others are not ready until the eleventh or the twelfth. Because of uncertainty about the time when the bitch actually started, it is more likely that the correct mating date will be earlier rather than later than is planned. Even for experienced owners it is very difficult to know what a bitch's pattern will be. At mating time the vulva should still be large, expanded and malleable, the discharge just ceasing or becoming pallid. It is possible to determine the optimum time for mating by taking a bitch to a veterinary surgeon who will take vaginal swabs for microscopic examination; clinical changes will show when she is ready to accept the dog. This will, however, mean several visits at daily intervals which is expensive in time and money, and it is probably only worth doing after failure to conceive at two matings.

In recent years it has become the custom to take a bitch to the stud dog only once, to wait with her or to assist at the mating, and then to take her home immediately – a rapid sequence of events tailored to fit our crowded lives. The latest advice of veterinary fertility specialists is to revert to the more old-fashioned method of boarding the bitch at the stud premises for several days. In this way she becomes acclimatized to the dog so that they

can mate as and when they will over several days. This is the optimum method for maximum conception, but not all stud dog owners have facilities for boarding bitches. If this is so, you would be well advised to make two visits to the dog, not more than 48 hours apart. It is a good idea to allow the bitch an hour or two to rest after mating before taking her home, although a bitch used to travelling is more likely to take the whole episode calmly. Bitches are sometimes sent unaccompanied to distant studs by air or rail but this is not a kind action with a companion bitch. Unless the owner is nervous and tense, it is best to be present at the mating, except where the bitch may have been so humanized that she dissociates herself from dogs and will not indulge in typical canine behaviour unless away from her human family.

It is courteous to arrive on time for your date with the stud dog. Be dressed in reasonably old clothes in case your assistance is needed, and bring a cheque book for the stud fee. The fee is for the mating and carries no guarantee of puppies, although most stud owners will allow a free mating at the next heat if no pup results. If only one pup is born of the mating, the dog is considered to be fertile. The failure to carry more pups to term is likely to be due to the bitch or to the wrong time of mating. If two visits are made to the stud, the one fee covers both, but when the bitch is boarded there will perhaps be an extra charge for her keep. It may be more convenient for the dog to visit the bitch, in which case travelling expenses are usually asked in addition to the normal stud fee, which varies according to the status of the dog and the rarity of the breed.

You may think that it would be pleasant and cheaper to use a friend's dog, but not all pet dogs take to stud work. Some have been conditioned to believe that the expression of sexual instinct is unacceptable behaviour, as it certainly is in a male kept as a household companion. You may find that such a dog is either uninterested in the bitch or too inhibited to complete a mating. It is not wise or kind to use a pet dog at stud merely on one occasion, or only very rarely. It is unsettling and increases the urge to urinate over furniture and fences, and the inclination to wander and to be aggressive to other males. The professional stud dog is introduced to his work at an early age and usually

has sufficient bookings for him to learn a routine of behaviour which his owner can control. Owners of pet male dogs are often unfortunate, for there is little demand for their use at stud unless they are show or obedience prize-winners. Not being used at stud has no adverse effect on the health or temperament of the male dog, and a stud experience makes no difference to obedience or any other facet of canine behaviour.

During the journey to the mating, it is best to allow the bitch out in some quiet spot to urinate, so that she arrives with an empty bladder. It is also advisable that she should not be fed. If any scent or other lotion has been used to disguise the odour of the bitch, remember to leave it off for a day or two before the mating.

The mutual attraction which dog and bitch have for each other at the time of mating is governed by scents known as pheromones, which are based on body secretions, the urine, faeces, saliva and products of skin glands. The most common site of scent glands is in the ano-genital region and the scent may be mixed with faeces or urine. Stud dog owners like to stage-manage the mating in their own way, but there is no doubt that some time given to free play and scent recognition is more satisfying for both parties to the mating. Moreover, it is more likely to produce a large and happy litter. The dog and bitch will perform a stylized ritual mating sequence of movements not seen at other times. This performance is useful both physically and mentally to get the parties 'warmed up' to the idea.

Breeders are beginning to revert to the idea of free matings of this kind, although some will still insist on staged matings, holding dog and bitch in position and literally forcing a mating to save time and trouble. One of the disadvantages of the 'free play' mating is that it really needs to be undertaken outdoors. The dog will want to urinate often during the preliminaries and some dog owners will not have the premises necessary to let dog and bitch loose safely. Some owners, particularly of toy breeds, are afraid that the dog will be hurt; they like to arrange matings on a table, holding the parties in position, and they may want the bitch's mouth tied with a bandage to prevent her biting. If the day for mating has been accurately predicted, the bitch should, after the preliminary play, stand with tail turned to one side

to allow the dog free penetration. The dog then mounts the bitch from the tail end, gripping her with his front legs behind her ribs, bringing his penis close to the enlarged and raised vulva. At this stage it is permissible, particularly if there is a difference in the size of dog and bitch, for human help to be given: the owner will steady the head of the bitch and perhaps support her underneath to stop her sitting down, while the stud dog owner either raises the dog a little or guides the penis to effect penetration. When the dog has entered the bitch, his penis enlarges and thickens, becoming engorged with blood, and he performs thrusting movements to ejaculate his semen. Movement is also taking place in the female vulva; the bitch's sphincter muscles will grip and hold the penis, even after ejaculation is finished, in a 'tie' lasting 30 minutes or longer. After ejaculation, which is performed in three fractions, at intervals of 10–20 seconds, the dog will descend from the back of the bitch and turn himself, with or without help, so that they stand back to back during the tie. It is usual to hold the animals on leads at this stage to prevent them pulling each other around, as bitches are apt to be very restive at this time. If the tie is very prolonged, verging on

60 minutes, a small smooth sliver of ice may be inserted alongside the penis into the bitch's vagina, causing the tissues to retract. The tie is a phenomenon peculiar to dog, fox and wolf. It is more satisfactory if it takes place but conception is possible without it, provided that the dog remains in position on the bitch's back long enough to ejaculate the final fraction of the emission.

Stud dogs should be used regularly. If a dog has not been used for two or more weeks, there is the possibility that the semen may be stale and inactive at first mating, so that it is wise to have two matings with several hours, up to 48 hours, between them. There is little risk of a stud dog being over-used as, in his prime, he is capable of four or five matings a week.

After the mating, the stud fee should be paid and the receipt and the dog's pedigree handed over, together with any papers necessary to register puppies at the appropriate Kennel Club; these require the signature of the stud dog owner.

Fertilization may not take place in the bitch until about a week after the mating. Ovulation only takes place 24–48 hours after the bitch is first willing to stand to the dog and the sperm of the dog will live in the

For large breeds, such as the Great Dane and the Bloodhound, it is better that mating should be under control. Ideally, there should be three handlers, one to supervise the bitch, one to supervise the stud dog and the third handler should be in a position where he can observe what is going on and direct proceedings. The loop of the lead can act as a muzzle as a precaution against the bitch attacking the dog.

bitch's reproductive tract for several days. There can therefore be almost a week's divergence in the expected day of whelping, although it is normal to calculate 63 days from the day of mating. The fertilized egg reaches the uterus (womb) about 10 days after mating and does not become attached to the uterine wall until 20 days later. At this stage the foetus is very small indeed, from 6 mm ($\frac{1}{4}$ in) to 30 mm ($1\frac{1}{4}$ ins) in diameter. No alteration of the diet for the bitch should take place until she is five to six weeks pregnant.

A vet can diagnose pregnancy by palpation of the abdomen between 24–30 days. It is easier with the smaller breeds and with a thin bitch, but difficult whenever a bitch is nervous and tense. Where diagnosis by palpation does not prove possible, other signs will become visible. It is seldom worth paying for a veterinary consultation to diagnose pregnancy, which at most will be an educated guess. Diagnosis by X-ray is only possible in the last week, when calcium is laid down in the little skeletons.

Whether the bitch has been mated or not, changes continue to take place within her reproductive organs. In some bitches these will mimic all the natural stages of pregnancy. The degrees to which bitches have a 'phantom pregnancy' vary, but there is a familial tendency in some strains to exhibit these symptoms to an abnormal degree. Such a bitch will have an enlarged abdomen and teats, and will secrete milk. She will also make a whelping bed and go through all the trauma of labour pains. She will guard and care for puppies which no one else can see, often using toys or other inanimate objects as substitute puppies, or she may take kittens or other puppies to fill her maternal need. Some bitches suffer acutely in a phantom pregnancy after every heat but this condition is never cured by having an actual litter. A vet may give the bitch hormone treatment and, in mild cases, less food and drink, with more exercise and diversion, may take her mind off her troubles. Phantom pregnancies seldom last more than two weeks if no encouragement is given, and this is one time when sympathy and indulgence are out of place. The only complete cure is to have the bitch sterilized.

Signs of pregnancy in the bitch are not easy to distinguish from a phantom pregnancy, which may be taken for a real pregnancy right up to term unless the puppies can be seen moving within the uterus during the final week. Signs to notice after the fifth week will be an enlargement of the abdomen, underneath, high up behind the ribs, the enlargement and pink coloration of the teats, and also the fact that the vulva has never completely returned to its normal size since mating. From five weeks onwards, your bitch herself should be telling you her secret by changes in behaviour. She may appear quieter, more loving and sentimental, and more careful of herself at play. It is unwise to allow her to romp with other animals or to jump fences and a gundog should not be expected to work, but in all cases controlled exercise should go on right to the end. The bitch's figure and teats will be enlarging all the time and milk may be present some days before the whelping takes place.

During the last four weeks of pregnancy the bitch will need about a third more food than normal, with an appropriate increase in the usual amount of mineral and vitamin supplement. Give the food in three or more small meals to avoid undue pressure from the stomach on the enlarged uterus. Cheese and fish are useful additions to the diet. Give milk in pellet form as liquid milk is not usually well tolerated. The bitch may find it difficult at this stage to be continent of urine for long periods, for example overnight, and should be excused any lapses from house training. She will revert to normal behaviour when the pressure of the full uterus is off her bladder.

During pregnancy any sign of illness, however slight, should be reported to the veterinary surgeon. An infection could mean that the bitch might lose some or all of her puppies and make for additional complication at whelping time if she carries them all to term. The bitch's appetite may be capricious, but otherwise she should be well and cheerful, capable and willing to take gentle exercise up to the end. It is wise to have the bitch examined by the vet about three days before the expected date of birth, and to find out how to get in touch with veterinary help day or night during the time the bitch might be in labour. It is also helpful to have telephone communication with either the breeder of the bitch or the owner of the stud dog to be reassured that the things which take place are normal for the breed, for bitches vary a great deal as do the peculiarities of each breed.

Beware of taking advice from too many conflicting sources; it is better to adhere to one lay adviser and the veterinary surgeon.

When you are sure that the bitch is pregnant, prepare the whelping room and the necessary equipment. A certain amount of capital is necessary to buy what is needed, to pay for the stud fee and veterinary consultations, to feed the bitch and her puppies and pay for advertising – for you will not see any money in return until the pups are at least six weeks old. It is wise to have an amount equal to the cost of three puppies of your breed as floating capital. In the event of a disastrous whelping, perhaps a Caesarian section and no puppy surviving, you could lose the greater part of this money. This must be taken into account when you set out to breed a litter. The same applies whether you are breeding a rare animal commanding a high price or a cross-bred litter which may have to be given away. Equipment, feeding and veterinary attention will all be necessary whatever the case and will all cost the same.

Preparing the Whelping Room

If the bitch is to whelp in a spare room, take up the carpet or cover it with plastic sheeting. If the bitch will have to traverse corridor or stairs to go outside after whelping, it is wise to have protection for this floor covering also as the discharge after whelping can be profuse and stain badly. The room should be shaded from strong light by blinds, but provided with a good, flexible electric light. If a garage or sunroom is to be used, a partition should be built to enclose the bitch and puppies in a mini-environment of their own and this enclosure should be roofed. The room should be capable of being heated to a steady temperature of 24°C (75°F) for a short-coated breed. In addition to the whelping box, you will need a table or trolley for all the equipment you will use, and another strong table on which the bitch can be stood for veterinary examination. You will also need facilities for handwashing, both for the vet and yourself, a chair and a camp bed, for whelpings may take all of 24 hours with long intervals between periods of activity. A small basket or box in which to place the puppies while the main box is cleaned is necessary, and a pail with a lid containing disinfectant into which the after-births (placentas) can be placed.

On the trolley, you should have on

the lower shelf the following items:
  Water bowl for bitch
  Jug of glucose water (1 tablespoon
  of glucose to ½ litre (1 pint) of water)
  Small bottle of brandy and spoon,
  size according to breed
  Pile of old towels and drying cloths
  for puppies
  Well-covered hotwater bottles
  Large pile of newspaper for putting
  under bitch
  Plastic or paper sacks for soiled
  paper and towels
  On the top shelf of the trolley:
  Surgical disinfectant
  Surgical scrub for hands, or soft
  cake of soap
  Roll of soft kitchen paper, or tissues
  Jar containing disinfectant in which
  to stand blunt-ended and
  sharp-pointed scissors
  Similar jar for blunt-ended
  thermometer
  Clock, notebook and pen for
  recording times and details of each
  birth and timing large expulsive
  pains in the bitch
  Scales to weigh pups (not usually
  needed to weigh more than 1 kg
  [2 lbs])
  Premature baby feeding bottle, with
  very small teats, or medicine dropper,
  and bitch milk substitute
  Teats in sterilizing solution
  Something to occupy owner, e.g.
  reading, letter writing etc. It is not
  wise to concentrate on the bitch all
  the time, but to be present if she
  needs reassurance and help.

The whelping box is essentially a place where the bitch can feel secure, shaded, away from draughts and able to exercise her primitive instincts to make a nest, to hunch up and expel her pups and to stretch out on her side to feed them. It is most important that the box should be clean of all visible dirt, as well as the invisible micro-organisms which may do so much harm and introduce disease. If a secondhand box is used, it should be scrubbed and stood out in the sunlight or leant against a radiator in order to kill any bacteria. In size the box must just fit the bitch when stretched out from nose to tail root. A box which is too large will allow the pups to get too far away from her, and if it is too small, the pups will be squashed when the bitch moves around. A whelping rail, fixed a few inches above the floor of the box to hold the bitch away from direct contact with the sides, provides an area into which the pups may creep to save them being squashed behind the bitch. It has the disadvantage, however,

that a pup remaining in this area all night may become chilled.

The insulated whelping box illustrated, with a heating pad sandwiched in part of the floor, is an investment, but it provides the most satisfactory whelping place of all. This box is not yet commercially available but can easily be made from the instructions given. A less luxurious box, not shown, is available from some kennel manufacturers ready-made. The open-tray type of whelping box is only suitable for Arctic or other heavily coated breeds which cannot endure enclosure. A small bitch may be whelped in a cardboard carton or in her own bed. If the whelping is to take place in a bedroom which is in use, a degree of seclusion may be obtained by draping a screen or towel rail with sheets. Background heating should be provided in the room but with due regard to safety, as in the early stages the bitch may be restless and could overturn anything not fixed. Extra heating is needed for the puppies, especially in a big litter or if for any reason they are separated for long from the dam. Newborn puppies cannot control their own heat loss and can only keep warm when in contact with a source of heat. When they are born, their wet state allows their temperature to drop rapidly. If, however, they are dried by the dam and kept in contact with her mammary glands, they will regain their temperature in about one and a half hours. If the bitch is dealing with other puppies, or distracted by her own distress, or if the pups are continually soaked in fluids from the rest of the litter being born, they can become deeply chilled to a state from which they will never recover. It is therefore important to have some additional source of heat for the pups—the heated area of the whelping box floor, a loose heated pad on which they may rest, well-covered hotwater bottles, or an infra-red lamp positioned not less than 1·2 m (4 ft) from the bitch and her puppies and not directly above them. Infra-red lamps are not much favoured, as they give a drying heat which is not good for the coat and if they are hung too low, the back of the bitch may be burnt. Heat from under the pups is preferable.

The birth should take place on clean newspaper, and vast quantities are needed for a big bitch with a large litter. While newspaper is too slippery to be a good surface for the pups, it is difficult to find any other material which can be changed so frequently

and disposed of so easily. Corrugated cardboard may also be used. A false floor of the whelping box may be encased in an old pillow-slip, but the number of changes needed makes this impractical for a large litter. If the whelping is to take place in an external room, it is possible to use a layer of wood-wool or shredded computer tape; straw and hay should not be used as they may have been contaminated by rats or may harbour parasites. If wood shavings are used, they should not be from coniferous trees or from trees which have been treated with chemical compounds. Although the room must be warm, it should also be well ventilated so that the bitch does not become overheated. She will pant a good deal during the whelping and you will want to be able to distinguish 'hot panting' from 'worried' or 'in pain' panting.

The genital apparatus of the bitch consists of:
(i)   The *vulva*, to be seen externally, which is also the urinary outlet
(ii) Internally, a relatively long *vagina*, which ends in a constrictive ring (the cervix)
(iii) the *Cervix* at the neck of the uterus. It is usually tightly closed except during oestrus and when whelping
(iv) the *uterus*, or womb, a Y-shaped structure with two projecting arms. Normally, the uterine wall is of thick tissue, but it can stretch to the texture of transparent paper when distended by growing puppies.

At 21 days of pregnancy, the fertilized ova implant themselves along the uterine horns, each attaching by its own placenta, by which it is nourished and waste products excreted. Each puppy is enclosed in its own bag of membrane, cushioned by amniotic fluid. At about the sixth to seventh week of pregnancy, depending on the size and number of puppies present, the uterine horns are so enlarged that they fold upon themselves, forming two layers. When this happens the bitch's outline alters dramatically, sometimes overnight. Her abdomen drops and there is a hollowness in her flanks, giving no doubt at all that she is pregnant.

When the time comes for whelping, some hormonal signal is given to start the movement of the puppies one at a time down the uterine horn and through the cervix. They must reach the cervix at the correct angle. Even when this is fully dilated there is not

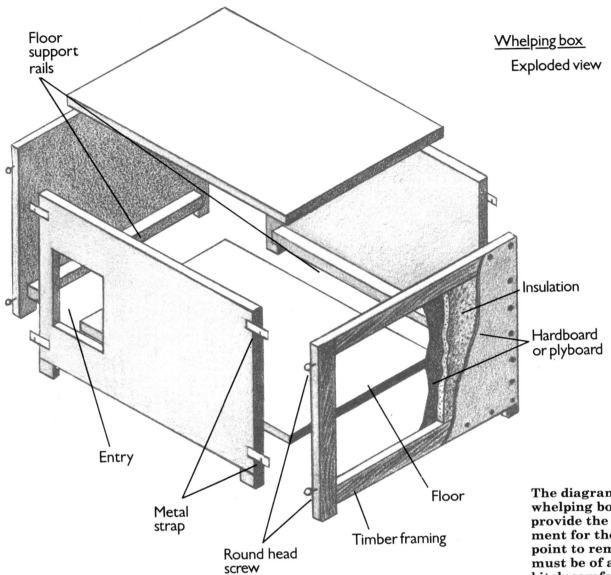

Floor
support
rails

Insulation

Hardboard
or plyboard

Entry

Metal
strap

Round head
screw

Timber framing

Floor

The diagram shows how to make a whelping box at home, which will provide the best possible environment for the bitch. An important point to remember is that the box must be of adequate size to fit the bitch comfortably when she is lying down. It is also essential to block out any draughts as this could endanger the lives of the newly born pups. The sides should be insulated with a non-fibrous, inert material.

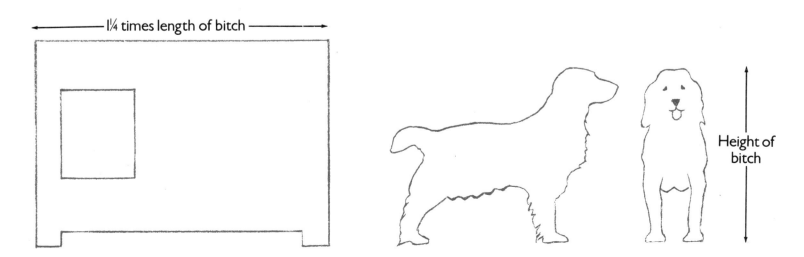

I¼ times length of bitch

Height of
bitch

123

much space for the average-sized puppy to pass through. Ideally, the blunt head of the puppy, still in its bag of membrane, should just engage at the centre of the cervix, so that the subsequent contractions of the uterus will urge it through by hydraulic pressure down into the vagina and out through the vulva. It is also very common for a puppy to present feet first and this way does not involve much more difficulty. The real whelping difficulties arise when the pup misses the cervix and presents with one shoulder or one leg, if the pup goes partly over into the opposite horn, blocking the cervix, or if the puppy is so oversize that it cannot be born naturally. In these cases you will need the help of a veterinary surgeon who may be able to deliver the obstructing puppy with forceps, or you may have to take the bitch to surgery for delivery by Caesarian section.

Whelping

The first sign of imminent whelping is likely to be the refusal of food; the bitch nearly always abstains completely for 24 hours, but there are exceptions. There will also be a drop of 1 or 2 degrees in anal temperature but, of course, you will only notice this if you have been taking temperatures and plotting a chart for a week or more previously. There may be an escape of a little fluid from the vulva when the bitch sits down but any greater loss of fluid must be reported to the vet. The bitch will work at making a whelping bed, so it is not wise to leave her with good furniture as she will shred up newspaper and material vigorously. This stage may go on for 24 hours or more, or it may start and then stop, behaviour returning to normal for some hours. From this time onwards it is important to keep all other animals away, even those to whom the bitch is normally devoted. The natural instinct is to seek solitude and protect herself and her pups. She will regard other dogs and cats as enemies and predators, so they should not even be allowed to sniff under the whelping room door. A bitch which feels threatened may hide her pups and injure them, or she may go into a state of hysterical excitement and hold up the whelping. The presence of too many onlookers can have the same effect. It is best, therefore, to restrict her helpers to not more than two people, and this is certainly not a time to call in children or interested neighbours. During this stage of labour the bitch will probably pant dramatically, a natural sign of excitement and early pain. Take this opportunity to cut the coat away from vulva and teats and to sponge her down with a weak non-toxic disinfectant, drying her well. A long-coated dog should also be groomed at this stage. The pet bitch is likely to be very demanding of the owner's company, especially at her first whelping.

Internally the whelping will have begun already, the cervix will have started to relax and dilate and the pups, which are on their backs during development, are rotating so as to be in the correct place for their journey down the uterine horn. Pups are not born in any special order and all the contents of one horn may come first, or all the pups may in fact be in one horn. The puppy is propelled by the waves of contraction of the uterus and the fluid pressure in its own bag. The fluid is the dilating and distending medium when the uterus relaxes in front of it and contracts behind it.

A canine whelping takes time and it is not realistic to suppose that a veterinary surgeon will be able to stay the whole time with a bitch or that he could spare a veterinary nurse for so long. The owner must be prepared to watch the bitch and to report to the surgery both progress and any hold-ups which may occur.

The first important sign of whelping – and careful note must be taken of the time – is the first really strong straining pain, which may make the bitch grunt or cry out. From the veterinary surgeon's point of view, whelping starts with this pain and the preliminary pantings and bed making are of little consequence. After the first strain the bitch should get on with having her puppies and within half an hour should produce the first. Delay is not uncommon, however, perhaps from physical or psychological reasons, for example if the bitch is worried or not suited by the conditions in which she is asked to whelp. If you feel that she would very much rather be in some other place, for example, in her bed in the kitchen or on her owner's bed, it might be best politically to give in, providing suitable protection for whatever place she chooses at least for her first puppy. You will find that once the first has been produced, if you take it to the prepared whelping room, the bitch will stay there with it and get on with having the others.

Soon after the first straining pain, a black water-filled bag will appear at the vulva. This is the bag of amniotic fluid which precedes the puppy. You may not see a bag as such, but merely a gush of greenish black fluid if the bag has broken inside. Normally the bitch will break it by licking or with her teeth, or in the case of a maiden bitch it may appear and retract for some time at the entrance to the vulva. When the green fluid has been spilt – it badly stains anything which it touches – the puppy itself should soon flop out on to the whelping box floor. The bitch may be standing or crouching or lying for this final expulsion. The pup will be encased in a membrane which must be broken. This is done by the bitch or by the attendant's fingernail or, very carefully, with scissors; in whatever way, it is very important to remove the bag from the puppy's head as it is no longer breathing via the placenta. If it remains in the bag it could get amniotic fluid into its lungs, causing a pneumonia, and at worst the pup could suffocate if it is not freed quickly. Some maiden bitches are half afraid of their newborn pups and the maternal instinct is not evident until several have been born. In exceptional cases, a bitch lacks any maternal instinct whatsoever and will totally disregard her pups for the company of her owner. The pups will then have to be reared entirely by bottle, fed two-hourly day and night. They should not be sold to anyone hoping to breed from them, as lack of maternal instinct is a hereditary fault which is cumulative and grows more intense down the generations.

When the pup's head is free, clean the mouth and nostrils of mucus and, if necessary, hold the head down to allow the fluid to drain. Should the pup appear limp and lifeless through delay in being born, resuscitation will be needed: swing it gently by the hind legs. It does not matter that the pup is still attached by its umbilical cord or that the bag is not off its hind quarters, the important thing is to get the puppy to breathe. When it has given a vigorous cry, you may sever the cord as far as possible from the puppy, leaving a long end which will drop off later. There is no need to tie or suture the cord. The bitch herself may attend to all this and proceed to lick the puppy dry and, if she will allow you to help, it means less temperature loss for the pup. Rub the newborn puppy vigorously with your old towels. When the placenta appears, the bitch will probably want to eat it as well as the membranes surrounding the puppy.

This is the natural primitive behaviour in a bitch and undoubtedly placentas, which resemble pieces of liver, provide good nourishment. They are, however, laxative so you should take as many as you can away from the bitch and put them in your pail.

When the pup has been dried, put it to a teat, squeeze a little milk for it and press on the lower jaw to make the mouth open. The sucking action encourages milk production and also contraction of the uterus in the bitch. The small amount of milk ingested will make the puppy pass its first motion, the meconium, so that it is better to let pups be with the bitch as much as possible during the whelping and not to take them away until all have arrived. The bitch may start to make expelling movements quite soon or she may rest for up to two hours. There is no need to worry. In the interval, you should weigh the first puppy, make notes of timings and distinguishing marks and examine it to see that its tongue and feet are a good pink, that there is no deformity of the toes or feet, no cleft palate, no hare lip and no dislocation of any joint. A puppy with blue or mauve appendages is not likely to thrive. If there is any deformity it should be marked down for destruction by the vet, but it should remain with the bitch until you can tactfully remove it when more pups have arrived.

In between births, put more clean paper under the bitch and get rid of soiled bedding, and try to save the dry pups from getting soaked again by the new arrivals. Make sure that each new pup is put to a teat so that it gets its share of the colostrum; this is the early milk which contains the maternal antibodies against disease, protecting the pup from distemper and other diseases until it is about six weeks of age. Offer the bitch a drink between puppies and if there is a long hold-up take her out into the garden to be clean; this often helps to speed developments.

If the interval between pups approaches two hours, this is an indication that some delaying factor is operating and putting the lives of the unborn pups in danger. You may feel that you can offer the vet more useful information if you make an internal examination to see if there is another pup nearly through the cervix. If you feel at all squeamish about making the examination, do not attempt it. Ask the vet to call or drive the bitch to his office if he suggests it. If you are able to make an internal examination, trim your nails down really short and smooth and remove any varnish and rings. Scrub your hands well for five minutes with the surgical scrub, leaving them wet and soapy, and apply the scrub also round the vulva of the bitch. Supporting the bitch with one hand under her

The diagram shows the first stage of labour. The pups have rotated in order to be in the correct position to begin their journey down the uterine horn.

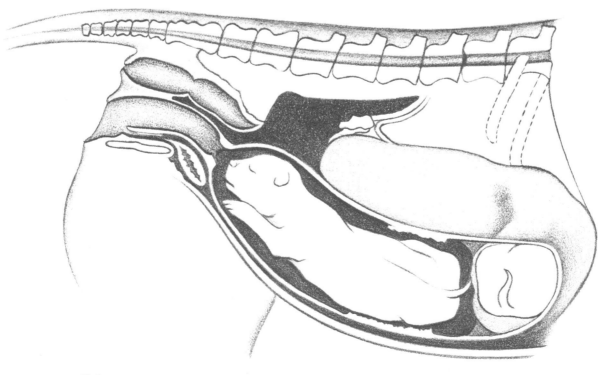

1st stage of labour

Birth of whelp

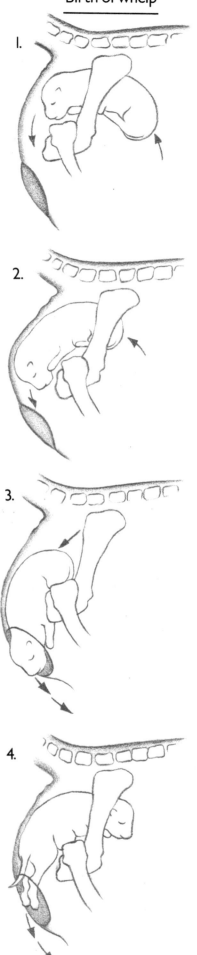

These diagrams show the birth of the whelp. In the first three diagrams the pup is in the correct position, but the fourth diagram shows the hind legs foremost in a breech position.

abdomen, insert one or two fingers into the vulva. Feel gently as high as your fingers will reach; this is unlikely to be as high as the cervix in all but the tiniest breeds. Once one or more fingers are in, keep them there; do not keep going in and out, and do not repeat the examination more than is strictly necessary as there is always the risk of introducing bacteria. By lifting the bitch's abdomen you may bring a foetus within reach so that perhaps you can touch a head or a hind foot, or perhaps no puppy anywhere at all. Your fingers inside the vulva will cause the bitch to strain, and you may be able to assess the strength of her effort and determine if she is becoming too tired to be much help in extruding other puppies. You may recognize that the foetus on the way is too large to be born naturally, or that the bitch has inertia and has stopped straining entirely. Your vet can help her begin again by giving an injection, or he may have to act surgically. Any information which you can give him can be a time- and money-saver.

Hopefully, however, at your first whelping your bitch will produce all her puppies quite naturally. When you think that she has finished producing, it is wise to have her examined by the vet to see if the uterus is contracting again and to ensure that all the placentas are out. If the bitch has had two matings, it is possible that she will start to whelp again 24 or more hours later, having conceived at both matings. If she was mated to a different dog, there may be puppies by the two different sires.

When whelping is finished, it is a courtesy to the vet to let him know and to arrange for him to check the bitch the following day. The bitch will have to be forced to go outside to pass urine and faeces, and someone should take her and compel her to stay long enough while another pair of hands cleans up the whelping bed. Drinks should again be offered, with a little light food, as the bitch will not voluntarily leave her pups for the first week or more. After the whelping there will be a dark discharge from the bitch's vulva which will clear gradually to a light red and persist for up to a month if the litter was large. Any return to foul-smelling or dark, tarry discharge should be reported at once to the vet. The bitch will not require a great deal of extra food for the first three days after whelping, and it is not wise to feed her too much as this may cause a diarrhoea which will affect

the puppies. She will normally lick her pups and clean all urine and faeces from them; if she neglects them, it is a sign that something is wrong. The bitch that is well and content should be stretched out on her side with all her babies feeding, or with one or two full and satisfied puppies lying under her neck or her ears.

If the bitch has had a lengthy whelping or is ill, or if for some reason her milk has not developed well, you may need to give some supplementary bottle feeds to the pups; sometimes it is also necessary to do this for early arrivals during a lengthy whelping. Any pup looking thin and empty may be fed by a premature baby bottle several times a day. Give each pup as much as it will take eagerly. It is always better to bottle-feed as a supplement to the mother's milk, rather than to take some pups away from her entirely. Make the milk strictly in accordance with the instructions given with a special dog preparation. Human babies require a completely different composition of milk and this is not rich enough for puppies. The pups should make no more than a warm humming noise, and any wailing cry or restless crawling about the box means that something is wrong.

Very few puppies are born looking like the breed standard; dalmatians are born all white; some grey dogs are born black; brindle markings are not easily distinguishable; dogs known as 'red' look a mousy colour; in all cases the proper coat colour develops later. When the eyes open they are blue and this colour, too, will alter later.

After the first few days following the whelping, the bitch will begin to want extra food in order to produce enough milk for her pups. This should be well balanced, served at four meals a day and generous in amount. At maximum milk production time, when the pups are three weeks old, the bitch will require three to four times as much food as normal, with vitamin and mineral supplements in proportion. By now you will find you are spending a great deal of money on your litter, but this is essential in order to rear strong and healthy puppies and to avoid the bitch 'feeding the puppies off her back' so that she becomes pitiably thin and loses all her coat.

If the puppies' tails need to be docked, this should be done when the pups are 3–4 days old, and ear cropping, if desired, comes at about 12 weeks of age. Toe-nails should be clipped soon after birth and a tiny amount taken off twice weekly thereafter in order to stop the pups scratching the bitch's teats. Navels should be inspected daily, and when the eyes open on the eighth to tenth day they should do so in a clean manner, without pus at the corners or lids. Although the ears are only just developing and hearing does not come until later, you should talk to the pups every time you see them, to accustom them to the human voice and to give them confidence. Until the pups are 20 days old, they and the bitch should remain in seclusion and not have visitors, nor should the bitch go into the street for exercise. The noses of the pups will remain bright pink in most breeds. Black pigmentation begins as little dots which later fuse together to give the jet black nose desirable in all but the grey and liver breeds and the yellow labrador.

The health of the bitch must be watched all the time she is feeding the pups as any poor appetite or refusal of food is a danger sign at this time. She should also be groomed and kept free of fleas and lice, but any powder or substance which the pups may lick must not be used. The great calamity which may overtake the bitch is eclampsia, a failure of her body to mobilize calcium which can, if neglected, lead to her death in a few hours. The symptoms are best described as 'odd behaviour' – hiding under furniture, eating plaster off the walls, continually glancing at walls and ceiling, paralysis of hindquarters, or any deranged and unnatural demonstrations. The next stage will be convulsions, prostration and death. Immediate veterinary help, day or night is essential from any vet if your own is not available. The reversal of the condition is quite dramatic and the bitch will be perfectly all right if you get help in time. This condition occurs most frequently when the pups are around three to four weeks old but it may come at any time, even just before the birth.

At 20 days, the pups should be getting on to their feet. They can see and hear and are therefore ready to be moved to a more sociable place, where they can find out about living with people. It is wrong to keep pups in seclusion after this age, as they will then have no opportunity to learn to become good pets. From three to nine weeks is the time when their minds are most open to socialization.

You will, perhaps, have begun to feed the pups from the age of two weeks with little balls of pulverized meat placed on the back of the tongue. They probably do not need this feeding, but it makes a useful basis for weaning if the bitch should suddenly dry off her milk. If you intend to wean the pups on to a complete soya-based dog diet, it is best to wait until they begin to stand quite firmly or otherwise they will fall into the dish. Meal for the puppies should be well soaked and mashed. Offer the first meals on a flat tray, large enough for all the heads to go round it, as this encourages competition. Very little is eaten at first but by four to five weeks all the pups should be eating strongly and not requiring much from the bitch. They will then be on four meals a day, with as much as they are willing to eat at any one time, indeed, some restraining hand will be needed on those which are greedy. If the pups get diarrhoea, your vet can probably supply you with an antibiotic paste. If they get bloated, try a gripe water as used for human babies and pat their backs to burp them.

The bitch should not be shut up with the pups at this stage but should be free to come and go at will. She has a lot to teach the pups in the way of deportment, fighting play and cleanliness, apart from feeding them. You can talk to the pups now, allow visitors to see them and let them hear radio and household noises, but you must still allow long periods of quiet and rest when they are not disturbed by anyone. Pups which can move about must be provided with a little playpen-type run so that they can get away from their bed to be clean. If they cannot exercise this natural instinct, they will be much harder to housetrain later on.

The pups should be wormed for the first time on their 21st day of life, and after that at five, seven, nine and twelve weeks and then at six and twelve months. You will then have done everything possible to avert the slight chance of a child being infected by worms. Your veterinary surgeon will supply the vermifuge and the instructions for giving it according to the weight of the puppies. The pups will almost certainly have worms, for these will have migrated to them out of the bitch's tissues via the placenta; their movement from the bitch is triggered by the hormonal changes of pregnancy. To preserve the health of pups and humans, get rid of the worms at 14-day intervals whether there are any visible signs or not, as even one unexpelled egg can start up another worm cycle. Worming does not upset pups at all and there is no period of starvation. Burn all the worms so that they are destroyed completely. Worm the bitch twice at 14-day intervals after she has finished feeding the pups. It is wise not to let tiny children handle the pups, and to insist that everyone else washes their hands immediately after they have been in contact.

Once the pups discover solid food, you should feed them four times daily in the way of your choice. Remember that feeding must be balanced with carbohydrates, fat and protein, and that cow's milk must be enriched with egg yolk or cream. Weaning should be a natural and gradual process and any aim of 'all off the bitch by a certain date', practised by some exhibitor-breeders, is a great mistake. As the pups take more food, the bitch's allowance should be reduced. There is seldom any problem of her milk drying off too early or persisting too late if she is in good health.

By the time they are six weeks old, the pups should be walking firmly. Their docked tails should be healed and they should be attending to their own defaecation – the dam will have stopped cleaning them. The baby teeth, which start to come through at about two weeks, will be firmly established and should not begin to be lost until the pups are nearly four months old. The bitch should be allowed free access to her litter, but she should not be shut up with them unless she has a bed where they cannot reach her. Pups can be put outside in good weather to play, but until they are about eight weeks old they seem to dislike bright daylight. Pups of this age can do a lot of damage to plants in a garden, they are very inquisitive and up to all sorts of mischief. Make sure that they cannot get at such items as garden chemicals, slug bait, weed killers, anti-freeze and household cleaners, and that they cannot chew electric wiring or cut off the telephone. Some house plants are also poisonous to pups, so take care that they cannot get at anything of this nature. They love cloth to pull between them or a ball, as long as it is big enough not to be swallowed. Do not give them nylon tights, for these are dangerous, nor plastic toys which may be chewed into pieces. A really large marrow bone is not only good exercise for the jaws and teeth but causes a lot of amusement. Make sure that the bone is large enough and do not leave it out overnight where it may be soiled by rats or mice. The pups should be offered water several times a day until they are old enough to have a dish down all the time – and realize that it is not a paddling pool!

Defects may show in the pups when they are more active or are eating solid food. For example, a pup which cannot get on to its feet, which is much smaller than the others or tired out by exercise before its fellows, or which vomits regularly after food, needs a vet's opinion to see if there is some deformity. If this is the case, the pup should be put down straight away. There is no sense in keeping a sub-standard puppy, not even if it is given away. It will never be a cheap or satisfactory pet, and its life is inevitably shorter than the average for the breed.

At about six weeks you can see the characters of the pups emerging – the bold ones, the cuddly ones, the escapers and the clowns. From the time they first walk, pups should be groomed and have their ears cleaned, and they should learn that they must, for a short while at least, submit to a pack leader who is a human being. In this way you are beginning to condition the puppy to becoming a companion and a responsible member of the household, one which does not need stern discipline. Puppies must be kept clean from fleas and lice, which they may pick up from the dam or in the garden. At worst, lice can cause anaemia in a tiny puppy and, at best, they can lead to derisory remarks from a vet to the new owner. Lice are often found around the ear margins and fleas in the groin. Another pest, cheyletiella, looks like scurf on the coat, and itch badly. The natural desire to be clean will be reinforced if the puppies are taken outside immediately after they have finished eating and also when they get up from sleep. In bad weather or at night they should be trained to newspaper.

You will already have started the process of registering your pups with the Kennel Club. Unless they are registered, it may be difficult for a purchaser to exhibit them or breed from them if they should prove of the required quality. If there are any surplus pups which have not been reserved, you should advertise these when they are five weeks old. Prospective buyers should visit several times so that you can get to know them and be assured that the homes are suitable. When a firm choice of puppy

is made, take a deposit of at least one third of the purchase price as a guarantee of good faith. The time when puppies are attractive to sell is short, and you do not want to find yourself in a quandary if a puppy is not collected. If buyers want you to act for them and to have the puppy vaccinated against various diseases, this must be understood to be an extra cost. It is also usual to charge board for retaining the puppy beyond eight weeks of age. Vaccination is not usually performed until after eight weeks, as the maternally derived antibodies may not have waned until then. Pups must be kept within house and garden until two weeks after their first inoculation, so that they do not run any risk of infection from other dogs.

When the puppies leave you, they should take with them a full diet sheet of their menu, with notes to guide the new owner on how meals will alter as the pup grows. You should also give a signed pedigree and a certificate of worming, stating when the pup was wormed, what substance was used, how much was given each time and

directions for later wormings. It is also helpful to make a note of any books which have been useful to you, the addresses of the secretaries of canine clubs and training clubs, a few hints on the most useful type of collar and bed and, perhaps, as a special bonus, a photograph of dam and sire, so that the new owner may have as much pride as you in your lovely and successful litter.

A bitch and her newly born pup. The whelp is attached to the cord, and this in turn is attached to the placenta. After her ordeal the bitch rests for a few seconds and then proceeds to break the membranes and cord with her teeth (see page 124). Puppies are normally strong and healthy, and they will be licked and stimulated by their dam. She will nose them and turn them over. This is excellent because it stimulates the puppies in every way, in particular to breathe and to get their circulation going.

All About Puppies

DOG breeders sometimes maintain that all problem dogs are made that way by their owners. This is often only an excuse for the unsuitable or untrainable puppies they have sold. We believe that the finished article depends about 50% on inherited characteristics and 50% on acquired ones. As you hope that the animal you are about to buy will be a member of the family for the next ten to fifteen years, it is worth going to a great deal of trouble in choosing it.

Once you have decided on which breed to have, you should try to find a seven- to eight-week-old puppy of that breed. Temperament is by far the most important factor in choosing a puppy. In dogs a good temperament is one that is bold, friendly and not afraid of noise or people; a bad temperament is one that is shy or nervous in any way. The majority of puppies may appear to have good temperaments, but only a minority end up as bold, friendly dogs. In choosing a puppy, its own behaviour is less important than the behaviour of its parents, grandparents and even great grandparents. It is unlikely that you will be able to see all those, but do try to see the parents and as many relatives as possible. If they are not the sort of dog you would like to own, try somewhere else. You should pay particular attention to the temperament of the dam. Geneticists believe that an animal inherits its various characteristics 50/50 from sire and dam, but by the time it is weaned a puppy will also have acquired other characteristics from its mother, or foster mother as the case may be. Experiments have been carried out where puppies from a bold bitch have been fostered onto a shy bitch and vice versa. These show quite conclusively that fear of any sort, and gun shyness in particular, is transmitted to the puppies by the time they are three or four weeks old.

Recent study has shown that in the first few weeks of their lives puppies learn much more than was previously believed. This has nothing to do with training, but simply with the conditions surrounding the puppy in its early life. By the time the puppy is eight weeks old, its instinct to keep its 'nest' clean can either be well developed or completely killed. Socialization with human beings should be developed from the time the puppy's eyes are open. At one time it was considered bad for puppies to be petted and fondled by children, but a puppy which is used to being handled from an early age will settle into its new home much more quickly. Provided it goes to the right home, the sooner the puppy leaves its brothers and sisters the better. The best age is usually between seven and eight weeks old.

Supposing that you have found a litter of puppies of your chosen breed, that you like the parents and that the pups have been well reared under reasonable conditions, what should you look for in the puppy itself? First of all remember that, although the puppies may look very much alike now, they will all grow up with very different characters, just like any family of brothers and sisters. And if you have just lost one of the same breed, don't expect any of these puppies to grow up just like your old dog.

In nearly every litter there is a dominant puppy which is quicker to learn than the others – very often learning how to escape! It is usually, but not invariably, a dog and as soon as the pups can crawl it will be first out of the nest, first to the feed bowl and almost certainly first to greet you on arrival. In later life this puppy will probably be a good worker, but it will also often be very dominant and wilful, making it difficult to train. The second, or even third, puppy in the social scale is often a better choice, but a lot depends on the parents. If the parents are hard dogs, choose the most submissive puppy, but if they are very amenable, soft dogs then you want to go for a bold puppy, even the number one puppy. Take plenty of time looking at a litter of pups and discussing them with the breeder, who knows, or should know, each puppy individually. The puppy to choose is the one which comes to you when you squat down to speak to it, which snuggles up to you when you take it in your arms, and which does not run away if you clap your hands or make an unexpected movement. The puppy you should leave behind is the independent dog which stalks off, minding its own business, which struggles to get out of your arms when you pick it up, and which runs away when you clap your hands. And the puppy you should not have on any account is the one which, on seeing a stranger, runs into its kennel or hides in a corner. Many people, especially women, feel sorry for a shy puppy and buy it, only to regret having done so for the rest of the dog's life. It is also very cruel to keep a nervous dog in a house full of rowdy children or any other noisy conditions. To force an animal to live in constant fear of everything around it is surely just as cruel as if you were to beat or starve it.

Always look for a dog with a bright, bold eye which looks straight at you honestly, and avoid any dog with a shifty, furtive look. Bright eyes are a guide to physical well-being as well as temperament, and it is equally important to start with a healthy puppy. Its skin should be soft and pliable when picked up in the hand and its coat should be glossy, although some types of coat do not look glossy even when in the best condition. The skin should be free from sores and bare patches, which can be due to fleas or lice, usually easily cured, but sometimes caused by a type of mange which may be impossible to cure. If the puppy is potbellied it is probably due to worms which are also easy to treat, but it is a sign of neglect, or ignorance, on the part of the breeder as the pup should have been wormed before this stage.

Below: A Spitz puppy with its young owner in Finland.

Right: A young Sealyham puppy, rather uncertain on its feet.

Below: Young Dalmatians at play.

Opposite page: This Poodle bitch suckling her puppies is obviously a contented and affectionate mother.

Right: A Beagle puppy setting out on the path of life.

Below: Golden Retriever puppies are very appealing at this age.

The most important point to remember with a young puppy is that it is still a baby. It is surprising how many people overlook this fact. They have some idea that if they don't start training their puppy right away, it can never be trained. At this age, however, the puppy does not need a replacement pack leader so much as a replacement mother. This is why women are so much better than men at rearing puppies. There is no such thing as giving a puppy too much affection, but don't forget that, like all babies, it needs a lot of sleep. Much suffering is caused to puppies which go to new homes where children are allowed to maul and play with them continuously. Many people would do well to train their children before attempting to cope with a dog!

New owners often make the mistake of starting to house train the puppy the moment they get it home. They take this infant from its brothers and sisters and its familiar surroundings, probably on a long car journey, then put it down on the kitchen floor, whereupon it does what any sensible person would expect it to do and the owner immediately smacks it for leaving a puddle on the floor. But animals do not reason as we do, they learn by association of ideas, and rather than associating the punishment with the 'crime' as the owner intended, the puppy is more likely to associate the punishment with the person who administered it and with its new home in general. This kind of treatment turns many bold, friendly puppies into timid, nervous wrecks within a few days of going to a new home. It never ceases to amaze us that mothers will wrap their own child in nappies, yet expect a canine infant to go through the night without relieving itself.

The best way to learn how to take over from the puppy's mother is to study her behaviour. She is constantly licking and caressing her puppies and pushing them about in play. We are not suggesting that you start licking your new charge, but a tense or worried puppy will often relax immediately in response to the touch of a sensitive and sympathetic hand. The bitch also 'talks' to her puppies in very soft tones, usually inaudible to human ears, so try to talk to your puppy in a quiet, reassuring tone of voice. This does not mean subjecting it to a barrage of meaningless chatter; talk to it when there is a reason for doing so and try to get some response.

If a puppy annoys its mother, say by biting too hard in play, she will growl at it and, if that has no effect, snap at it. Next time she growls at the puppy, it will associate the sound with correction and stop whatever it is doing. A sudden snap from the bitch is reserved for more serious misbehaviour. It nearly always frightens the puppy, and it will almost certainly draw back and may even run away. But very soon it will come back and probably roll on its back in front of her. Her response to this is to lick and caress the puppy, making friendly noises and reassuring it in every way she can that she still loves it – so long as it behaves itself.

The human 'mother' can, and should, learn several things from this behaviour. The bitch corrects the puppy *as and when* it is doing the wrong thing; not several seconds or even minutes after, as so many humans do. And once the puppy has been corrected, it is over and all is forgiven. Very soon the puppy associates a growl with correction, and will stop whatever it is doing. A puppy reacts instinctively to a growl, and it is very seldom that a puppy will go right up to a strange dog which growls at it. This instinct can be, and should be, used in training.

To give a practical example of how this treatment should work with your puppy, imagine it is chewing the hearth rug. You should say 'No' to it in a harsh 'growling' tone (never shout – the puppy has better hearing than you). A sensitive puppy will probably react to this growl and stop chewing, whereupon you should praise it by stroking it and encouraging it in a friendly tone. If it does not respond to the growl, follow immediately with correction which, for a puppy of this age, can be a light tap on the nose or gripping the scruff of its neck. As soon as the puppy responds, praise it well. A lively puppy will probably take some time to learn, but repeat the whole performance more severely each time until it gives up.

It is important to remember that 'No' is not the first sound a puppy should learn to understand. Dogs do not understand words, only sounds; it is just as easy to teach a dog to lie down by saying 'Stand up' as it is by saying 'Lie down'. The first sound a new puppy should learn is its name. It should learn to associate its name with pleasure and your first object should be to get it to come to you every time it hears its name. One of the most usual of all dog problems are dogs which will not come when they are called. Most of these dogs have been taught *not* to come, because the owner has created

Above: A working sheepdog puppy.

Left: Contrary to common belief, cats and dogs are not necessarily natural enemies.

the wrong associations. Some have been taught to run away by the owner's efforts to train them. For a young puppy in a new home, every effort should therefore be made to make it associate its name with pleasure. Later on the name can be used in different tones, but for the present it must always be spoken in a friendly, reassuring tone. Never shout the puppy's name and never use its name to scold it. Use a harsh 'No' or 'Ahh' which can be growled rather than spoken. Don't keep repeating the puppy's name, as that will simply accustom it to a sound which it will learn to ignore, like the radio or conversation. And don't call it when there is no chance whatsoever of it responding – for instance, when it is digging a hole in the garden or sees a dog in the distance. Call it when it happens to be coming in your direction of its own accord. When it reaches you, praise it enthusiastically and offer it some food. Next time the puppy hears its name, it should show more inclination to come towards you. The more you shout a puppy's name without getting any response, the more you are teaching it not to come when called.

The first thing most people want to teach a puppy is to be house clean. To the majority of owners it is much more important that the puppy should be clean in the house than that it should be happy, but a lot of people overlook the fact that a happy puppy is more likely to be clean than an unhappy one. There are two important points to remember here. First, that we are dealing with a baby, and second that, unlike some other babies, the puppy has a natural instinct to keep its living quarters clean. Babies cannot go for any length of time without emptying both bladder and bowels, and an instinct cannot develop if given no opportunity to do so. In other words, if the puppy cannot relieve itself outdoors, Nature will force it to relieve itself indoors. And once this becomes a habit, it is very difficult to break.

The first few days in a puppy's new home are vital for teaching good habits. Vigilance and time spent in the early days will be more than repaid later on. You should notice when the puppy feels uncomfortable, but you may get very little warning with a young puppy. Pick it up gently and quietly and take it out. Don't *put* it out, but *take* it out and stay with it until it does what you want it to do, then praise it and bring it indoors again.

Puppies nearly always want to relieve themselves when they wake up and after they have had a meal. So take yours out at these times, whether or not it shows any desire to do so. A puppy which has been brought up under clean conditions will soon go towards the door when it feels uncomfortable. All you have to do then is to open the door. But remember that the puppy cannot open the door itself, and it cannot wait until you come back from shopping or finish a long telephone conversation. To punish a puppy which makes a mistake under these circumstances is pointless and cruel.

Few people, however, have the time to keep a constant eye on a puppy. The answer to this is a playpen, very similar to a child's playpen, an essential piece of equipment for the average puppy owner. The pen should be placed as near as possible to the door, with a bed in one corner, and the floor should be covered with newspaper. When you are too busy to keep an eye on the puppy, all you have to do is pop it in its pen. There might appear to be a disadvantage in that the puppy will get into the habit of using the newspaper in its pen and will not want to go outside. But when the puppy is outside its pen, it will tend to go towards the pen if it wants to relieve itself. This should be fairly obvious and you can easily put it outside – hence the reason for the pen being near the door. When eventually you remove the playpen and the newspaper altogether, the puppy will still head for the same spot and you can then open the door so that it can go outside.

So far we have been dealing with the puppy brought up under good conditions, but all puppies are not brought up under good conditions, and if the instinct to be clean is not strong enough in itself, something more drastic is necessary in an effort to develop it. You will need to teach the puppy what to do and what not to do by correction and reward. If the puppy just squats down wherever it happens to be, without any warning, pick it up quickly, 'growl' at it with a harsh 'No' and take it outside. Don't smack it, but don't be as gentle as you would be with a puppy which is trying to be clean. Being picked up firmly and quickly is a severe enough correction for a young puppy. A reasonably sensitive puppy will now associate feeling uncomfortable with correction, and this will worry it and make it hesitate the next time. Now is your opportunity to pick it up gently, talking to it in reassuring tones. This will help it to understand that it is doing the right thing, and also that you are still a nice person even if you did have to correct it for doing wrong. With a less sensitive puppy, you may have to repeat the correction several times before it gets the message and you may have to be more severe, even to the extent of grabbing it by the scruff of its neck and giving it a good shake. But don't slap the puppy and don't correct it if you go into a room and find a puddle on the floor. Just wipe the mess up and wait for an opportunity to catch the puppy in the act.

The sooner a puppy is taken out to meet the great wide world, the easier it will be for it to accept it. Very young puppies are much less likely to be afraid of strange people, noise and so on, than older ones, and they are less likely to be carsick. But if you take a young puppy out before it has

been inoculated, at about the age of eight weeks, there is a grave risk of it picking up an infection. You can take a puppy out in the car from the age of six weeks, but take care not to put it on ground where other dogs have been. It can be handled and made a fuss of, but try to avoid people with dogs of their own. If you take care, the risk of infection is very small and certainly less than the risk of the puppy becoming shy of traffic and people if kept away from them for too long.

Car sickness is in itself quite a problem. Start by taking the puppy out as young as possible, as frequently as possible and for very short distances. But don't take it out just after a meal! Some dogs are never carsick but if yours is, try to get it over the problem as quickly as possible. There are a great many tranquillizers available which will help. It is wise to consult your veterinary surgeon, who will advise on the correct drug and dosage for your particular puppy. But you should not regard drugs as a cure, only as an aid to help the puppy. Always give the minimum dose, and if it does not work, you can give a little more next time. Reduce the dose as soon as possible until you find that the puppy is quite happy without being given anything. You can also help your puppy to overcome car sickness by trying to persuade it to associate the car with pleasure. A puppy's first car ride usually takes it away from its own familiar surroundings to a new home, which it inevitably finds very bewildering. And all too often its next trip is to the vet, who sticks a needle in it. So make a regular car journey, such as driving the children to school, take the puppy with you and feed it when you get home. The children should prevent it thinking too much about itself on the way there, the journey back will be short and it will have its breakfast as a reward. It is also worth taking the puppy out in the car before giving it a walk. If you take it even a short way in the car and then let it have a romp which it enjoys, it should very soon associate the car with pleasure and be anxious to go in it. When you do have to go on a longer journey, it is often a good idea to stop after the first half hour or so and let the puppy have a good run.

Once your puppy is old enough to be inoculated (eight to twelve weeks), you should consult a veterinary surgeon as there are various types of inoculation. Two inoculations are normally given, which will protect your puppy against distemper, hardpad, hepatitis and two forms of leptospirosis.

Remember that it is not a good idea to take an uninoculated puppy into a waiting room with other dogs which may be infected; if possible, try to find a vet with an appointment system so that you can be seen immediately, or wait outside in your car.

Above left: A Norfolk Terrier puppy in a light, portable playpen.

Dogs in Miniature

TOY dogs? The very mention of them makes many people bristle, especially the owners of giant breeds. They conjure up visions of snuffling, yapping nuisances, of shivering Chihuahuas, of spoilt, bad-tempered Pugs slobbering all over their doting owner's laps. Not a very nice picture but fortunately a very wrong one. The dictionary defines the word 'toy' as a 'plaything, a trifling thing, not meant for real use'. So to call all the tiny dogs 'toys' is to do them a grave injustice. Many of these diminutive breeds pack more courage and intelligence into their small frames than some of the lumbering giants weighing 45 kg (100 lbs) or more.

Toy dogs are by no means a recent introduction. Many have been with us for centuries and it is worth first of all taking a look at some of these dogs from the past.

Probably the toy breed with the most ancient lineage is the Pekingese, or Lion Dog, of the Chinese Emperors. Dogs of very much the same type as the modern Pekingese can be identified from Korean bronzes dating back to 2000 BC. Their history was recorded by artists on scrolls now known collectively as the Imperial Dog Book. The Peke seems to have made its journey from East to West with its royal dignity untarnished, and still looks on other lesser breeds with great disdain. Incidentally, while the Pekingese is known as the Lion Dog of the East, the Maltese Terrier was in the past called the Lion Dog of the West.

Below: Lion Dogs, the ancestors of the modern Pekingese, were bred to resemble dragons so that they would drive away evil spirits.

Below: Begging is an easy trick to teach a Pug – most have a good solid base to balance on!

Right: Two young King Charles Spaniel puppies.

Opposite page: Two dainty little Papillons.

Other toy breeds with a history behind them are the Toy Spaniel, famous for their connection with the Stuart King Charles II. These little dogs were often called 'Comforters' or 'Spaniels Gentle', probably because they were credited with special powers of healing if clasped to the bosom of a sick person. Toy Spaniels were firm favourites with many famous European artists long before they became accepted at the English Court.

The Papillon, or French Butterfly Dog, was also at one time called a toy spaniel. The name arises from the large, butterfly-shaped ears which are a feature of this breed. Oddly enough, they were at one time shown with drop ears, when it could hardly be said they resembled butterflies, or at best very sad ones. These little dogs were very popular as models for such painters as Rembrandt and Van Dyck.

Having seen how long many of the toy breeds have been in existence, one can refute the argument that they are very delicate and difficult to breed, although it must be said that some of the larger-headed, short-nosed breeds do have whelping troubles. So also do some of the scaled-down miniatures, such as the Toy Poodle, but chiefly because their ancestors were, until quite recently, possibly three times as large and throwbacks sometimes crop up. But taken all round, most toy dogs are tough, hardy little characters.

Soon after World War II people began to buy smaller dogs. Food was expensive and in short supply, and many people in towns lived in small houses with little opportunity to exercise a large dog. Toy

Charles and Cavalier King Charles Spaniels with their long silky coats and attractive colouring still retain their sporting instincts, and some are even used to work to the gun. They are cheerful, carefree little dogs, equally happy to share a city flat during the week or join you for a country ramble at weekends. Perhaps you will prefer the stolid Pug or quicksilver Chihuahua, both with nice easy-to-care-for coats. A quick rub over with a damp chamois leather and a final polish with your hands and these little dogs are neat and tidy, ready to take anywhere.

So take your pick from short coats, long coats, rough coats or fluffy coats, snub noses or almost no noses at all, medium noses and long pointed ones, small eyes or large eyes. Large protruding eyes must be

not have to go to such extremes with your own small house dog. It will not, of course, grow such a splendid coat as its brothers and sisters in the show ring but it will probably have a lot more fun in life. In fact, most toy dogs are very adaptable and, treated like dogs, not playthings, they are happy to go for a walk in the park, play ball in the garden or guard the car when you go shopping. (A word of warning about leaving dogs in cars, especially short-nosed breeds such as Pugs, Pekes and King Charles: even with the windows open, a car left in or out of the sun on a hot day can heat up to a very high temperature in a very short time.) As far as guarding is concerned, many of these tinies do a very good job indeed. They may not look as formidable as a German Shepherd, but the

dogs cost a great deal less to feed than a large breed, take up less room in a small house or car, cost less on public transport, need far less exercise and usually take less time to groom. But do not be misled into thinking that they cost less money to buy than a large dog. The opposite is probably true, one reason being that, while a larger breed may have ten to fifteen puppies in a litter, a bitch of the toy breeds will be more likely to produce four puppies at the most.

If you are thinking of buying a toy dog, the best place to see most of the breeds together is a large championship dog show. Dogs at shows are divided into groups to make it easier to judge them, and the group you will want to look out for will be the toy group. No matter what you are looking for in your small dog you should be able to find it here, all in miniature. The little King

treated with a little extra care if they are not to cause trouble. These eyes can pick up dust, cigarette ash or anything else floating around in the air, all of which will cause irritation. If it is only simple irritation the trouble can often be soothed by bathing the eye in a saline solution, 1 teaspoonful of salt to $\frac{1}{2}$ litre (1 pint) of water, making a solution very like the natural fluid of tears. Any serious scratch or blow to the eyes should be immediately referred to a veterinary surgeon.

If you are looking for a dog as a pet and companion rather than a show dog, do not be put off by all the preparation you see at dog shows. These dogs are entering what is really a canine beauty contest. The show Yorkie may well wear curlers every night and the Maltese be brushed and powdered to show off its profuse coat, but you will

noise they make will scare off any would-be car thief.

The pet toy dog will still need regular grooming, of course: brushing to keep its coat tangle-free, and a bath when necessary. What your little dog will also need is a thorough drying after being out in the wet, even if it is short-coated. The water itself will do it no harm while it is running about, but a small, low-to-ground dog will pick up an awful lot of moisture in a short time and must be well dried when it comes inside again. As good a way as any is to soak up the moisture with a chamois leather and give the dog a final rub with a rough towel; pat rather than rub dry if it has a very long coat.

Most dogs have small stomachs, and toy dogs especially should not be overfed. For the really tiny ones, two small meals a

Above: These attractive little long-haired Chihuahuas are sometimes confused with the Papillons shown on the previous page.

Opposite page: A proud King Charles Cavalier bitch with her litter of puppies.

day are often better than one large one. Some small dogs also have a tendency to develop bad teeth, possibly because their tiny mouths are pushed to the limit to accommodate the required number. You can help to remedy this by letting them have large raw bones to chew on and a hard dry dog biscuit occasionally. You should also check for tartar forming on the teeth, which will cause them to decay; if there does appear to be a thick deposit forming, then check with a veterinary surgeon. But most of the larger breeds have a few troubles too and, taken all round, a well-bred, well-reared and sensibly treated toy dog should be just as healthy and active as its bigger brothers.

One of the most popular toy breeds is the Toy Poodle. Small, chic, intelligent and a non-coat-shedder, it makes a good choice for the town flat. They first became popular

– indeed, almost over-popular – in the 1950s. This led to indiscriminate breeding by unscrupulous breeders and resulted in a great number of neurotic, nervous Poodles with slipping patellas, ingrowing eyelashes and many other unpleasant constructional faults. The popularity boom now seems to have worn off, however, and the Toy Poodles of today have greatly improved.

If you can manage to find a well-reared Toy Poodle puppy bred from sensible, healthy parents, you should have a pet to be proud of. They are usually jaunty, chic little chaps, willing and able to learn all sorts of tricks. Most Poodles have a very active brain as well as an agile body, and they have frequently been used in the circus to perform tricks. They seem to appreciate an audience and the more you teach them, the more they enjoy it. Their small size is no bar to working them in obedience classes

and quite a few have made a name for themselves in this sort of work. So if you want your Poodle to be a happy little dog, let it use its brain and give it plenty to do. If you treat it like a lapdog and fuss over it, it will probably develop into a neurotic little horror, but you will only have yourself to blame.

Poodles have the advantage over other breeds in that they do not shed their coats, but on the other hand they do need careful and regular grooming and clipping. They have a tendency to grow excess hair in the entrance to the ear canal, and this must be regularly plucked out or it will get matted and block the ear, causing endless trouble. If you start when the dog is a puppy and gently pluck out the hair with forefinger and thumb, it should never get to the stage where it causes trouble. White poodles also tend to get 'tear marks' below the eyes. These cause little harm but they look most unattractive. The eyes can be bathed in a saline solution or even cold tea, and there are special preparations on sale at good pet stores which are most effective. Always check to see that the dog has not got ingrowing eyelashes which are causing this trouble; if so take it to your veterinary surgeon.

Poodles can be professionally clipped at beauty salons, or you can learn to do it yourself if you simply want a smart pet. In either case, the earlier clipping is started the better. Treated firmly but gently as a puppy, the dog will soon accept clipping as part of its general routine and will even look forward to it.

If you decide to clip the dog yourself, have a look round the poodle benches at dog shows and chat to the exhibitors. Buy an illustrated book on the art of clipping and make a start with a good pair of electric clippers. Always be very light-handed; most cases of 'clipper rash' and of dogs disliking clipping are due to a heavy-handed clipper. Should a rash develop, dab baby lotion or cream over the affected part and dust with talcum powder. Be very careful clipping the tail for the first time; it is very sensitive and if you have the clippers adjusted too finely you can cause the dog a lot of pain and irritation.

You can start clipping when the puppy is about eight weeks old. All that is necessary at this stage is to clip the feet, face and tail. As the coat gets longer, it will need 'tipping' slightly with scissors to keep it even. If you only intend to keep the pup as a pet and not for showing, it is best to shape the topknot into a neat round. Puppy hair is very soft and breaks easily, so do not leave ribbons or rubber bands on for very long. Never do too much at once; far better to clip two feet and then let the puppy have a rest, than subject it to a long session. Be extra careful when the pup is teething at about the age of five months; it is best not to clip round its face at all for a while as its mouth might be sore.

The Japanese Chin, or Japanese Spaniel as it was once known, came from Japan in about 1882. The breed caught the public's fancy and soon a considerable number were being imported and exhibited at dog shows. They soon became a great favourite with Queen Victoria and she had her portrait painted with one. Although fairly new to the Western world, the breed has existed in the East for centuries. No one seems to know its exact origin, but it is thought that it had as ancestors the Pekingese and a now extinct feathered variety of Pug called the Loong Chua.

Weighing about 3 kg (7 lbs), the Japanese Chin is a very smart little dog, black and white or red and white, marked in distinct patches. Its coat is long and straight, with a pronounced ruff and feathering on the legs and feet. The tail is well plumed and carried proudly over the back. Slightly higher on the leg than the better-known Pekingese, the Japanese is noted for its energy and love of life. Its gait is high-stepping and graceful. It enjoys jumping and both you and your pet will get a lot of fun from some small 'hurdles' put up in the garden.

Japanese Chins are usually good house dogs. They have a deep bark for their small size, but they are not usually 'yappers', like some other tinies. Most owners of Japs find they are very good mixers and get on well with dogs of other breeds. As the standard calls for rather prominent eyes, particular care should be taken to keep these clean and free from dust and grit, if necessary washing them with saline solution (see above). Their silky coats should be kept in good condition by brushing; use a wide-toothed comb if the dog is shedding its coat or has got some tangles, but don't overdo the comb work as it will tend to pull out too much coat. Make sure there are no mats between the toes or behind the ears, and always keep the feathering on the hindquarters particularly clean.

When the dog is casting its coat, a bath can be a help in loosening the dead undercoat and giving the new one a better chance to grow through. Use a towel to sop up the surplus water, then use a hairdryer and gently brush the dog dry at the same

Opposite page, left: This Poodle in a pet trim is obviously enjoying his country outing.

Opposite page, right: A well-balanced little Toy Terrier.

Right: A large and lively family of Japanese Chins.

time. This way the coat will not get broken and will lie much flatter.

Japs are intelligent little dogs and, like all dogs, are the better for some training. It gives them a chance to use their brains and makes for a better and closer relationship between dog and owner.

The English Toy Terrier has had quite a few different names in the last century, including Toy Manchester Terrier, Toy Black and Tan, and Miniature Black and Tan, but English Toy Terrier seems to be the final choice. It is a very old British breed, and many years ago a great deal of money was won and lost on these little terriers in the rat pits where their record stood second to none.

Toy Terriers make delightful house dogs, especially for the smaller house or flat. Most are undemanding little dogs, but they are very keen and alert and will soon give warning if strangers are about. Although quite small, the ideal weight being between 2.7–3.6 kg (6–8 lbs) in Britain and up to 5.4 kg (12 lbs) in America, they still retain their sporting instincts and remain real terriers. Sturdy as well as elegant to look at, most would still welcome the chance to have a go at a rat, or even a mouse.

These miniature terriers have a sleek, glossy coat and longish legs which keep them well up out of the dirt, so they need the minimum of time and trouble spent to keep them looking well groomed. All that is necessary is a good brushing with a short, stiff brush or glove, a wipe with a damp chamois leather and a final polish with your hands to give a good gloss. In colouring, they are a clearly defined pattern of jet black and rich mahogany tan. The colours must never run into each other, but

should appear quite separate. The head is black with two tan cheek spots, tan spots over each eye and a tan muzzle. The legs from the knee down are tan, but the toes are pencilled in black. No white is allowed. They have fairly large upright ears, and stand about 28 cm (11 ins) high, making a smart, distinctive little dog.

Another good point in the Toy Terriers' favour is that they are not usually fussy feeders and have small appetites. They are not shivery little dogs but, only having very short coats, they do tend to feel the cold and wet. If kept on the move they will enjoy a run in bad weather, but they should not be allowed to stand around and should be well dried on return. A warm comfortable bed will also be appreciated and this could be combined with a small travelling box, lined with a warm blanket.

The smallest breed of dog in the world, and one of the most popular, is the Chihuahua. The standard states their weight as being under 2.7 kg (6 lbs) and even more diminutive is preferred. Unhappily, although they usually weigh 1.8–2.7 kg (4–6 lbs), some have been recorded weighing as little as 450 gm (1 lb). If you shrink a breed to a third of its size or less in a few generations, you are almost bound to breed trouble. Some of these very small Chihuahuas have a considerable amount of hip trouble and the bitches often have very difficult whelpings, requiring caesarean operations to enable them to have their litters. So should you decide on one of these fascinating small dogs, try to find a slightly larger one and you will find it a lot easier to manage.

It is generally accepted that these little dogs originated in Mexico in the state of Chihuahua, from which they take their name. The first one was registered with the American Kennel Club in 1904. Chihuahuas still exist in their original form, slightly larger and tougher than the pet dog we know, in Indian villages in Central America. Travellers have brought back tales of packs of fifty or more enthusiastically hunting wild pigs in the forests! I doubt if the show dogs would appreciate that pastime, but they are still agile, alert little dogs, usually very intelligent and devoted to their owners but none too keen on strangers. This is not a bad thing as it generally makes them good house dogs and less likely to be stolen.

If you do not like the short-coated Chihuahua, there is also a long-coated variety. The standard is the same for both types except that the longer coat should be soft, often with a slight wave. The tail is well plumed and the feet and legs are well feathered. The ears are fringed and there should be a large ruff round the neck. As with the smooth variety, any colour or combination of colours is permissible. The smooths may feel the cold a bit and some appreciate a warm polo-necked sweater on a cold winter's day, but their coats take very little looking after to keep them soft and shining. A good daily massage with the hands and a brisk rub with a damp chamois leather to remove dirt and loose hairs are about all you need to do. The long-coated Chihuahuas are also easily kept in good condition by a short daily session with brush and comb. Their teeth need watching carefully as their mouths are very small and the teeth may be a bit cramped, so try to get

the dog used to having its mouth handled while it is still a puppy. Brush the teeth with a toothbrush and scale them if necessary, thus avoiding any build-up of tartar. The dog's nails also need an eye kept on them and should not be allowed to grow too long.

Yet another smart, smooth-coated tiny is the Miniature Pinscher. Usually black and tan, red or chocolate in colour, it makes a lively companion. Although often described as a small edition of the Doberman Pinscher, this is not correct. Min Pins were in existence long before Herr Doberman introduced his namesake to the dog world. A rather different toy breed is the rough-coated Griffon, which with its quaint monkey face has a charm all its own.

A newcomer to the West is the pretty little Bichon Frise, a small white dog with a double coat, the outer hair long and silky. Its ears are sometimes tinged with cream, apricot or grey. These little dogs have a lot of character and are very lively.

Above left: Three smart Miniature Poodles in a 'lion clip', the usual trim used for showing.

Right: A young Bichon Frise pup ready for a game.

Advanced Grooming

The conception of advanced grooming by largely mechanical means may at first appear to be somewhat complicated and beyond the average person's scope. If you intend to exhibit a dog in present day show rings, then for the long-haired breeds you will certainly have to seek professional help.

Up to a point nevertheless, by observing a few simple rules and scrupulously following a clear set of directions you yourself can present your dog so that he is a pleasure to look at.

When making the initial outlay of buying equipment, do not count the cost. Cheap, unsuitable or makeshift tools will prove to be more expensive in the long run. Obviously, the choice of grooming tools will vary according to the breed of dog which you own. For any breed, however, your first and foremost requirement will be brushes and combs. Of the many types of brushes, the most common and versatile is that with wire bristles set into a rubber pad. This variety is both strong and efficient.

Invaluable for many long-haired breeds is the slicker brush, again with wire pins set on a rubber pad, the whole attached to a curved base with a handle in the shape of a rake. The curved is preferred to the flat base as it gives greater play to the operator. This slicker brush will loosen matts and tangles which the ordinary brush cannot. It must, however, be used with due care.

For the smooth-haired breeds, hound gloves are most useful. These are employed for removing dead coat or undercoat and will give that final shining, burnished appearance.

Combs are also in many sizes and varieties. Steel combs are by far the most effective. It is advisable to have at least two, even three, with a big-coated dog. For really large tough coats you will want a long steel comb with very widely spaced teeth. A long comb with fairly widely spaced teeth is necessary for all long-haired dogs.

Finally, for perfecting the job, especially in the case of Poodles, use a small steel comb, half of it with very fine teeth, the other half with teeth a little more widely spaced.

Scissors should be carefully selected and should never be too small – seven inches in length are the most suitable. Hairdressers' scissors are ideal and should be chosen with a view to their easy manipulation by you yourself. For pet Poodle trims, scissors where the blades have a slight curve are an advantage as they help to round off hair with less effort.

Many breeds, for instance terriers, should be stripped. Most beauty parlours will not strip these in the approved way as they do not have the necessary time to spend on the individual dog. It is more normal to use clippers, with scissors for the final shaping. The end result can be neat and workmanlike and the whole effect is as if the dog had been stripped.

A stripping comb is a tool with a razor blade encased in its serrated teeth. A stripping knife fulfils the same purpose, having a nicked blade of steel fastened to a wooden handle.

To use a stripping tool grasp it firmly with the blade touching your forefinger. To remove the hairs turn the blade slightly in a twisting motion. Do not try to strip large areas of hair at one time.

Advanced grooming of many breeds involves the use of clippers. Hand clippers are not only difficult to use but are very slow in comparison with electric clippers. Apart from the clipper itself, you will need blades which can be attached very easily at will, according to the amount or length of hair to be left on the dog's coat. These blades are marked in numbers in some makes and in millimetres on others. Four blades are essential. Firstly, there is the number 5, or 5 millimetre blade, and this leaves about half an inch of hair on the body. Next comes the number 10, or 2 millimetre blade, which has teeth that are not so coarse and are set closer so

Opposite: The Pekingese, as the name suggests, originally came from China. They combine great dignity with personality plus.

145

that a clean smooth surface is left and the skin is not revealed to excess. Thirdly, the number 15, or 1 millimetre blade, is used mostly on feet, faces and tails for a closer effect than that given by the 10/2 m blade. Finally, there is the number 30 or $\frac{1}{4}$ millimetre blade. This is more drastic in that it produces a closely shaven effect and should therefore only be used where dogs are to be exhibited and then by an expert. Practice is needed before its use, for if handled indiscriminately it can cause a rash.

The modern method of holding a clipper–i.e. grasping it on *top* of its case rather than beneath it, so that the whole hand is *over* the clipper–means that there is less risk of dropping it. The wrist is flexible because the hand is held in a position where it has maximum strength and will be better able to make detailed ins and outs.

For the owner with one or two dogs only, a good hand dryer is adequate–preferably of metal.

As far as the actual process of advanced grooming is concerned, it will seem less complicated if dogs are divided into three grooming groups–easy, moderately easy and difficult.

Easy Grooming

This first category involves those breeds of dogs with smooth coats. Beagles, Smooth-haired Dachshunds, Greyhounds, Whippets, Italian Greyhounds, Smooth-haired Griffons, Dalmatians, Labradors, Great Danes, Dobermans, Mastiffs, Bull Mastiffs, Bull Terriers, Miniature Pinschers, Manchester Terriers and Chihuahuas, all can be included in this section.

A dog should always have a glossy look to his coat and this can be achieved by rubbing down daily with a hound glove. The glove can be used quite rigorously and if a special sheen is required, try smoothing over the whole coat with a piece of silk.

For many people, the clean uncluttered outline of a smooth-coated breed is its main appeal. Try to keep this neat picture by scissoring off any odd hairs sticking up from the surface of the coat. Such hairs should be trimmed from around the edges of ears or from the area of the eye. Whiskers can be snipped off together with any errant hairs protruding from the muzzle or drooping from an otherwise smooth tip of a tail.

The smaller, more fragile type of dog such as the Italian Greyhound or Chihuahua should also be rubbed down with a hound glove to keep them spick and span. You will probably find, however, that a glove made of fibre instead of the heavier duty variety made from boar hair or wire will not feel so harsh for a tiny dog.

An occasional shampoo with either a dog preparation or a human hair product is not amiss. A dog cannot grow a coat glowing with health if the skin underneath is dirty.

Moderately Easy Grooming

As they have long coats, dogs in this category necessarily need more specialized grooming. It is still, however, more or less a tidying up process, ensuring that neat outlines are preserved.

In all three sections mentioned, only those breeds which are more commonly kept as pets are listed.

The Afghan Hound, is a dog which requires a great deal of attention. Daily brushing is essential together with occasional bathing. Never bath an Afghan before removing all matts and tangles, because if you do, you will merely make matters worse and will risk causing pain to the dog. Large matts need easing out by brushing first with the wire brush, then combing with a wide-toothed steel comb. Work gradually from the ends of the hair to the roots, gently loosening the tangles between your fingers. Put your hand at root level on the coat so that you do not accidentally pull at the skin.

Grooming an Afghan as a pet owner, you are primarily concerned with keeping the long flowing coat free from all entanglements. Help this by scissoring between the pads of the feet being careful not to nick the skin. Trim round the feet so that they acquire a club-like appearance. Taper the tail feathering carefully. The Afghan's coat is parted from head to tail and the hair must be brushed from that parting in a downward direction. The long lean face should be kept free from straggling hairs. This is done by taking errant hairs between finger and thumb and carefully plucking them out. Stripping combs or knives should never be used on the Afghan. Odd hairs appearing along the centre parting should be plucked out to leave the divide smooth and neat.

The Saluki, an exotic hound, has attractive fringing on ears, tails and legs. Taper the tail feathering and keep the leg feathering trimmed. Follow the natural line and do not remove too much. Scissor the paws so that they have a rabbit-like look and keep the face and muzzle free from odd hairs.

The German Shepherd Dog (Alsatian) should be brushed daily, then rubbed down with a hound glove and finished off with a chamois leather. Trim the whiskers and tidy the hair on his feet. The St Bernard, Pyrenean, Samoyed, Corgi, etc. are all cared for in a similar way but pay due attention to the small differences in their outline. Remember that the grooming procedure of these breeds is not only essential towards keeping a well cared-for appearance. The more you groom regularly and properly, the less you will suffer at moulting time, when brushing out dead or excess hairs.

The Old English Sheepdog is more of a problem. Trimming establishments simply do not have the time to cope with the great thick coat, so they usually run a clipper down the body from top to toe. One should try to preserve that most typical aspect by regular use of a brush and scrupulous attention to removing matts. Hair round the eyes should be trimmed into a squarish shape to reveal the eyes. Whiskers should be trimmed squarely so that the whole face acquires a box-like look. Paws can be scissored round and hair cleaned from between the pads of the feet. Grooming in layers is advisable when brushing these dogs. Beginning at the ankle level, part the hair a few inches up and across the leg and brush the lower hair down and comb. Take a section above and repeat the procedure. Teach the dog to lie down on his side on the table and part the hair on the body from neck to tail. Proceed as for the legs.

The Collie is a different proposition in that, to maintain its coat in condition, one should not groom daily. Of course it cannot be left entirely without grooming. Groom initially so that the entire coat is free from knots, not forgetting those danger spots behind the elbows and inside the hind legs. Bath only when strictly necessary as too much can destroy the natural oils. Be very chary of using a comb, otherwise you will break off the hairs and end up with a sparse coat. There is one area, however, on which you must use a fine-toothed comb–the hair behind the ears, which is fine and of a silky texture. A certain amount of scissoring is necessary and such trimming can, if you wish to take the trouble, make all the difference to a Collie's appearance. This is done with straight scissors held so that the points face the feet. The hair on the legs is brushed or combed so that it stands out away from the legs. It is then scissored downwards. Trim hair away from between the pads of the feet. Scissor round each paw. Tidy up hair in the ears, which for exhibition purposes is done by careful plucking between finger and thumb. Whiskers can be trimmed, or not, as you prefer.

Treat the appealing little Shetland Sheepdog more or less the same as the Collie.

The fox-like little Pomeranian with its great ruff of hair needs frequent grooming with the wire bristle brush. First, brush *with* the growth of hair, then brush in the *opposite* direction and finish off by brushing again *with* the growth of hair. Free the coat of tangles by judicious use of a steel comb with wide-spaced teeth. Scissor round the paws to give a trim outline and trim under the tail to help that cobby look. Ears should be shaped to a point with scissors, following the true line of the ear.

The Papillon should be groomed sparingly. Taper the tail hair very slightly with scissors and round off the paws. Tidy up odd face hairs.

Brush the Yorkshire Terrier *with*, *against* and finally *with* the growth of hair. The coat is parted down the middle of the back and falls straight until it sweeps the ground. After grooming, trim the hair between the legs under the belly in a straight line just enough to prevent it trailing along the floor. Trim around the feet to the shape of the paw. Gather up the head hair and fasten it with wool or ribbon, never tug it as this can break the hair. Scissor the ears from the tips to where they widen out.

The Maltese Terrier has its coat groomed on either side of a central parting and its head hair is tied up. Keep the hair under the belly trimmed in a straight line and scissor neatly rounds the paws.

The delightful Shih Tzu must be brushed regularly to keep free from matts and to give a glossy sheen. Again, make a central parting and tie up hair on the head. Keep the body hair underneath scissored in a straight line and clean off the hair from between the pads of the feet.

The Pekingese's hair should be brushed out from the sides of the body and the brush then taken upwards in a lifting motion. This gives the impression of fullness. It makes grooming easier to spray the coat first. Sprays are in many varieties and a matter of personal choice. Ears are

A Maltese needs special attention if it is to be perfectly groomed for the show ring.

groomed towards the face. The coat beneath the ears is brushed outwards to give a ruff-like effect and the hair on top of the head is brushed smoothly back. The tail is parted down the middle and the hair brushed to fall either side of the body in a fan shape.

The thick coat of the Chow Chow is brushed in the reverse direction to the growth of hair. Never allow the hair to become matted and use a widely spaced steel comb to prevent this. Scissor round the paws until the feet have a cat-like look. Trim round the edges of the ears and give them the appearance of standing away from the coat. Remove errant hairs from the face and over the eyes. Trim the breech hair on the hind legs. Do this in a straight line so that the requisite stiff-legged look is preserved.

The huge coat of the Keeshond is groomed in the same manner as that of the Chow Chow.

The Elkhound has a heavy coat which should be brushed regularly. Whiskers can be trimmed, and also any hair growing out of line on the ears.

Difficult Advanced Grooming
The grooming of dogs in this section requires considerable knowledge and should be patterned on a good picture of the particular breed concerned. It is impossible in a limited space to give more than a general description of the grooming procedures. The care of the terrier family, for example, is given only in outline. If stripping tools

are used, their job is made easier by the prior use of a chalk block on the coat but, naturally, this can only be employed on a white coat.

Ideally, the Scottish Terrier should be stripped and plucked, not clipped. Trimming establishments clip Scotties and this is enough for domestic purposes. The Scottie has several main features – his whiskers are luxuriant, the eyebrows bushy, the tail tapers to a point and his body hair, smooth along his back, merges into the long skirts which form the 'apron'. The head is trimmed cleanly on the skull, leaving large eyebrows. Cheeks are trimmed or stripped from the outside corners of the eyes to the mouth, leaving huge whiskers. The edges of the ears are scissored to give a sharp outline, the whole ear area being neatly trimmed. Whether strippers or clippers are used, the back and neck hair should appear even and should gradually merge into the profuse belly apron. Shoulders should be stripped to the chest, the hair on the chest being trimmed to prevent any shagginess. Hair under the tail is rounded off, the tail itself being tapered with no escaping hairs to spoil it. Try for a final box-like, chunky appearance. Use scissors to round the feet.

The overall appearance of the Sealyham should be chunky, with full hair under the belly. The skull between the ear and eye corners to the mouth corners should be stripped or clipped with a 10/1 m blade. Long whiskers are blended into the cheeks and heavy beetling eyebrows are desirable. The ears are shaved both inside and out, their edges being trimmed carefully. Neck and shoulders are stripped closely. Legs are left with a profuse growth of hair and the coat on the back of the hindquarters is stripped carefully to achieve a straight aspect. Paws are rounded and hair between the pads is removed. The tail is stripped cleanly and allowed to taper.

The West Highland White Terrier is similarly stripped. This is done sparingly on the skull between the ears and, also sparingly, under the eyes. The ears are scissored and their edges trimmed around to finalize in the sharply pointed tips. Straggly hairs are cleaned from the tail. The coat on the back is tidied up to culminate in the long hair hanging underneath the belly. Strip the rump under the tail to give the impression of a short-bodied dog. Paws are scissored into a rounded

shape. His ruff is blended in with his whiskers.

The Cairn Terrier also has that distinctive ruff. Dead hairs from cheeks, between the ears and above the nose are stripped slightly. Curly hair is removed from the body to give a flat effect, the hair on the chest being left full. Shaggy eyebrows are combed downwards before the eyes and ears and then trimmed and scissored so that they stand away from the head. Down from the hocks, the hair is stripped closely and the paws are rounded off. The tail should be thick and brush-like, but odd hairs must be disposed of so that a neat outline is preserved.

The Kerry Blue Terrier should appear as short-coupled as trimming can make it. Eyebrows and whiskers are forward sweeping and profuse, with ears trimmed both inside and out, their edges neatly scissored to the points. The tail is tapered and the paws scissored into a club-like shape. Body hair should end up in a comparatively short, thick mass of curls. Be guided by a really good picture.

Airedale, Welsh and Lakeland Terriers resemble one another as to their presentation; clean ears; scissoring on front legs to give a really straight look; eyebrows trimmed closely at their outer edges, gradually lengthening to the inner corners. Trim the face so that a straight line is obvious from between the eyebrows to the nose. Forward pointing whiskers must be squared off. Hair on the body follows the bone formation and should blend imperceptibly into the leg hair. Make the legs really straight by snipping off any odd hairs.

The Wire Fox Terrier should be stripped, but for utility purposes a clipper is used. Stripping or clipping is taken closely round the cheeks as far as the mouth, the hair between and just under the eyes being plucked out. Brows are left heavier towards the

inner corners and ears are shaved with scissored edges to form into the final V. The tail is stripped to a somewhat rounded point. All four legs are left with plenty of hair but shaped to give a straight, uncompromising appearance. Paws are trimmed around and the coat on the neck is taken off comparatively closely, blending into the more heavily coated shoulders and back. A fringe-like effect is left beneath the belly, shaped to arch up to the hind-quarters.

The face of the Irish Setter is cleaned of whiskers and untidy hairs so that the entire head is smooth and uncluttered. The clipper can be used on the throat as far as the chest, where the hair is tapered to eventual fullness. A 10/2 m blade shaves the ears from their tops at skull level to about a third of the way down, the inside of the ears being shaved as well. Paws are scissored and a stripping comb used on the shoulders to obtain an even aspect. Beneath the belly, scissor the hair into the arch of the loins to accentuate this curve. Tidy up the tail feathering.

The Cocker Spaniel should be stripped. Spaniels owned as pets are clipped for practical reasons. Strip this breed following the body line leaving long hair underneath the body and on the legs. Feathering on legs and tails is trimmed so that the hair does not appear 'endy' and the skull between the ears is smooth and flat. The American Cocker has far more coat than his English relation. His whole picture is an exaggeration of the English Cocker. With both, it is wise to consult an expert as their presentation is a specialist's job.

Whereas the lion trim of a Poodle, which is used for show purposes, takes a whole day or more, your own pet poodle can be kept in the basic lamb trim. Clipping of the face, feet and tail is done against the growth of hair. A 30/¼ m blade is used on the feet of a black and mature brown Poodle, while a 15/⅓ m is suitable for the pastel colours as this is not so drastic. Do not take your clippers too far up the leg or you will end up with an untypical look. Hair is cleaned with the clippers from between the pads. The clipper line should extend round the foot in a straight line with no diversions into the leg hair. The head is clipped with the 10/2 m blade in a straight line from eye corners to the tops of the ears and from under the Adam's Apple to the outer corners of each ear. A moustache is optional. The entire face is clipped until it is smooth. Differentiate between the hair on the head and that on the ears by making a scissor line between the tops of the ears and the head hair. The fine hair is taken off the stomach as far as the navel using the same blade as for trimming the face. Still with this blade, clip the tail, leaving enough hair to form a comprehensive pom pom. Do not clip too far up the tail towards its tip. The 5/5 m blade is taken from head to tail all over the body and continues beneath the stomach. Do not let this line dip down too low over the forelegs or hind legs. Leave enough hair so that this can be blended in with the body in an unbroken continuous line. The Poodle is then bathed. It is advisable to bath *after* clipping as this helps to guard against clipper rash. This also ensures that you will be able to give a better finish to the hair when you come to scissor it. Now comes the finishing, and this is where the curved scissors are more efficient. Firstly, run the 5/5 m blade down the body. With scissors, trim round the bottom of each leg in a straight line. Scissor each leg into a sausage-like shape. Blend the hair at the top of each leg into the short body hair, leaving no ridge or step. The tail pom is rounded, as is the moustache if this has been left. The topknot needs time and care as this, together with the tail pom, is the focal point of the Poodle's presentation in the pet trims. Scissor the topknot in a straight line from eye corners over the tops of the ears, being careful not to touch the hair of the topknot itself. Comb forward the whole of the head hair, shake the head gently to settle the hair and then cut across the front in a slightly curved line. Next the back of the topknot is scissored to merge in with the short hair at the back of the neck and the top is rounded off. The whole effect should be of a big, rounded pom and each leg should match the other in width and shape.

Opposite page: From a domestic point of view, it is more practical to keep a poodle in the basic lamb trim. Before you begin working, make sure that all your tools are within easy reach. You must from the outset establish that you are master. Never hold the dog in an indecisive, half apprehensive manner. Clipping of the face is done against the growth of hair, until the entire face is smooth.

Below: A dog's whole appearance can be greatly enhanced by the careful use of various tools and aids applied to its coat. A wide variety of equipment is available today, but it is important to use only good quality tools to ensure that the job is well done.

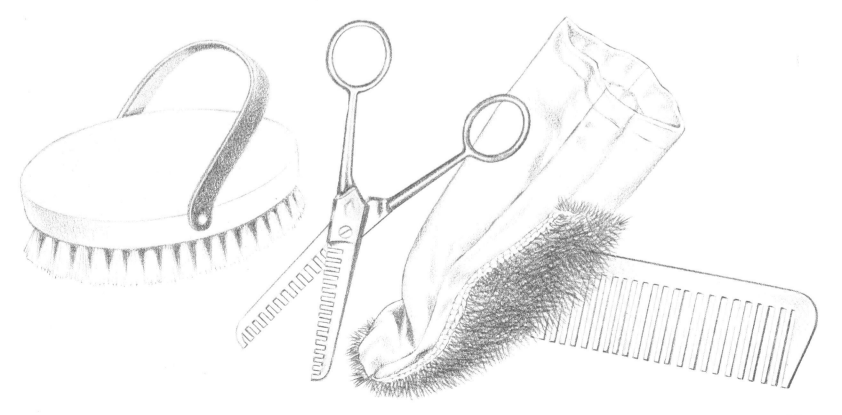

A-Z of Breeds

Each Kennel Club issues breed standards, i.e. verbal descriptions of the ideal specimen of a breed. These may differ in detail from one country to another. Where weights and heights are included in the following list, these are the maximum for male animals; bitches are normally slightly less.

Affenpinscher
A toy dog whose name means 'monkey terrier', the Affenpinscher is an energetic, alert and comical little dog with a vivacious personality. The colour should be black, the height 26 cm (10¼ ins) and the weight 3·6 kg (8 lbs). The breed originated in Germany but it is rare both there and in the U.S. It is practically unknown in Britain.

Afghan Hound
This is a hound bred for the chase and therefore wilful and independent in temperament. Its beautiful coat can be of almost any colour but time needs to be spent on it to keep it free of matts. Its height is 69 cm (27 ins) and weight 27 kg (60 lbs).

Airedale Terrier
The largest of this group and nicknamed the 'King of Terriers', the Airedale was formerly used as an army, guard and rescue dog but is now usually found only in the show ring. Males can be up to 61 cm (24 ins) in height. Bred originally in the Yorkshire dales, this breed enjoys popularity in the U.S. and has a steady following in Britain.

Akita
The Akita is one of those breeds expanding rapidly in North America. This is a Japanese spitz-type dog with a dense coat of medium length, which can be any colour except white. In their native land they have been used as guard and army dogs. The males stand up to 70 cm (27½ ins) in height and can weigh up to 50 kg (110 lbs). They are unknown in Britain.

Alaskan Malamute
These are among the top 40 breeds in the U.S. but they remain practically unknown in Britain. Their very dense coat is usually in various shades of grey. Their height is 64 cm (25 ins) with a weight of 38 kg (85 lbs). A cap or mask of dark shadings on the head is a desirable and distinctive feature of the breed.

Alsatian *see* German Shepherd Dog

American Cocker Spaniel
By the 1940s the American Cocker had become the most popular dog in the U.S. The head is domed, a feature which is accentuated by clipping. The coat is profuse and often long enough to touch the floor. The height is about 38 cm (15 ins). The American Cocker now has a steady following in Britain.

American Water Spaniel
As the name suggests this is a breed developed in the U.S. as a gundog for the inland waterfowler. This is a brown dog with a curly, oily coat. Its height is up to 46 cm (18 ins) with a weight up to 20·5 kg (45 lbs). It is still rare in the U.S. and is unknown in Britain.

Anatolian Karabash Dog
This is a Turkish shepherd's dog, a few of which have been imported into Britain in an attempt to popularize and stabilize the breed. It is mastiff-like in appearance, pale fawn or striped brindle in colour with a black facial mask and ears. It is up to 74 cm (29 ins) in height and 56 kg (124 lbs) in weight.

Australian Cattle Dog
This dog has a wedge-shaped head, pricked ears and a short, dense coat either blue mottled or red speckled. Its height is 46 cm (18 ins) with a weight of 18 kg (40 lbs). It is rare in the U.S. and unknown in Britain.

Australian Terrier
This is a compact, agile and short-legged dog with a straight, harsh coat either blue and tan or red in colour. It is about 25 cm (10 ins) in height and weighs between 4·5–6·5 kg (10–14 lbs). It is not well known in Britain but enjoys a certain popularity in the U.S.

Basenji
The Basenji was a hunting dog of the Congo basin. The breed has a number of distinctive features including an inability to bark. Its short, lustrous coat is usually red or black and tan and normally it has white feet and tail tip. Its height is 43 cm (17 ins) and its weight about 11 kg (24 lbs). It is not very common in Britain but it is moderately popular in the U.S.

Basset Griffon Vendéen
This is a rare breed in Britain and unknown in the U.S. Although similar in outline to the more popular Basset Hound, the Griffon Vendéen is less exaggerated in form and has a harsh, wiry coat with bushy eyebrows and whiskered jaw. Its height is about 38 cm (15 ins).

Basset Hound
This popular, low-to-ground hound is deceptive in appearance as it is really a somewhat hefty dog on very short legs. The solemnity of the domed and wrinkled head belies the character of the dog which is that of a hearty extrovert. Originating in France, the breed is popular everywhere. It has a normal height of 38 cm (15 ins).

Beagle
A 'smart as paint' little hound which originated in Britain and, though still very popular there, is even more widely kept in the U.S. Heights vary around 38 cm (15 ins). It can be any recognized hound colour.

Bearded Collie
The 'Beardie' was formerly a Scottish sheep and cattle dog. It is a shaggy, energetic and intelligent breed firmly established in Britain and has recently been granted breed recognition by the American Kennel Club. The harsh, shaggy coat is in all shades of grey, or brown with white collie markings. The height is up to 56 cm (22 ins) with a weight of about 23 kg (50 lbs).

Bedlington Terrier
Developed in the Border country between England and Scotland, the Bedlington has a small following on both sides of the Atlantic. It is a graceful, muscular dog, with a pear-shaped head and a light, springy gait. The coat is thick and linty in texture, either blue or sandy in colour. Its height is up to 41 cm (16 ins) with a weight of up to 10 kg (23 lbs).

Belgian Sheepdog (Groënendael)
This is the black variety of three closely related breeds. The others are Malinois and Tervueren. In Britain the term Belgian Sheepdog is used for all three. The coat is medium in length, straight and abundant, black and shiny. A male dog can be as high as 66 cm (26 ins).

Bernese Mountain Dog
The dog's soft, silky coat should have a natural sheen, jet black in colour with tan and white markings. Its height is up to 70 cm (27½ ins) and its weight up to 54 kg (119 lbs). Originating in Switzerland, the breed is established in the U.S. but extremely rare in Britain.

Bichon Frise
The coat is profuse, silky and pure white so that the dog looks like an animated powder puff. It can vary in height between 20–30 cm (8–12 ins). European in origin (possibly Spanish), the breed is firmly established in the U.S. and has recently been introduced into Britain.

Black-and-tan Coonhound *see* Coonhound

Bloodhound
This breed, because of its size and remarkable appearance, is more widely known than kept. Its smooth coat is either red, black and tan, or liver and tan. With a height of up to 66 cm (26 ins), it weighs up to 50 kg (110 lbs).

Border Collie
Perhaps the most widely used working sheepdog in the world, the Border Collie has been exhibited in Australia for a number of years and has recently been accepted as a show dog in Britain. Its moderately long coat is dense and weatherproof, usually black with white or tricolour collie markings. It has a height of about 50 cm (20 ins).

Border Terrier
A natural-looking terrier which needs no stripping, the Border is a workmanlike, sporting little dog with a harsh coat, usually red or grizzle and tan. It weighs up to 7 kg (15½ lbs). It is well established in Britain, its homeland, but uncommon in the U.S.

Borzoi
One of the most spectacular and aristocratic of the coursing hounds, the Borzoi comes from Russia. Its silky coat can be of any colour but is usually white with coloured patches. Its height is about 76 cm (30 ins) and its weight up to 47 kg (105 lbs).

Boston Terrier
The Boston is the national breed of the U.S. where they are much more popular than in Britain. Its top weight is 11·5 kg (25 lbs). In the U.S. classes at shows are divided into light-, medium- and heavy-weight categories.

Bouvier de Flandres
A rugged, hardy, powerful cattle dog from Flanders, the Bouvier is well established in the U.S. where its virtues as guard, companion and police dog are appreciated. It can be up to 70 cm (27½ ins) in height and weigh 40 kg (88 lbs). It is extremely rare in Britain.

Boxer
A very popular dog everywhere, the Boxer originated in Germany where it was used as a police and army dog. Its height is up to 61 cm (24 ins) and its weight up to 30 kg (66 lbs). Its coat is usually red, fawn or brindle, often with white markings.

The body formation of the Borzoi gives a clear indication of great speed, combined with strength and agility.

Briard

One of the French sheepdogs, the Briard is now well established on both sides of the Atlantic. The long, stiff, shaggy coat should preferably be of a darkish solid colour, although fawn and tawny shades are acceptable. A breed peculiarity is a double dew-claw on the hind leg. Its height can be up to 69 cm (27 ins).

Brittany Spaniel

Among the 20 most popular breeds in the U.S., the Brittany Spaniel is valued for its hunting abilities. As the name suggests, it is in origin a French breed. Its dense, flat coat is orange and white or liver and white. It can be up to 52 cm (20½ ins) in height and weigh 20 kg (44 lbs). The first four of this breed were imported into Britain in 1975.

Buhund

The Norwegian Buhund is one of the smaller spitz breeds. The coat is smooth and harsh and usually wheaten or sandy in colour. It is a handy size, up to 44 cm (18 ins) at the shoulder. It is not common in Britain and rare in the U.S.

Bulldog

The national breed, the British Bulldog is now an animal of amiable disposition and devotion to the human race. The smooth coat can be of any colour except black. Its weight can be up to 25 kg (55 lbs).

Bullmastiff

Another British guarding breed, the Bullmastiff, though not numerous, maintains a steady position in the registration tables of both the British and American Kennel Clubs. The short coat can be any shade of brindle, fawn or red. The height can be up to 69 cm (27 ins) and the weight as much as 58 kg (130 lbs).

Bull Terrier

Jaunty dogs with an eye full of wicked humour, Bull Terriers make excellent companions for active energetic families. The coat is short, harsh and glossy. In the U.S. the breed is divided into white—where any marking other than on the head disqualifies—and coloured—where the main body colour must predominate over the white. In Britain both classifications compete together. Britain also recognizes a Miniature variety of not more than 35 cm (14 ins) in height or 9 kg (20 lbs) in weight.

Cairn Terrier

The Cairn is a short-legged terrier breed from Scotland. It stands about 25 cm (10 ins) at the shoulder and weighs 6·5 kg (14 lbs). Colours include sandy, grey and brindled, often with dark ears and muzzle.

Canaan Dog

A very old Palestinian breed, the Canaan dog is almost unknown in Britain but has an enthusiastic specialist club in the U.S. supporting a nucleus of the breed. It has a wedge-shaped head, pricked ears and a bushy tail carried curled over its back. Its height is up to 61 cm (24 ins) with its weight up to 27 kg (60 lbs).

Cavalier King Charles Spaniel

One of the most popular of the toy group in its British homeland, the Cavalier has yet to make much headway in the U.S. Its long, silky coat can be black and tan, solid red, white with red patches or tricolour. Its weight can be up to 8 kg (18 lbs).

Chesapeake Bay Retriever

This, as befits an American breed, is a dog of rugged individualism, hardy, courageous and needing firm handling. Well known in America where they are valued as gundogs for the duck shooter and wildfowler, they are practically unknown in Britain. Height can be up to 66 cm (26 ins) with a weight of up to 34 kg (75 lbs).

Chihuahua

The world's smallest dog has two varieties, long-haired or smooth-coated. The smooth coat should be soft and glossy and of any colour. The long coat is flat, slightly wavy with fringed ears, feathered legs and a plumed tail. The weight can be as much as 3 kg (6 lbs) but most are smaller than this.

Chinese Crested Dog

The hairless breeds have always been rare and this is an uncommon dog in Britain and even rarer in the U.S. The Chinese Crested is entirely hairless except for a crest on the head, a plume on the tail and hair on the feet. The skin can be of any colour, often mottled and patched. The weight may vary between 3–5·5 kg (7–12 lbs).

Chow Chow

This is a cobby, powerful dog of leonine appearance, moderately popular on both sides of the Atlantic. Originally from China, the Chow is distinguished by its bluish black tongue and its stilted gait caused by the almost straight formation of the hind legs. Red is the most common shade but black and blue are also acceptable. The minimum height is about 46 cm (18 ins).

Clumber Spaniel

The heavyweight of the spaniels, Clumber Spaniels are uncommon in their homeland, Britain, and even more so in America. The straight, silky coat is white with lemon or orange markings, which should be confined to the ears, head and muzzle. Its height is about 46 cm (18 ins) and the weight up to 31·5 kg (70 lbs).

Cocker Spaniel

The English Cocker Spaniel is the most popular of the spaniel group in Britain but less well known in the U.S. where it has been eclipsed by its descendant, the American Cocker. The flat, silky coat comes in a wide variety of colours. Its height is up to 41 cm (16 ins) and its weight up to 14 kg (32 lbs).

Coonhound

Unknown in Britain, there are six breeds of Coonhound in the U.S.—only one of which, the Black-and-tan, is recognized by the American Kennel Club. The other five breeds are the Redbone, the English Coonhound, Bluetick, Treeing Walker and Plott. Racoon hunting is a popular sport in the U.S. and it is reckoned that some 40,000 of these dogs are bred annually. The height varies between 56–66 cm (22–26 ins).

Corgi *see* Welsh Corgi

Curly-coat Retriever

A British retriever breed now rare everywhere, the Curly-coat is either black or liver, the coat from the skull backwards being a mass of short, crisp curls. The height is normally 69 cm (27 ins) and the weight 36 kg (80 lbs).

Dachshund

One of the most popular of all breeds, Dachshunds come in three coats (Smooth-, Long- and Wire-haired) and two sizes (Standard and Miniature). The Smooth-coated tends to be a one man dog, aloof with strangers. The Long-haired is glamorous and friendly to all. The most usual colours in these two coats are red or black and tan. The Wire-haired Dachshund is the least known and the most extrovert in character. Its coat is commonly a shade of brindle. Sizes vary between different breeds in different countries, but top weight for a Standard dog is around 11 kg (25 lbs).

Dalmatian

Originating possibly in Yugoslavia, the Dalmatian was first appreciated in Britain and is now a well-known breed throughout a large part of the world. Its sleek, glossy coat is pure white with round, well defined spots of black or liver. The height is about 61 cm (24 ins) with a weight of 25 kg (55 lbs).

Dandie Dinmont Terrier

A short-legged, long-bodied, muscular little sporting terrier, the Dandie Dinmont is another breed from the Scottish Border country. The crisp body hair is grey (pepper) or sandy (mustard). Its height is from 20–28 cm (8–11 ins) with a weight of 8–11 kg (18–24 lbs).

Deerhound

The Scottish Deerhound is a gentle, dignified animal whose size and bearing need a spacious setting to be appreciated to the full. A hound built for galloping, the harsh, ragged coat is usually grey. Its minimum height is 76 cm (30 ins) with a weight of up to 47 kg (105 lbs).

Doberman Pinscher

In the U.K. this breed is known as the Dobermann. It is an agile, powerful, quick-thinking dog with a smooth, hard, glossy coat which is usually black and tan. Its height is up to 69 cm (27 ins).

Elkhound

The Norwegian Elkhound is one of the more popular of the great family of spitz breeds. Compactly built with an alert expression, it is usually bold, energetic and friendly. Its thick, coarse coat is in various shades of grey. It is almost 52 cm (20½ ins) in height and weighs about 23 kg (50 lbs).

English Setter

The English Setter is deservedly popular as a companion and show dog and is one of the most beautiful of the medium-sized breeds. The long, silky white coat is softly flecked with black, lemon, liver or tricolour markings. About 69 cm (27 ins) in height, it weighs about 30 kg (66 lbs).

English Springer Spaniel

The English Springer is one of the gundog breeds which still has plenty of working ability. It is popular in both Britain and the U.S. as a dog for the rough shooting man as well as a companion. It stands about 51 cm (20 ins) at the shoulder and weighs some 23 kg (50 lbs). Its colour is normally liver and white or black and white.

English Toy Spaniel *see* King Charles Spaniel

English Toy Terrier

There seems no very good reason why the numbers of this minute terrier should be as low as they are. Its weight is between 2·7–3·6 kg (6–8 lbs), and its height between 25–30 cm (10–12 ins). In the U.S. the breed is known as the Toy Manchester and the weight limit is 5·5 kg (12 lbs).

The Finnish Spitz has an overall square build and a wedge-shaped head. It is a hunting dog with an independent character.

Estrella Mountain Dog

This Portuguese sheepdog is nearing extinction but a handful are in Britain where enthusiasts are struggling to establish the breed. The coat is either long- or short-haired and the colouring black and tan, tan, grey or fawn. Its height is about 67 cm (26½ ins).

Field Spaniel

The numbers of this Spaniel are very low. Resembling a stoutly built Cocker, the flat silky coat is usually solid-coloured. Its height is up to 46 cm (18 ins) and its weight up to 23 kg (50 lbs).

Finnish Spitz

Though still uncommon this breed is firmly established in Britain but rare in the U.S. It is more lightly built than many spitz and the colour is usually a brilliant reddish brown. Its height is up to 51 cm (20 ins).

Flat-coat Retriever

This is another retriever whose numbers have declined drastically. It is a bright, active, docile dog with a flat, dense coat of medium length, either black or liver. It weighs between 27–32 kg (60–70 lbs).

Foxhound

The English Foxhound is never kept as a pet or showdog and it would be most unsuitable in either role. It possesses incredible hardness and stamina, is a specialist in the field of foxhunting and is best suited by kennel and pack life. The American Foxhound is a leggier and more versatile hound. Foxhunting takes many forms in the U.S. Foxhound trials are probably the most popular and many hundreds of these are run annually.

Fox Terrier

The two breeds of Fox Terrier, the smooth- and the wire-haired, have the same basic construction differing only in their coat. Both types are popular, the wire-haired possibly being a slight favourite, even though its coat has the disadvantage of needing to be stripped frequently. Their background colour is usually white with black or tan markings. The height is 39 cm (15½ ins) and the weight 8 kg (18 lbs).

French Bulldog

The smooth, short coat can be brindle, white, pied or fawn. Its weight can be up to 13 kg (28 lbs). The French Bulldog has some likeness to the Boston Terrier but is a much less popular breed than the latter in the U.S. In Britain the two breeds are about the same in number.

German Shepherd Dog (Alsatian)

The most versatile and widespread of the working breeds is the German Shepherd Dog. Active both physically and mentally, it does not suit a lazy or indifferent owner. The coat is dense, about 4 cm (1½ ins) in length and the colour is not regarded as important. The height is up to 66 cm (26 ins).

German Short-haired Pointer

This breed is an immensely popular sporting dog in the U.S. and firmly established in Britain. The coat can be solid liver or liver and white. It can be 63 cm (25 ins) at the shoulder and weighs 32 kg (70 lbs).

German Wire-haired Pointer

The coat is harsh and wiry, forming bushy eyebrows, a beard and whiskers on the head. The colour is liver and white and its height is up to 66 cm (26 ins). Well established, though not common, in the U.S., it is very rare in Britain.

Golden Retriever

The Golden Retriever is a good tempered, gentle breed with a high reputation for trainability. Like all retrievers it is a large dog requiring plenty of exercise. Its flat, wavy coat can be any shade of gold or cream. The height is about 61 cm (24 ins) and the weight 34 kg (75 lbs).

Gordon Setter

The Gordon Setter maintains a moderate following in the U.S. and Britain. Originally a Scottish breed, it is a handsome dog with a silky, flat, black-and-tan coat. Rather heavier than other setters, it stands 66 cm (26 ins) at the shoulder and weighs about 29·5 kg (65 lbs).

Great Dane

The Germanic Great Dane is one of the most popular of the really large breeds. The short coat can be brindle, fawn, black, blue or harlequin. The minimum height is 76 cm (30 ins) and the minimum weight is 54 kg (120 lbs).

Great Pyrenees

This large white dog is known as the Pyrenean Mountain Dog in the U.K. It makes an excellent guard and companion dog but it has an independent nature which needs firm and patient training. The minimum size should be 71 cm (28 ins) and the minimum weight 45 kg (100 lbs).

Greyhound

Most Greyhounds are racing dogs with a few kept for coursing and fewer still for show and as companions. The show and the racing Greyhound differ in looks. The latter is a plainer, slightly smaller animal with a somewhat coarser coat. The show Greyhound is up to 76 cm (30 ins) in height and can be almost any colour.

Griffon Bruxellois

The Griffon is among the most independent, humorous and cheeky of the toy dogs. The two coat varieties, the rough and the smooth, are often born in the same litter. The colours are red, black and tan or black. It is a sturdily built dog up to 4·5 kg (10 lbs) in weight.

Groënendael see Belgian Sheepdog

Harrier

The Harrier is best described as a hound intermediate in size between a Beagle and a Foxhound. Its use in Britain for hunting the hare is declining as Beagle packs are more popular for this sport. The hound stands up to 53 cm (21 ins) high.

Husky

Though recognized in Britain under this name, elsewhere the breed is sometimes known as the Eskimo Dog. The breed is rare in Britain. As it is a working sledge dog, with the strength, obstinacy and independence needed for Arctic freight hauling, this is not a dog for any but the experienced owner. The coat can be any colour and is thick and dense. Weight and height are variable up to 69 cm (27 ins) and 47 kg (105 lbs) respectively.

Ibizan Hound

The Ibizan Hound comes from the Balearic Islands and is rare in Britain and unknown in the U.S. It is a fast and efficient sporting dog, hunting with scent, sight and hearing. Most in Britain are smooth-haired and either white or chestnut-red with white. Its height is 74 cm (29 ins) and its weight up to 23 kg (50 lbs).

Irish Setter

The Irish or Red Setter is the most popular of the three setter breeds. It is a big, racy dog, high-spirited, scatterbrained, but always affectionate and kind. Its long, flat, silky coat, lustrous and glowing, is a brilliant chestnut-red.

Irish Terrier

Exceptionally sweet tempered towards humans, this dog is equally cocky and touchy where other dogs are concerned. It is a racily built terrier with a hard, wiry, red coat. Its height is 46 cm (18 ins) and it weighs 12 kg (27 lbs).

Irish Wolfhound

The owner who can afford to rear and house a dog whose minimum height and weight are 81 cm (32 ins) and 54 kg (120 lbs) respectively is rewarded by the devotion of a gentle and noble animal. The coat is rough, harsh and wiry, and the colour usually grey or fawn.

Italian Greyhound

This Greyhound in miniature presents a slender and fragile appearance but is as active and as hardy as the rest of the toy group. The maximum weight in Britain is 4·5 kg (10 lbs). In the U.S. there are classes for under and over 3·6 kg (8 lbs).

Jack Russell Terrier

This is a breed without Kennel Club recognition and unknown in the U.S. Nevertheless it is a very popular small terrier in Britain. It is short-legged with a docked tail, dropped ears and either a smooth or a harsh coat. The colour is usually white with tan or black markings.

Japanese Chin

This toy dog is known as the Japanese Spaniel in the U.S. It is a dainty, stylish little dog with an Oriental snub nose and a soft, straight, silky coat. The colour is white with black or red even markings. Its weight should be about 3 kg (7 lbs).

Keeshond

A Dutch breed of the spitz-type, the Keeshond is popular in the U.S. and moderately so in Britain. The ash or wolf-grey coat is harsh and off-standing. Its height should be 46 cm (18 ins).

Kelpie

The working sheepdog of Australia is the Kelpie, a breed unknown in Britain and very rare in the U.S. This is a smooth-coated dog with upright ears and a thick brush of a tail. The colours are black, red, fawn, chocolate or blue with or without tan markings. The height is up to 50 cm (20 ins) and the weight 14 kg (31 lbs).

Kerry Blue Terrier

The Kerry Blue is a terrier from Ireland, possibly more of an exhibitor's dog than a favourite with the general public. Though the puppies are born black, the adult coat is blue. The height is 48 cm (19 ins) and the weight 17 kg (37 lbs).

The Kerry Blue was bred as a vermin killer, sheep herder, retriever and guard. A medium-sized dog, its most striking feature is a soft and abundant coat in beautiful shades of blue-grey.

King Charles Spaniel

This snub-nosed toy spaniel is known in the U.S. as the English Toy Spaniel, and its numbers are even fewer there than in its British homeland. As with the Cavalier there are four colour varieties, black and tan, solid red, tricolour, and white with red markings. Its weight is up to 6·5 kg (14 lbs).

Komondor

This is one of the Hungarian sheepdogs It is regularly exhibited in the U.S. and there are a small number in Britain. It is a large white guard dog with a remarkable adult coat of long felted cords. Its height is up to 80 cm (31½ ins) and the weight up to 61 kg (135 lbs).

Kuvasz

This white Hungarian guard dog has a small following in the U.S. but there are none in Britain. The breed tends to be suspicious of strangers. It has a soft, medium-length, rather fluffy coat. Its height is 66 cm (26 ins) and its weight about 32 kg (70 lbs).

Labrador Retriever

Originally from the east coast of Canada, this breed was developed and popularized in Britain. It is included in the top ten breeds both in the U.S. and in Britain. In the U.S. the height is 62 cm (24¼ ins), in Britain 57 cm (22½ ins). The weight is up to 34 kg (75 lbs).

Lakeland Terrier

The Lakeland has a moderate following in Britain and the U.S. The usual colours are black and tan or red. Its height is 37 cm (14½ ins), the weight 8 kg (17 lbs). As with most other terrier breeds this is a British product.

Large Munsterlander

This is a German gundog recently imported into Britain. It is an energetic and enthusiastic working dog with a dense and moderately long coat, black on the head and with black patches on its white body. The height is 61 cm (14 ins) and the weight 29·5 kg (65 lbs).

Lhasa Apso

The Lhasa Apso is the most popular of the Tibetan breeds in the U.S. and the second most popular in Britain. This is a solid little dog with a height of 25 cm (10 ins) at the shoulder. Its profusion of coat needs a certain amount of care. Golden or honey colours are preferred but most colours are acceptable.

Lowchen

Introduced into Britain from the continent in 1969, the Lowchen or Little Lion Dog has made a great deal of progress in a very short time. The long and wavy coat, which can be of any colour, is clipped in the traditional lion fashion with a plume left on the end of the long tail. The height can be up to 36 cm (14 ins) and the weight up to 4 kg (9 lbs).

Malinois

One of the three varieties of the Belgian sheepdog, the Malinois is rare both in Britain and the U.S. It has the same standard as the Groënendael with a height of 66 cm (26 ins) but differs in coat and colour being a short-coated, dark fawn dog with a thick, bushy tail.

Maltese

This toy dog is of Mediterranean origin and enjoys a fair degree of popularity on both sides of the Atlantic. The white, silky coat resembles spun sugar and is set off by the dark eyes and black nose. The height is 25 cm (10 ins) and the weight under 3 kg (7 lbs).

Manchester Terrier

The Manchester is a smooth-coated British terrier. It is better known in the U.S. where the drop ears are cropped. The short, glossy coat is black with rich tan markings. The height is 41 cm (16 ins), the weight 10 kg (22 lbs). In the U.S. there is a Toy Manchester Terrier known in Britain under the name English Toy Terrier.

Maremma Sheepdog

The Maremma is an Italian sheepdog present in small numbers in Britain. It is a large white dog with rather a suspicious temperament. The coat is moderately long and the minimum size is 65 cm (25½ ins) with a weight of about 34 kg (75 lbs).

Mastiff

Though kept in moderate numbers in both the U.S. and Britain, the Old English Mastiff's size precludes it ever being enormously popular. The short coat can be apricot, silver-fawn or dark fawn brindle. Muzzle, ears and nose should be black. The minimum height is 76 cm (30 ins).

Miniature Pinscher

This dog is moderately popular in Britain and the U.S. Smooth-coated, with erect ears and a short, docked tail, its smart appearance has much to recommend it. The colours are usually red or black and tan and the height is between 25–32 cm (10–12½ ins).

Newfoundland

A massive, water-loving dog originating in Newfoundland but standardized in Britain, the Newfoundland enjoys a steady support from owners who appreciate its protective loyalty and devotion. The long, flat coat is waterproof and usually black, but white with black patches (known as Landseers) and solid bronze are also known. Its height is 71 cm (28 ins), its weight 67 kg (150 lbs).

Norfolk Terrier; Norwich Terrier

In Britain these are accepted as two different breeds, the difference between them being a matter of the ear carriage. The Norfolk has a dropped ear and in the case of the Norwich it is upright. In the U.S. both compete under the title Norwich Terrier. The wiry, straight coat is commonly red and the ideal height is 25 cm (10 ins).

Old English Sheepdog

A very popular breed everywhere, the Old English Sheepdog or Bobtail is no longer used for working but makes an excellent guard and is a devoted companion for those who are prepared to cope with its coat, its size and its energy. The coat colour is grey, grizzle or blue with white markings. The minimum height is 56 cm (22 ins) but most are larger, weighing as much as 41 kg (90 lbs).

Otterhound

The Otterhound, probably British in origin, is in danger of extinction. One pure-bred pack exists in Scotland and a few are exhibited and used for general sporting purposes in the U.S. It has some resemblance to a rough-coated Bloodhound. The hair is crisp and oily with a thick, woolly undercoat. The height is 61 cm (24 ins).

Papillon

This is one of the European toy spaniels, the name Papillon being derived from the resemblance of its large, fringed ears, which are carried obliquely, to the wings of a butterfly. The silky coat is white with coloured patches and the plumed tail is carried over the back. The height is up to 28 cm (11 ins) and the weight about 3 kg (7 lbs).

Pekingese

The Pekingese has been a most popular toy dog for many years. It is a sturdy, dignified and determined little dog with a regal bearing and a character to match. Its profuse coat needs care and can be almost any colour. Surprisingly heavy for its size, 6·5 kg (14 lbs) is the upper limit.

Pharaoh Hound

Unrecognized in the U.S., the Pharaoh Hound is exhibited regularly in Britain. It is one of the Mediterranean greyhound breeds, a fast, agile dog with a strong hunting instinct. The large ears are carried erect and are very mobile. The coat is short and of a rich tan colour with white markings. The height is 63 cm (25 ins).

Pointer

Probably Spanish in origin, the Pointer remains a moderately successful dog even though changing times have much restricted its use as a gundog. The smooth coat is usually white with lemon, orange, liver or black markings. American Pointers are slightly larger than those in Britain—up to 71 cm (28 ins) in height and weighing up to 34 kg (75 lbs).

Pomeranian

This is a dwarf German spitz with a foxy head and a long, stand-off, harsh coat. It is a perky, vivacious little handful making an excellent watchdog and is also popular both as a pet and a show dog in the U.S. and in Britain. Most weigh considerably less than the American upper limit of 3 kg (7 lbs). There is a wide range of colours but orange or sable is by far the most common.

Poodle

The highly successful French Poodle comes in three sizes. In order of popularity they are Toy, Miniature and Standard. The Toy must be under 25 cm (10 ins) in the U.S. and 28 cm (11 ins) in Britain; the Miniature under 38 cm (15 ins); and the Standard over—and usually considerably over—38 cm (15 ins). This is an intelligent breed which, despite becoming highly fashionable, has managed to preserve a love of life and a clownish sense of humour. The Poodle coat, which has to be trimmed to lion or continental clip for the show ring, does not shed hair but unfortunately matts easily. The coat can be any solid colour.

Portuguese Water Dog

Although unknown in Britain and near extinction in Portugal, there is a nucleus of this breed in the U.S. where it is hoped that it will become established. As the name suggests, the dog is an excellent swimmer with a long, oily and wavy coat frequently clipped in a lion clip. Its colours are black, brown or parti-coloured. The height is 56 cm (22 ins) and the weight 21 kg (46 lbs).

Pug

Like many other short-nosed toy breeds, the Pug is believed to have originated in the Far East. It is one of the heavyweights of the toy group—up to 8 kg (18 lbs). Popular everywhere, the Pug has a smooth coat, either fawn or black.

The elegant and graceful Saluki is a hound with exceptionally keen sight. It is fashioned for speed, rapid turning and endurance.

Puli

This is another Hungarian sheepdog with an extraordinary coat. It is well established in the U.S. but rather less common in Britain. The coat, often rusty black, can be floor length and it must be corded so that it hangs in thin ropes rather than matting or felting together. The height is 46 cm (18 ins) and the weight 15 kg (33 lbs).

Pyrenean Mountain Dog *see* Great Pyrenees

Rhodesian Ridgeback

This is a hunting dog from South Africa. Although firmly established in Britain and the U.S. it has never achieved much popularity. The short, sleek coat is red and the name of the dog comes from its unique feature, a ridge of hair along the spine growing in a direction opposite to the rest of the coat. The height is 69 cm (27 ins) and the weight 36 kg (80 lbs).

Rottweiler

The power and strength of the breed is evident. It was as a German police and army dog that the Rottweiler first became known to the rest of the world. The smooth coat is black with mahogany markings. The height is up to 69 cm (27 ins).

Rough Collie

The Rough Collie remains a favourite with the pet-owning public everywhere. The abundant coat with its head-framing mane and frill, is usually sable and white, tricolour, or blue merle. The breed is slightly larger in the U.S., up to 66 cm (26 ins) in height and 29·5 kg (65 lbs) in weight.

Saint Bernard

The size of this Swiss dog keeps its numbers low in Britain but it is amongst the most popular ten breeds in the U.S. The coat is moderately long, dense and flat, although there is also a smooth-coated variety. The colours are orange, mahogany brindle, red brindle, or white with patches of these colours. The standard states that the taller the better, provided that symmetry and substance are not lost.

Saluki

Although the nickname 'Gazelle Hound' indicates the Saluki's natural quarry, it also suggests the grace and elegance of this greyhound from the Mediterranean deserts. Although there is a smooth variety, most have feathering on the ears, legs and tail. It can virtually be of any colour and up to 71 cm (28 ins) in height.

Samoyed

The Samoyed is one of the spitz group. The straight, harsh, outer coat stands away from the body and is pure white. One engaging feature is the slight turning up at the corner of the mouth which gives the breed a smiling expression. The American Samoyed is slightly larger than the British being up to 60 cm (23½ ins) in height.

Schipperke

The Belgian name means 'little skipper' and, although popular in the U.S., numbers in Britain are not great. Usually jet black, the coat is dense, straight and slightly harsh in texture, forming a ruff round the neck and culottes on the hindquarters. Its weight is up to 8 kg (18 lbs).

Schnauzer

The German Schnauzer comes in three sizes of which the smallest, the Miniature Schnauzer, is by far the most popular. The two smaller Schnauzers are usually pepper and salt in colour, i.e. a mixture of dark and lighter grey hairs. The Giant Schnauzer is often darker, sometimes black. Maximum heights for the three breeds are Miniature Schnauzer 36 cm (14 ins), Standard Schnauzer 51 cm (20 ins) and Giant Schnauzer 69 cm (27 ins).

Scottish Terrier

This popular terrier with the rather dour expression is thick set and short-legged. The trimming necessary for a modern show dog seems almost to caricature the animal but less exaggerated coat care is wholly adequate for the pet. The most fashionable colour is black but wheaten and brindle are acceptable. The height is 28 cm (11 ins) and the weight 10·5 kg (23 lbs).

Sealyham Terrier

Sealyhams come from Wales. Although never in the limelight, they have maintained their moderate numbers overs the years both in the U.S. and Britain. The medium-length, hard coat is usually white. The height is up to 30 cm (12 ins) and the weight 9 kg (20 lbs).

Shetland Sheepdog

As popular everywhere as its larger cousin the Rough Collie, the Shetland Sheepdog has a look of sweet, alert, gentle intelligence which is particularly endearing. The usual colours are sable, tricolour or blue merle. The American 'Sheltie' is bigger than the British with a height of 41 cm (16 ins).

Shih Tzu

This is the most popular of the Tibetan breeds in Britain and is also a well known dog in the U.S. It is an active and hardy little dog with an arrogant appearance. The long, dense coat is profuse and all colours are permissible. The height is 27 cm (10½ ins) and the weight 7 kg (16 lbs)

Siberian Husky

The Siberian Husky is a popular breed in the U.S. where not only is it kept as a companion but also to take part in the popular sport of sledge dog racing. The coat is dense rather than long and the usual colouring is wolf or ash grey with white points. The height is 60 cm (23½ ins) and the weight 27 kg (60 lbs). A few are registered annually in Britain.

Silky Terrier

The alternative name of 'Sydney Silky' for this breed indicates Australia as its country of origin. Although unknown in Britain, it is a popular toy breed in the U.S. Ears are upright and the tail is docked short. The coat, about 15 cm (6 ins) long, is silken in texture and blue and tan in colour. The height is 25 cm (10 ins) and the weight 4·5 kg (10 lbs).

Skye Terrier

This terrier from Scotland has the disadvantage of a floor length coat. The colour is usually either grey or cream with black points. The Skye Terrier is a very long animal. While its height at the shoulder is only 25 cm (10 ins), the length from nose to tail tip is about 100 cm (40 ins). Its weight is 11 kg (25 lbs).

Sloughi

A few Sloughis are registered in Britain and they are one of the Mediterranean greyhound breeds. They are racy and lean with heads slightly heavier than an English Greyhound. The short coat can be of any colour. It is up to 76 cm (30 ins) in height.

Smooth Collie

The Smooth Collie, a Scottish breed, as are all the collies, has exactly the same physical conformation as the Rough Collie except for its coat. In place of the profuse hair of the Rough, the Smooth variety has a short, harsh, dense jacket. The height is 61 cm (24 ins) and the weight 29·5 kg (65 lbs).

Soft-coated Wheaten Terrier

One of the Irish terrier breeds, the Soft-coated Wheaten has only recently been recognized by both the American and British Kennel Clubs. The coat should be wheaten in colour and soft and silky in texture, falling in light, loose curls or waves. The height is up to 50 cm (19½ ins) and the weight 20 kg (45 lbs).

Staffordshire Bull Terrier

This is the British version of an old fighting breed developed in the mining communities in the Midlands. Courageous by nature, with an ability to ignore pain, it is sweet-tempered in the home and usually excellent with children. The short coat can be any colour. The height is 41 cm (16 ins) and the weight 17 kg (38 lbs).

Staffordshire Terrier

This is the American version of the same breed as that described above. Both breeds appeal to those who admire courage to the point of rashness. The Staffordshire Terrier is taller and heavier, up to 48 cm (19 ins) in height and 23 kg (50 lbs) in weight.

Sussex Spaniel

The Sussex is a thickset, low-to-ground British Spaniel, few in numbers anywhere. The coat is abundant and flat, a distinctive rich golden liver in shade. The height is 41 cm (16 ins) and the weight 20 kg (45 lbs).

Tervueren

This is one of the three Belgian sheepdogs. It is established in the U.S. but rare in Britain. The coat should be long, straight and fairly harsh, and red, fawn or grey in colour with a black overlay. The height is 66 cm (26 ins).

Tibetan Spaniel

A well liked and firmly established breed in Britain, the Tibetan Spaniel still awaits recognition by the American Kennel Club. Its height is about 25 cm (10 ins), its weight between 4–7 kg (9–15 lbs). The flat, silky coat can be any colour or mixture of colours.

Tibetan Terrier

The Tibetan Terrier is still a rare breed in both Britain and the U.S., although established in both countries. The long, profuse coat can be any colour except liver. The height is 41 cm (16 ins), the weight 13·5 kg (30 lbs).

Toy Fox Terrier

This is a breed unknown in Britain but widely kept in America, even though it is unrecognized by the American Kennel Club. The satin smooth coat should be white and black with tan trim. Its weight should be between 1·5–3 kg (3½–7 lbs).

Valhund

This Swedish herding dog has recently been introduced into Britain. The coat is harsh and close-fitting, the usual colour being some shade of yellowish or brownish grey. The height is 33 cm (13 ins) and the weight 13 kg (28 lbs).

Vizsla

The Hungarian Vizsla is Hungary's only sporting breed. It is well established in the U.S. but is not common in Britain. The smooth coat is russet-gold. The height is 63 cm (25 ins) and the weight 30 kg (66 lbs).

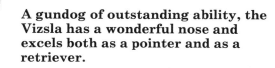

A gundog of outstanding ability, the Vizsla has a wonderful nose and excels both as a pointer and as a retriever.

Weimaraner

This German breed is well known in the U.S. where it is used as a working gundog. In Britain the numbers are modest but steady. The smooth coat is a metallic silvery grey and the eyes are light in colour. Its height is up to 69 cm (27 ins).

Welsh Corgi Cardigan

Of the two types of Welsh Corgi, the Cardigan is the lesser known, with only a modest following in Britain and the U.S. compared with the Pembroke. The Cardigan has rather larger, upright ears and a splendid fox-like tail. Although the short coat can be any colour except white, it is usually dark brindle, tricolour or blue merle. The height is 30 cm (12 ins), the weight 12 kg (26 lbs).

Welsh Corgi Pembroke

The more popular breed is slightly smaller with the same fox-like head but with a short, docked tail. The usual colour is red with white markings or tricolour. The height is 25–30 cm (10–12 ins), the weight 11 kg (24 lbs).

Welsh Springer Spaniel

Although rare in the U.S., this breed is currently enjoying a modest degree of popularity in Britain. It is a happy, active dog, big enough and willing to do a hard day's work in the field. The flat silky coat is a glorious rich red with pearly white markings. Its height is up to 48 cm (19 ins).

Welsh Terrier

This Welsh breed enjoys more popularity abroad than in its homeland. Smart and workmanlike when trimmed, its wire coat is usually black with bright tan markings. The height is 39 cm (15½ ins), the weight 9·5 kg (21 lbs).

West Highland White Terrier

Currently Britain's top terrier and also very popular in the U.S., the 'Westie' also comes from Scotland, the home of many short-legged terrier breeds. It has an easy-to-keep-clean, harsh, white coat. The height is 28 cm (11 ins), the weight up to 8 kg (18 lbs).

Whippet

The affectionate nature and elegance of form of the Whippet ensures its popularity everywhere. Every line indicates that it is built for speed and it has remarkable powers of acceleration. The fine, smooth coat can be any colour. The height is 47 cm (18½ ins), the weight 9·5 kg (21 lbs).

Wire-haired Pointing Griffon

This breed is unknown in Britain and rare in the U.S. The coat looks unkempt with the dry, harsh outer coat resembling the bristles of a wild boar. The colour is grey or dirty white with chestnut patches. The height is up to 60 cm (23½ ins).

Yorkshire Terrier

These diminutive scraps are the most popular of toy dogs in Britain and the second most popular in the U.S. The colour and length of the straight, silky coat is of great importance in the show ring. The height is 20 cm (8 ins). The weight is up to 3 kg (7 lbs) but most show dogs are considerably less than this. The colour must be a dark steel blue and tan.

'BEST IN SHOW' WINNERS

	WESTMINSTER (US)		CRUFTS (UK)		SYDNEY ROYAL (AUSTRALIA)	
	Name	Breed	Name	Breed	Name	Breed
1960	Chik T'Sun of Caversham	Pekingese	Sulhampstead Merman	Irish Wolfhound	Starya of Kobe	Samoyed
1961	Cappoquin Little Sister	Toy Poodle	Riverina Tweedsbairn	Airedale Terrier	Chetwyn Merthytidvill	Welsh Corgi (Pembroke)
1962	Elfinbrook Simon	West Highland White Terrier	Crackwyn Cockspur	Fox Terrier (Wire)	Foxwyre Flash Gem	Fox Terrier (Wire)
1963	Wakefield's Black Knight	English Springer Spaniel	Rogerholm Recruit	Lakeland Terrier	Mighty Rare of Ware	Cocker Spaniel
1964	Courtenay Fleetfoot of Pennyworth	Whippet	Silbury Soames of Madavale	English Setter	Rekcal Jiky	Miniature Poodle
1965	Carmichaels Fanfare	Scottish Terrier	Fenton of Kentwood	German Shepherd Dog	Mazari of Carloway	Afghan Hound
1966	Zeloy Mooremaide's Magic	Fox Terrier (Wire)	Oakington Puckshill Amber Sunblush	Toy Poodle	De Montfort Much Ado	Fox Terrier (Wire)
1967	Bardene Bingo	Scottish Terrier	Stingray of Derryabah	Lakeland Terrier	Almark Black Prince	German Shepherd Dog
1968	Stingray of Derryabah	Lakeland Terrier	Fanhill Faune	Dalmation	Baymor Famous	Foxhound
1969	Glamoor Good News	Skye Terrier	Hendrawen's Nibelung of Charavigne	German Shepherd Dog	Vondobe The Maharajah	Dobermann
1970	Arriba's Prima Donna	Boxer	Bergerie Knur	Pyrenean Mountain Dog	Furbari Shalakhan	Afghan Hound
1971	Chinoe's Adamant James	English Springer Spaniel	Ramacon Swashbuckler	German Shepherd Dog	Lourdale Tzarmark	Samoyed
1972	Chinoe's Adamant James	English Springer Spaniel	Abraxas Audacity	Bull Terrier	Fermoy Mahnfred	Afghan Hound
1973	Acada Command Performance	Standard Poodle	Alansmere Aquarius	Cavalier King Charles Spaniel	Tinee Town Talktime	Australian Terrier
1974	Gretchenhof Columbia River	German Short-haired Pointer	Burtonswood Bossy Boots	St Bernard	Kingsmens Witchcraft	German Shepherd Dog
1975	Sir Lancelot of Barvan	Old English Sheepdog	Brookewire Brandy of Layven	Fox Terrier (Wire)	Calahorra Turban	Afghan Hound
1976	Jonis Red Baron of Crofton	Lakeland Terrier	Dianthus Buttons	West Highland White Terrier	Regalen Saladin	Pekingese
1977	Dersade Bobby's Girl	Sealyham Terrier	Bournehouse Dancing Master	English Setter	Calahorra Benedictus	Afghan Hound

Above: Despite the scowling exterior, the modern Bulldog is an amiable and friendly dog.

Overleaf: Two handsome Boxers.

**Above: The German Shepherd Dog is
one of the best known dogs in the world
and is a very versatile and intelligent
breed.**

Left: An energetic young Lhasa Apso is quite a handful, but fun to own.

Above: The striking colour of the Weimaraner makes it one of the more easily recognisable of the gundog breeds.

Above: The melting eyes of this American Cocker is one of the breed's many charms.

Right: This Great Dane is showing a friendly interest in two orphan lambs.

Dogs on Show

FOR years the rat pit, the dog pit, the bear pit and the bull ring provided an opportunity for men to test their skill at producing dogs to beat the dogs belonging to other people. These were hard men who lived in hard times and we must excuse them if they appear to have had little feeling for the suffering of dumb animals. In the early nineteenth century dog fighting and the baiting of other animals were made illegal, and so, instead, some owners started matching their dogs against each other for appearance only. With the development of dog shows came an entirely new 'breed' of dog owner.

The first record of an organized dog show was at Newcastle-on-Tyne in June 1859, when there was one class for setters and one for pointers. In 1873 the British Kennel Club was founded and has been recognized as the ruling body in Britain ever since. Over 3,500 shows are held under Kennel Club rules every year in Britain, as well as about 300 field and working trials. All dogs shown at recognized shows, which means practically all dog shows in Britain, must be registered at the Kennel Club, and the same applied to field trials for gun dogs, working trials for police dogs and obedience classes. It does not, however, apply to sheepdog trials, which are held under the rules of the International Sheepdog Society; hound shows, which are run by the Masters of Foxhounds Association; and coursing matches, which are held under the rules of the National Coursing Club.

As the cult of showing dogs has spread throughout the world, governing bodies have been founded in each country to see fair play. Anyone contemplating showing a dog should contact their own Kennel Club to find out what shows are available and what rules and regulations must be adhered to.

Left: This handsome Rough Collie would make a beautiful pet.

Right: Preparations such as these are necessary if a Yorkshire Terrier is to look like a prizewinner.

The merit of dog shows has often been queried and opposing factions believe that many breeds have been either improved or ruined as a result of showing. Nevertheless, many breeds, such as the Irish Wolfhound and the Old English Mastiff, would be extinct if it were not for dog shows. And it is the people who exhibit dogs who breed the thousands of pure-bred puppies necessary to supply the pet market. Although there are also thousands of mongrel puppies which can be purchased much more cheaply, one has no idea what a mongrel puppy will turn out to be like; with a pure-bred puppy, one at least has a fair idea of what it will look like when grown up and what sort of characteristics it is likely to develop. For choosing the sort of dog you would like, dog shows are the best place to see a wide variety of breeds.

For people who criticize the whole idea of showing animals, it is difficult to explain the attraction. It is certainly not done for the money and very few people have ever made money by showing dogs. A lot of satisfaction is to be derived from producing an animal to such a high standard that it beats all the others in its class. To win best of breed or, better still, best in show at a championship show is a very real thrill and one experienced by comparatively few people. To those interested in genetics, the breeding of any animal to certain high standards of perfection is a never-ending source of pleasure and satisfaction.

Dog shows in Britain are graded from championship shows at the top through open shows down to matches and exemption shows. The classes at the shows are graded from open down to novice, with titles like

Below: Foxhounds have their own recognized shows, where, unlike most dog shows, the hounds are judged loose and not on a lead.

Opposite: Small dogs like this Yorkshire Terrier are usually judged standing on a table.

postgraduate and mid-limit to make it all very confusing for the uninitiated. The important point to remember is that when the dog has won a certain number of the lower classes at the lower shows, it can then only enter into the higher classes. If it eventually becomes a champion, it can only compete in open classes at championship and open shows. To become a champion in Britain, a dog must win three challenge certificates under three different judges, each of whom must sign a declaration saying that in their opinion the dog is 'clearly worthy of the title of champion', and these titles can only be won at championship shows which are chosen by the Kennel Club. In America, Canada and most other countries the principles are the same although the methods of carrying them out may be different.

To anyone with an inclination to take up pedigree dog breeding as a hobby or who feels like showing the dog they already have, the first advice is to go along to several shows and try to find out what it is all about. Go to one or two big championship shows, but also take a look at your local show because that is where you should start showing. Watch how the experts handle their dogs and don't forget that today's experts were yesterday's novices.

When you go to dog shows you will hear all sorts of stories about judges who 'judge the other end of the lead'. This is often the complaint of the owner who shows a dog unsuccessfully for quite a long time, then sells it to another owner who immediately starts winning with it. He has overlooked the fact that the second owner

Above: This long-coated Chihuahua looks justly proud of the huge cups it has won at Crufts Dog Show.

Above right: Canine beauticians carrying their art to extremes, to prepare a dog for a special occasion.

Top: The line-up at Crufts, perhaps the best-known dog show in the world – but this class of Pyreneans seems to find it all rather a bore.

is obviously an expert who has presented the dog to such perfection that it hardly resembles the dog dragged round the shows for so long by its previous owner. Presentation and showmanship won't turn a bad dog into a good one, but it can make it look a great deal better.

The dog's appearance depends a great deal on what has been done before the show. With so much difference between the various breeds, there must obviously be equally great differences in preparation. 'Breed books' devoted to each breed often give detailed advice on how to prepare that particular breed for the show ring, and experienced exhibitors are usually very pleased to help a novice. Nevertheless, there are several general points worth mentioning. Good condition, as we have already seen, 'goes in at the mouth'. No amount of grooming or trimming can make up for good health provided by good food and adequate exercise. I use the word 'adequate' deliberately; one does not want to get a show dog as fit and hard as, say, a racing Greyhound. The show dog should, in fact, carry more flesh to give a rather more rounded appearance.

To win in the show ring a dog must walk properly on a lead, stand to be handled by the judge and have a general air of self-possession. To do so it must have confidence in its handler, who cannot inspire such confidence if he or she is a bundle of nerves. This explains why a professional handler can often get more out of a dog he has never seen before than the owner, who knows it well. The advice given earlier on socializing puppies applies just as much to show dogs as to dogs kept as pets. It is important to take the dog out as a puppy to meet other dogs. Training classes can be a help and some canine societies run handling classes for 'beauty' dogs, as opposed to 'obedience' dogs.

Confusion is often created in the minds of newcomers to dog showing because the judge at one show will often reverse the placings of a judge at another show. Judging is done according to a standard of points laid down for each and every breed, but although the standard is always the same different judges interpret it in different ways. One judge's idea of what is 'moderately wide between the ears' may be very different from another's. It is a good thing, maybe, that judges do differ; if everyone could agree on the perfect dog, then that dog would win all the prizes and there would be no point in anyone else showing! Experienced exhibitors learn to know which judges like their type of dog and try to show under these. Big breeders will often show one dog under one judge and a different dog under another, but even

then they are not assured of automatic success.

Many people put their dog or dogs in the hands of a professional handler, who prepares and shows it for them. They then go along to see it win (or lose), rather like a racehorse owner goes to the races. To me half the fun of showing is in preparing and handling the animal oneself. Nevertheless professional handling is very common in America and for some breeds in Britain. Practically all Wire Fox Terriers and several other terriers are handled by professionals. It must be admitted that it is very difficult for a novice to win in these breeds against the experts, but amateurs do still win against the professionals and the satisfaction of doing so is even greater than when one wins against other amateurs.

Below: The hustle and bustle of the Airedale ring at Crufts.

Care and Grooming

THE dog has often been called 'Man's best friend' but, unfortunately, Man is not always the dog's best friend. A great number of pet dogs are either overfed, underfed, under-exercised, allowed to stray or kept in unsuitable conditions, and they suffer from various physical and mental disorders because their owners have not taken the trouble to find out more about the art of keeping a dog healthy and happy.

The dog was domesticated many thousands of years ago and, although it retains many of his natural instincts, it is now entirely dependent on Man for all its needs. So before deciding to take a dog into your home, think very carefully and make quite sure that you are willing and able to accept all the responsibilities that go with dog ownership. Small or large, the dog will need feeding, exercising, grooming, training and its health looked after. In case of illness your veterinary surgeon will be the person to consult, but any responsible owner should have some knowledge of first aid and know the symptoms of simple common ailments.

Feeding

Breeders often say that 'half the pedigree goes in at the mouth', and it is certainly true that the food a puppy is reared on will affect its whole future. Most adult dogs are adaptable animals and will usually eat a wide variety of foods, but any dog will be healthier and happier if fed a properly balanced diet. Dogs are by nature carnivores, that is to say meat-eaters, but today most are fed a mixed diet and appear to thrive on it. Our grandparents most likely fed their dogs on table scraps and left-overs, from which the dogs probably got sufficient nutrients, but today a lot of our food is processed, pasteurized, dehydrated, refrigerated, preserved and so on. If your dog is fed on scraps from these foods, its diet will very likely be short of a number of essential ingredients.

To keep in good health, your pet will therefore need proteins, carbohydrates, fats, minerals, vitamins and trace elements. Probably the simplest diet for your dog is meat and wholemeal biscuit meal, a diet which has been fed successfully to innumerable dogs for many years. But, as meat is so expensive, you may prefer to feed one of the many proprietary diets available. The pet food industry offers a

bewildering variety of diets for you to choose from. Most foods offered by the well-known firms contain all the essentials for your dog, but dogs, like people, are individuals and what suits one may not suit another. Some dogs like dry food, some like moist; some like tinned meat and some prefer raw meat. So if your dog does not like one type of food, try another, and don't forget that dogs like a change as much as we do. I can think of nothing more boring than being presented with the same food in the same dish at the same time every day. Proprietary foods are only as good as their contents and the care that goes into manufacturing them, so buy a reputable brand and if possible check on the label to see what the ingredients are.

Tinned dog food is usually cooked meat in various forms. Better-quality products have more meat than gravy, and as meat is

about 75% water, make sure you buy this type otherwise the poor dog is only having a meaty drink. If you find your dog prefers liver, chicken, rabbit or beef, let it have what it likes best. It makes very little difference what meat is in the tins, as most of the better-quality ones have vitamins and minerals added in the right proportions.

Another way of using meat, other than fresh, is dried meat. The good-quality product has a very high protein content and is very economical to feed. It must be well soaked in boiling water and allowed to cool before being mixed with wholemeal biscuit to make a balanced meal.

So-called 'soft-moist' foods are popular with many dogs. Usually bought in plastic bags, these are meaty foods which some dogs prefer to dry ones. The product keeps very well until opened but must then be used up fairly quickly.

One very dry type of food is called extruded or expanded. This is cooked under less heat than biscuit and has a very high food value. It looks like a rusk or very light biscuit meal and forms a complete diet on its own. If you are changing your dog to this type of food from a more conventional diet, do so gradually as it will need time to adjust to the change. Other dry foods are the pelleted and flaked diets, which are also complete feeds. The flaked diet has the same contents as the pellets, and has the advantage that it can be fed moist if the dog prefers. On the other hand, the manufacturers claim that the pellet form is more easily digested. It can be bought in large or small pellets, depending on the size of the dog.

When feeding any of these dry diets, it is essential that the dog should be supplied with water all the time. If you remember that meat contains about 75% water and these dried foods only have a water content of about 8%, you can see that the success of feeding them depends very much on water being available as required.

One meal a day is usually enough for most dogs, but if for some reason you prefer to split this and feed two smaller meals, it will do no harm. In fact, in some cases it is a good thing. Very small dogs, giant breeds and old dogs are probably better fed twice a day. This ensures that the stomach is not overloaded and makes digestion easier. It is almost impossible to advise people what amount of food to give their own pet dog. Like people, some dogs are good converters of food and some are bad, and, like people, most dogs are overweight. An active, high-spirited dog will eat far more than a stolid, lazy dog of the same size. It is easier to put weight on a dog than take it off, so if your dog has a tendency to get fat feed him a little less.

It is much better not to give dogs titbits. It only makes them bad-mannered, always begging for food, and upsets their stomachs. Special dog chocolate drops and other candy do no harm if they are given in moderation, as an aid to training or for some special reward. Dogs do not need bones in their diet, but if you want to give your pet a bone to gnaw make sure it is a large raw marrow bone. Cooked bones, especially poultry and chop bones, are very dangerous. The cooking makes the bones brittle and they can splinter and pierce the intestines, often with disastrous results. Hard nylon 'bones' or raw hide strips are good for dogs to chew and help to keep their teeth clean, or you could give a large, hard dog biscuit for the same purpose.

When you feed your dog does not matter, but do not give it a heavy meal and then take it out for a run. If you can steel yourself to do it, all dogs benefit from a 'fast day' once a week. It gives the dog's stomach a rest, and if yours is a fussy feeder it does help considerably in getting a clean plate.

Equipment

It is quite possible to buy your dog almost as large a wardrobe as your own. There are plastic raincoats, tweed winter coats, woolly football jerseys, leggings, rainhats, dainty beds with foam mattresses, and so on, but your dog will not thank you for, nor will it need, all these expensive luxury items.

There are certain essential items that

Left: Dogs enjoy chewing bones and it is good for their teeth. Large bones are best. They should never be cooked, as cooked chicken, rabbit or mutton bones can break into very dangerous splinters.

Below: Your dog's food and water bowls should be kept just as clean as the plates you use yourself.

Opposite: A young St Bernard on a long nylon lead, of the type often used in the show ring.

all dogs do need, however. Every dog needs a collar and lead. Collars can be the ordinary flat leather buckled type, narrow round ones, studded leather collars and, of course, fancy studded collars for poodles. You can also buy collars in nylon, which is very strong and durable, not to mention washable, and it is very light for the dog to wear. Chain collars are usually 'slip collars' and are often used for training. Slip collars should never be left on a dog, as the ring can easily get caught up in something like a car door handle and the dog could be strangled. They should be kept strictly for training. From the dog's point of view, a light collar is best and it is preferable to take the collar off at night. Your name and address will need to be fixed to the collar. This can be engraved on a plate or disc, or written on a slip of paper and put in a small barrel attached to the collar. The latter method is the most useful as you can change the address if you take the dog on holiday with you.

Leads are available in any of the materials already mentioned for collars. Chain leads are not very practical, unless the dog eats leather ones. Leather leads are ideal if they are made of good-quality leather and are kept supple. Nylon is very strong and has the advantage that it can be rolled up and put in your pocket. All leads should be a reasonable length (short leads encourage a dog to pull), with strong clips.

Your dog will also need its own food and water bowls. These are obtainable in a variety of shapes and sizes, usually in plastic, aluminium, stainless steel or earthenware. Make sure they are easy to clean. If you have a dog, like a spaniel, which has long ears, get one of the bowls specially styled for these dogs. They are much narrower at the top, and the dog will not get its ears in a mess when eating.

You will also need to give your dog its own bed. There are plenty of styles to choose from. but basically the bed needs to be raised off the floor to keep it out of draughts, easy to clean and comfortable. Although a lot of dogs sleep curled up. a bed should be large enough for it to sleep stretched out if it wants to. Baskets are not advisable as they tend to harbour dirt and fleas. A folded-up blanket or piece of carpet can be placed in the bed. This should be washable, and to keep it clean longer you can put a 'dog sheet' over it, either buttoned or zipped on. There are also heated dog beds on the market. Normally these are not necessary, but with old or sick dogs they

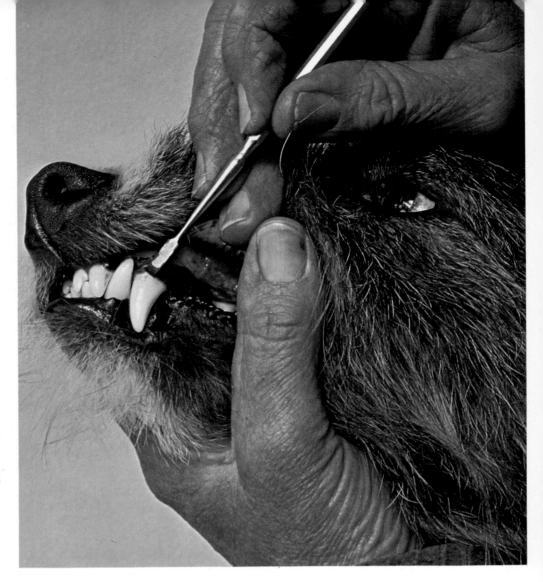

Right: Scaling teeth. If you have a firm, steady hand and dog which you can control this task is not difficult, but if you are hesitant to do it yourself you may prefer to visit a veterinary surgeon or dog's 'beauty parlour'.

Far right: Using a hound glove on a smooth-coated dog. You should exert plenty of pressure, which will tone up the dog's muscles as well as groom its coat.

can be very useful. Small dogs are often best kept in a small indoor kennel. It gives them a feeling of security and keeps them warm and cosy. The kennel can also be used as a travelling box.

Some grooming equipment will be necessary. All breeds need a brush and comb, nail clippers, a pair of scissors, a tooth scaler if you wish to look after the dog's teeth yourself, a rough towel and a chamois leather for drying. A hairdryer is useful for the longer-coated breeds as it is difficult to get their coats looking good if they are only rubbed with a towel. Short-coated breeds will need a hound glove or mitt instead of a comb. These are often made of rubber or double-sided, one side with very short wire pins or bristles and the other covered in some material, such as velveteen, to give the coat a final polish. Nail clippers can be bought in the shape of pliers or what is known as the 'guillotine' type. Most dogs seem to prefer the latter. A coarse steel nail file is also useful to finish off the rough edges on the nails. It is no good going to a lot of trouble grooming your dog if you are using a dirty brush and comb, so make sure these are washable and give them a wash at least once a week.

A great number of dogs are seen wearing coats, but very few actually need to. It may please the owner to put his pet into a pretty coloured jersey but the dog will probably be happier and healthier without it. Some of the very small, thin-coated breeds do feel the cold, however, and on wet windy days they may be better off with a little extra protection, and of course coats are a help if the dog is sick or has a touch of rheumatism.

Exercise

All dogs, small or large, need exercise, and most need far more exercise than they are given. They all need at least thirty minutes free running exercise daily, more if possible. Left to their own devices, very few dogs will take much exercise, so to exercise your dog properly you will have to exercise yourself. It will probably do you as much good as the dog!

Small dogs can get a lot of exercise in a confined space, but they will still appreciate a change and the chance to romp in the open. If you teach your dog to retrieve (most dogs learn quite readily), it can be a great help in exercising it. If time is short and you cannot get to a park or take it for a walk in the country, you can still give it a lot of exercise in a small garden. Hide various objects or its favourite ball and then send it to look for them, or use a tennis racquet and a couple of balls and bat the balls out in different directions, then send the dog for them one at a time. Dogs can get very keen on this 'game' and, apart from physical exercise, it teaches a dog control, concentration and gives it a chance to use its nose.

Another sport enjoyed by many dogs, especially gun dog breeds, is swimming. If a young dog is reluctant to go into the water, never force it or, worse still, throw it in. Encourage it by throwing a ball into the water, going in yourself, or having another dog that likes swimming to go in first. Choose a warm day and a calm lake or river with a gradually sloping bank. Swimming is excellent exercise and a short swim will do your dog as much good as a much longer period of running.

Some of the larger, active breeds, such as Dobermans and German Shepherds, enjoy running beside a bicycle, but don't overdo it and don't go too fast. And only let a dog run beside a bicycle on traffic-free roads.

You will probably find other activities for your dog to enjoy and the more varied exercise you can give it, the more it will benefit. On cold, wet days even small dogs will be all right if kept moving, but don't leave them to stand about doing nothing, and always dry a wet dog on return to the house. In very hot weather, exercise, except swimming, should be carried out in early morning or late evening when it is coolest, as dogs can suffer quite badly from heat stroke.

Grooming

Grooming should not be looked on as a chore, or a battle. Both you and your dog should enjoy it. Grooming is necessary for all dogs, short- or long-coated. It keeps the dog clean and tidy, tones up the skin and muscles, gets rid of loose hair and encourages the new coat to grow through more rapidly.

It is best to give the dog a few minutes grooming daily and a thorough groom once a week. Take the opportunity to give it a good check-over at the same time as the weekly grooming session. Starting at the head, open the mouth and check the teeth and gums. If the teeth show signs of tartar deposit, you can remove it yourself with a tooth scaler. The teeth must be scaled from the gums to the tip of the tooth. This is fairly simple to do if there is only a light deposit of tartar, but, if possible, it is

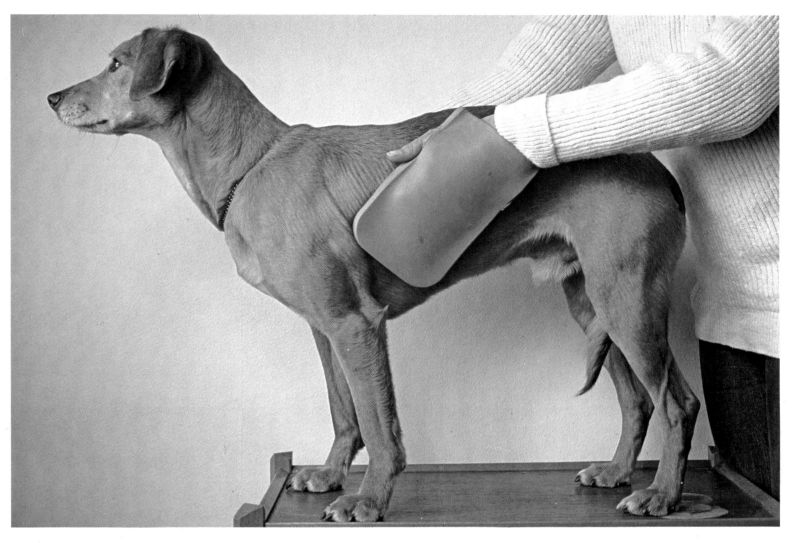

advisable to be shown how to do it correctly. Heavy tartar causes receding gums, bad breath and decaying teeth, so if the teeth have been allowed to become heavily encrusted consult your veterinary surgeon. When you are doing the weekly grooming, you can clean the teeth with an ordinary toothbrush which helps to keep the deposits down.

Next check the eyes. These should be bright and clear, and any discharge should be checked with your veterinary surgeon. Some breeds with protruding eyes or very deep-set ones seem to accumulate dirt and dust in the corners, causing irritation and often making the eyes water. One of the best and cheapest eye solutions is the normal saline solution. Just mix 1 teaspoonful of salt into $\frac{1}{2}$ litre (1 pint) of boiled water and allow it to cool.

While you are looking at the dog's head, you should also check the ears. Dogs with longish, hairy ears, such as spaniels and poodles, pick up all sorts of things on their ear flaps, which can mat the hair and cause discomfort. Have a look inside the ear, and if the inside of the ear flap is rather grubby, wipe it round with a piece of damp cottonwool. Never poke or probe into the ear itself; you cannot see down the ear without a proper instrument and if there is any obstruction you could easily push it down even further. If there is no discharge and the ear smells fresh but it seems to irritate the dog, try pouring a little warm olive oil down it. This should soothe the ear and if there is a bit of dirt inside it will help to float it out. Apart from this simple treatment, never mess about with ear troubles, but take the dog to the veterinary

surgeon.

Some dogs get cracked noses in very dry or very cold weather. A little oil rubbed in usually relieves this trouble.

Make sure the feet have no cut pads, thorns, cysts between the toes, or mats of hair. Some city dogs get cracked pads from too much walking on concrete. A little oil will often help and the dog can wear special boots for a few days until the pads heal. If there are mats of hair under the pads or between the toes, cut these out very carefully with a pair of sharp, blunt-ended, curved scissors. If these mats are left, they accumulate dirt and set up an irritation which can lead to eczema. This will need professional treatment.

Keep the nails short and do not forget the dew claws. These are small extra claws found on the inside of the feet, rather like a thumb in humans. They are usually in the forefeet only, but some breeds also have hind dew claws. As these claws do not reach the ground, they are not worn down and will need regular clipping. If not attended to frequently, they can grow right round into the foot and cause a nasty abscess. You may be lucky and own a breed in which the dew claws have been removed.

Use a nail clipper and file to keep the dog's nails in trim. The nails have a sensitive 'quick' running down the centre; in a white nail this shows up as a pink streak. Care should be taken to avoid cutting this, as not only is it painful for the dog, it also bleeds profusely. If you just cut the pointed tip of the nail, it should be safe even if the dog has black nails where you cannot see the tip. After you have clipped the nails, finish them off with a coarse file,

drawing down from the root of the nail to the tip. If you file the nails regularly, the quick recedes and you will not need to use the clippers so frequently.

Under the dog's tail are two small glands, called the anal glands, situated on either side of the anus. The wild dog does not just eat meat, it eats the skin and bones as well, and this helps to keep the anal glands emptied, but because the domestic dog has less roughage in its diet, these glands fill up and do not empty of their own accord. A very evil-smelling liquid collects and can cause an abscess if it is not removed. The glands can be emptied quite easily by holding a pad of cottonwool over them and squeezing firmly on either side. Although a simple job when you know how, it is a good idea to ask your veterinary surgeon to show you the first time.

Below: Spaniel eating from a bowl especially designed to keep ears out of food.

Right: Dogs with feathering, such as spaniels and setters, are better brushed with a stiff brush. If they are very muddy, however, it is easier and quicker to use a comb. Provided this is only done occasionally, and a wide-toothed comb is used, no harm will be done.

Below: Cleaning a spaniel's ears.

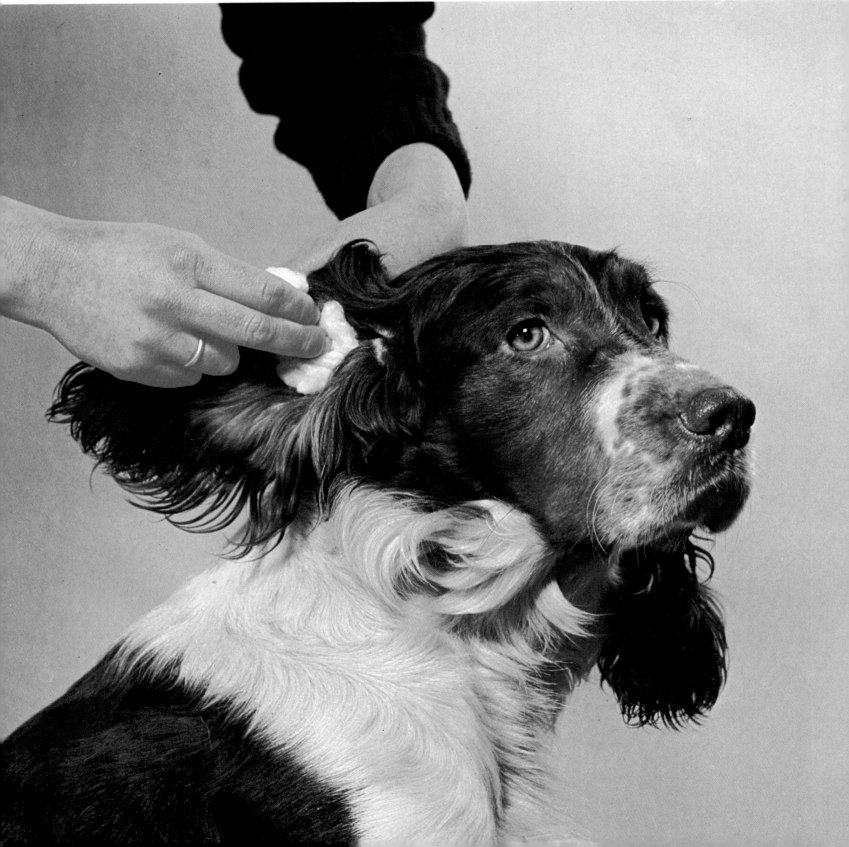

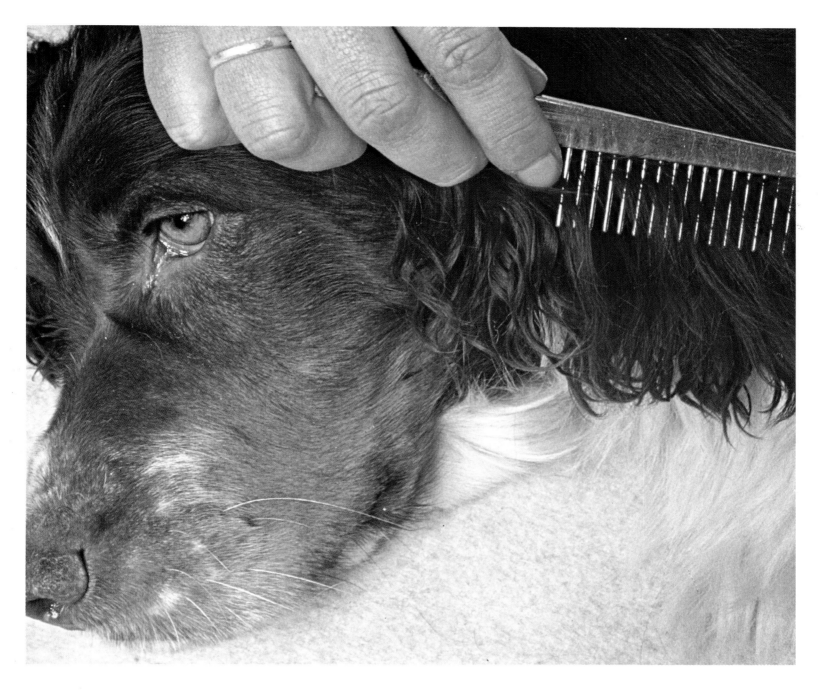

When your dog is dirty it will need a bath. How often you bath it will depend on the weather and how dirty it gets. Pour some warm water into a suitable container, either sink, bowl or bath, stand the dog in the water, pour on some shampoo and work up a good lather. Leave the dog's head to last; once it is wet, the dog will try to shake. Give the rest of the dog a good washing, and rinse it very well – at least twice in tepid water. Finally wash the head, being careful not to get shampoo into the eyes or to get the inside of the ears wet. If you are outdoors, let the dog out, on a leash, and once it has given a good shake rub it dry with a large rough towel. Indoors, it is best if you put the towel right over the dog to remove the surplus moisture. In either case, an electric hairdryer is ideal for drying the dog off completely, especially for long-haired breeds; brush and comb the coat as you dry it, otherwise it will dry into a tangled mass. If it is a warm sunny day, the dog can run about outside to dry itself, but take care that it does not try to roll on the ground and undo all your good work. Make sure you keep it busy playing, say with a ball, or be sure the surface of the ground is clean and dry.

Above: Combing the ears. The comb should be moved from the skin outwards.

Below: Nail-clipping, using 'guillotine' clippers.

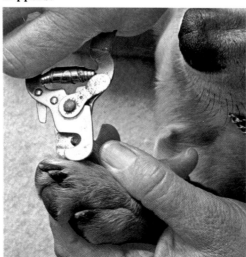

Below: Opening the dog's mouth, so that you can give it a pill or remove a bone or any other object which is causing it distress. Gently press its lips over its top teeth, which will make it open its mouth. If you are doing this for the first time, you may need to use both hands and have someone else to help you.

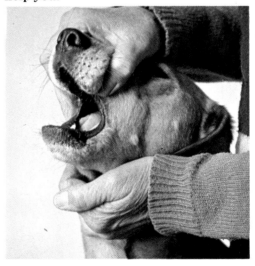

Above: Brushing a small, wire-coated dog. You can also stand the dog up on a table so that you can exert more pressure on the brush. This also teaches show dogs to stand up to be handled by the judge.

Opposite: Children should always be encouraged to groom their own dogs. Here we have an excellent example of a happy child/puppy relationship.

One very good way of freeing a dog from fleas, lice or other unwanted guests is to give it a medicated bath. Most pet stores have a good selection, and if you follow the instructions carefully they are usually most effective. Remember, though, that fleas do not breed on the dog but in its bedding or in cracks in the floorboards, so it is no use bathing the dog without also washing its bed, the bedding and the immediate surroundings.

There are other methods of getting rid of fleas, besides bathing the dog. 'Flea collars' are very effective. They are specially impregnated plastic collars which last up to about three months and really do seem to keep the dog free from fleas. Alternatively, there are aerosols which can be sprayed into the dog's coat. Be careful when you are using these to keep them pointed away from the dog's face. The coat can also be turned back and insect powders shaken onto the exposed skin.

Unfortunately, however well cared for your dog is, it is almost certain that it will pick up a few fleas from time to time, so when grooming it always check to see that there are no fleas or traces of flea dirt (little black specks) in the coat. If they are not discovered fairly quickly, fleas set up intense irritation which makes the dog scratch, and this in turn can lead to skin troubles which are much more difficult to cure than the odd flea.

General health care
There are one or two simple things you should learn to do to help the dog yourself before you need to call in a veterinary surgeon. The first is being able to take a dog's temperature. The normal temperature should be about 38.61°C (101.5°F) and anything over two degrees of fever should be regarded as a warning of something serious. The temperature should be taken in the rectum. Grease the end of a *snub-nosed* thermometer and insert it gently into the dog's rectum. Hold it there for the required time and then gently remove it. Do not let go of the thermometer once it is inserted, as it has been known for dogs to pull them right inside!

Next you need to know how to give medicine to the dog. If this is liquid, you will find it easier to put it in a small bottle rather than trying to tip it out of a spoon. Have the dog sitting and if possible have someone holding it steady. Insert a finger between the dog's lips on one side of the mouth, pull them slightly apart and outwards and you will find that this forms a most convenient 'pocket' into which you can carefully pour the liquid. Keep its head slightly back and only pour in a small quantity at a time which it can swallow easily. Continue slowly until you have poured in the whole dose. Keep the dog's mouth shut and gently massage its throat to make sure that it has swallowed all the medicine.

You may also need to give your dog a pill or capsule. Some people try to put it in its food, but this is inadvisable as the dog might spit it out in pieces, eat half of it or it may be the sort of medicine that should not be given with food. The best way is to place your hand over the dog's face and on either side press its lips over its top teeth;

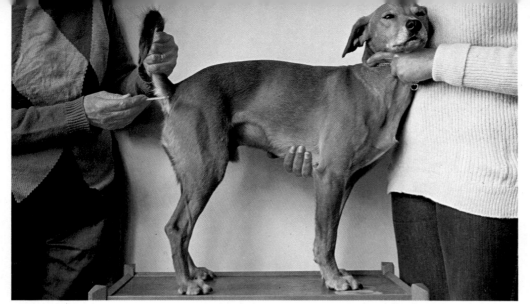

Left: Taking the dog's temperature. Hold the dog firmly and gently insert a blunt-nosed thermometer.

Left below: An emergency muzzle can be made from a length of bandage or any long piece of material. This is the belt of a dressing gown.

Below: Administering liquid medicine. Pull out the dog's cheek to form a pouch into which to pour the liquid.

Bottom: Dogs, like people, are more pleasant to live with if they have a bath when necessary.

Opposite page: A hairdryer can be a great help with long-coated breeds, especially if the weather is bad.

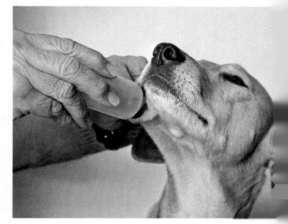

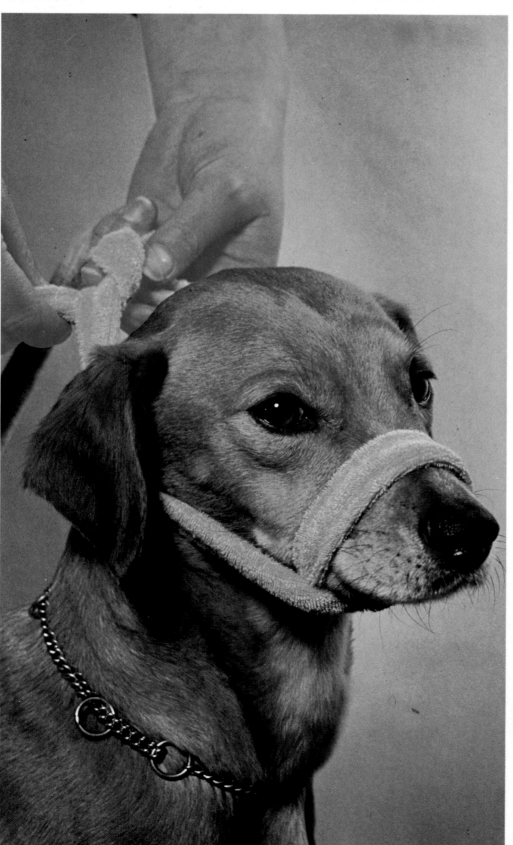

this will make it open its mouth. Tip its head slightly backwards, and with your other hand drop the capsule right at the back of the tongue. Withdraw your hand quickly, shut the dog's mouth and watch for it to swallow. If it appears to be holding the pill in its mouth, massage its throat gently or close its nostrils for a few seconds.

Something else every owner should know how to do is put an emergency muzzle on a dog. Any dog involved in an accident, in pain and frightened, is liable to bite in fear and it is only common sense to protect yourself. A large handkerchief, soft belt, tie, scarf or odd strip of cloth can all be used. Make a loop, slip it over the dog's nose and pull the knot tight under its chin; take both ends back and tie them firmly behind its ears. You should then be able to handle the dog safely.

By now you should know what a healthy dog looks like, your own dog in particular, so any signs of abnormality should be carefully watched. Look for dull

eyes instead of bright ones, an active dog that suddenly refuses to go for a walk, a placid dog which becomes irritable, excessive thirst, lack of appetite in a normally greedy dog, excessive scratching, especially round the ears, or the dog holding its head to one side. These are just a few of the more obvious signs that all is not well.

The veterinary surgeon should always be consulted sooner rather than later, but there are a few things that require his immediate attention. Very severe vomiting should never be allowed to continue for more than an hour or two at the most. Give the dog nothing at all by mouth and take it straight to the vet. Diarrhoea is often due to a change of food or a stomach upset of some sort and will often clear up quickly by itself, but if it continues for more than 24 hours the dog should be seen by the vet. In all cases where you suspect the dog is not well and the symptoms do not clear up quickly, do get in touch with your veterinary surgeon. A large number of illnesses if treated promptly cause little harm, but if left to get a good hold can be very serious indeed.

First Aid

Accidents. Traffic accidents are probably the most common accidents suffered by dogs. Move the dog as little as possible, as it is most likely suffering from shock and possibly internal injuries. If there is excessive bleeding, it must be stopped. First check that there is nothing in the wound, then apply a pad of gauze if any is available (if not, use a clean handkerchief, torn sheet or the most suitable clean covering you can find). Then bandage firmly over the pad. If blood seeps through, rebandage on top and take the dog to the vet immediately. To move a large injured dog with as little disturbance as possible, it is best to use a blanket. Slide it gently under the dog and, with one person at each end holding two corners, gently lift the dog into a car.

If the dog is suffering from internal bleeding, its breathing will be rapid and shallow, its skin will feel clammy, its pulse will be rapid and it may be unconscious. In this case, simply get it to the veterinary surgeon just as fast as you can.

Burns. Extensive burns are very dangerous. The only recommended first aid is to immerse the part in cold water and get professional treatment immediately.

Heat stroke. In very hot weather or if it is left in a closed car, even in warm weather, dogs can suffer badly from heat stroke. The dog will probably be panting, weak and near to collapse. It might be vomiting, and its temperature will be very high. Lower the temperature as soon as you can – if you are indoors immerse the dog in a cold bath; outdoors you may be able to find a hose, or failing that a tap, where you can get water to pour over it. Once the dog shows signs of recovery, dry it off, keep it in a cool place and encourage it to drink.

Poisoning. If you know the dog has taken poison, try to make it vomit. A small piece of washing soda pushed down its throat, or salt and mustard in water, will usually work quickly. Take the dog to the veterinary surgeon at once, and if you know what it has swallowed take along the packet or bottle.

Drowning. Contrary to general belief, not all dogs can swim. Even a dog that is normally a good swimmer may fall off a bridge and hurt itself, or get trapped in a steep-sided pond where it is unable to get out. The first thing to do is to place the dog's head lower than its body, pull out its tongue, try to drain out any excess water from its mouth and apply artificial respiration. Place the dog on its right side, tongue out and head forward, put your hand over its ribs behind the shoulder blade, press down on the ribs and release the pressure immediately. Repeat at intervals of about five seconds with short, sharp movements until the dog starts breathing normally.

Choking. Small rubber balls are the most usual cause of choking in dogs. The dog will be in considerable distress and, although able to breathe, will be unable to swallow and will salivate profusely. You will probably be able to feel the ball in its throat. The dog should be seen as soon as possible by a veterinary surgeon, who may have to anaesthetize it before removing the object.

Dogs sometimes also get a rubber ball stuck behind their molar teeth, causing an obstruction. If possible try to remove the ball, but be careful not to push it further down. Bones, pieces of stick and even stones can equally become lodged in the back of the mouth and cause a nasty wound. A dog with something wedged in its mouth usually paws frantically at its mouth or rubs it along the ground, slobbering profusely. Open its mouth carefully, taking care not to get bitten, and see if you can pull out the offending object. If you cannot get hold of it take the dog to the veterinary surgeon, who will give it an anaesthetic before removing the object and treating the wound.

Prevention is better than cure so try to keep your dog away from poisons, cooking stoves, unguarded fires, needles and sharp bones. Do not let it run loose on the streets, and never leave it shut in a closed car. And if it should be unlucky and suffer an accident, apply suitable first aid and then get it treated by the veterinary surgeon as soon as possible.

Above left: Picking up an injured dog on a blanket.

Right: A visit to the vet need not be an ordeal for the dog if it learns that it is being helped and is among friends. This Boxer is being gently held and comforted while its injured paw is bandaged.

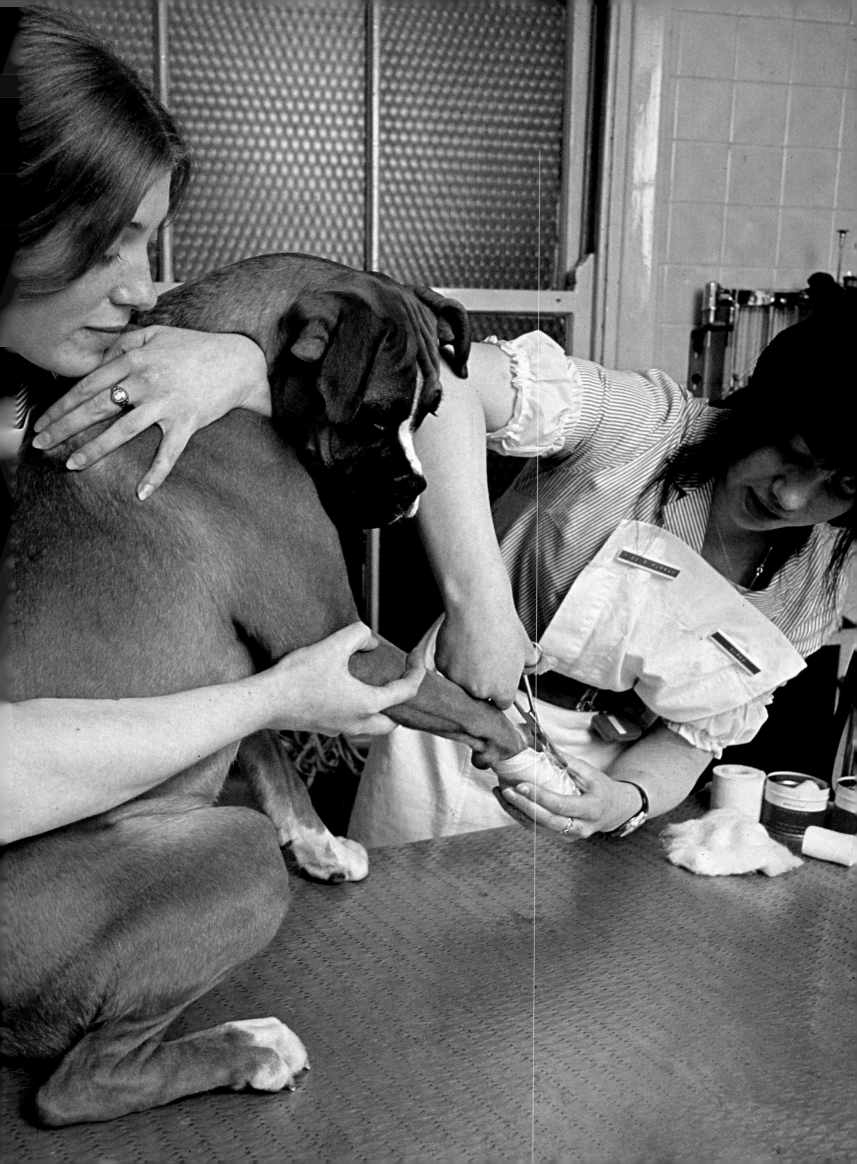

Index

Figures in italics denote illustrations

Acknowledgments

The publishers would like to thank the following individuals and organizations for their kind permission to reproduce the photographs in this book:

A.F.I.P.: 4, (A. M. Berenger) 6, (Gerard Mathieu) 133 left; Ardea: (Jean-Paul Ferrero) 1, 55 above, 62–3, 103 above; Australian News and Information Bureau: 87; Bavaria Verlag: 99 above; S.C. Bisserot: 112 above, 144; Camera and Pen International: (Max Wilkins) 46 right, (C. de Jaeger) 176; Bruce Coleman: (J. van Wormer) 12, (Hans Reinhard) 2–3, 86, 92, 95, 131, 132 above, 133 right; Bruce Coleman Inc.: (Leonard Lee Rue III) 63 above; Gerry Cranham: 174 above, 190; Anne Cumbers: 43, 49, 56, 93, 94 below, 110 below, 141, 161, 164, 167, 168, 171, 173; *Daily Telegraph:* (John Sims) 179; Gary Ede: 140 left; Mary Evans Picture Library: 21, 22, 26, 28, 31, 98 above; Will Green: 41; Sonia Halliday: 7; Robert Hallmann: 97; Michael Holford: 16, 25, 33, 44, 135; Jacana Agence de Presse: (P. Pilloud) 52 above, (B. Rebouleau) 54, (Soyamoto) 61, 143, (G. Trouillet) 89, 137, (B. Josedupont) 90–1, 101 left, (Nadeau) 103 below, (J. H. Labat) 166; Paolo Koch: 174 centre right: Frank H. Meads: 46 left; Jim Meads: 34–5, 35, 36–7, 38, 39, 40, 42–3; Metropolitan Police: 88 below; John Moss: 59 left, 91 above, 100, 110 above, 132 below, 170; Daniel O'Keefe: 112 below left; Mike Peters: 45; Pictor: (Tony Frissell) 14–15, 50–1, 64, 82 below, 96, 138, 139, (Alpha) 63 below; Dick Polak: 178, 180, 181, 183 below left, 183 below right, 183 above, 186 above right and below right, 186 above left, 187, 188; Popperfoto: 189; John Rigby: 60; Spectrum: 10 below, 44, 102, 109 below, 130 above, 162–3, 172; John Massey Stewart: 129; Tony Stone Assoc.: endpapers; Syndication International: 175; Sally Anne Thompson: 10 above, 11 above and below, 47 left, 48, 53, 55 below, 57 above, 58, 59 right, 82 above, 83, 84, 85 right, 94 above, 98 below, 99 below, 101 above right, 104, 105, 106, 107 below, 108, 109 above, 111, 112 below right, 136 left, 136 right, 140 right, 142, 165, 174 centre left 176, 177, 182, 184, 185, 186 below left; Tiofoto: 63 centre; Elizabeth Weiland: 52 centre, 52 below, 81, 85 left, 107 above, 130 below; Barbara Woodhouse: 8–9, 57 below, 169; ZEFA: 47 right, 88 above (W. Schmidt) 13.